AWAKENING
TO THE
SPIRIT
WORLD

Also by Sandra Ingerman

Soul Retrieval: Mending the Fragmented Self

Welcome Home: Following Your Soul's Journey Home

A Fall to Grace (fiction)

Medicine for the Earth: How to Transform Personal and Environmental Toxins

Shamanic Journeying: A Beginner's Guide (book and drumming CD)

How to Heal Toxic Thoughts: Simple Tools for Personal Transformation

How to Thrive in Changing Times: Simple Tools to Create True Health, Wealth, Peace, and Joy for Yourself and the Earth

Audio Programs:

The Soul Retrieval Journey

Miracles for the Earth

The Beginner's Guide to Shamanic Journeying

Shamanic Meditations: Guided Journeys for Insight, Vision, and Healing

Soul Journeys: Music for Shamanic Practice

Also by Hank Wesselman

Spiritwalker: Messages from the Future

Medicinemaker: Mystic Encounters on the Shaman's Path

Visionseeker: Shared Wisdom from the Place of Refuge

The Journey to the Sacred Garden: A Guide to Traveling in the Sacred Realms (book with CD)

Spirit Medicine: Healing in the Sacred Realms (with Jill Kuykendall—book with CD)

Little Ruth Reddingford and the Wolf (with Raquel Abreu—book for children)

Audio Program:

The Spiritwalker Teachings: Journeys for the Modern Mystic
(with Jill Kuykendall—six-CD set with booklet)

AWAKENING
TO THE
SPIRIT WORLD

The Shamanic Path *of* Direct Revelation

Sandra Ingerman
& Hank Wesselman

SOUNDS TRUE

BOULDER, COLORADO

Sounds True, Inc.
Boulder, CO 80306

Book design by Rachael Murray

Printed in the U.S.A.

ISBN-13: 978-1-61664-290-7

We dedicate this book to the next seven generations . . .
May this foundation help them to envision a new world . . .
And may a profound reverence alight on them.

Contents

Preface from Sandra Ingerman

Shamanism is an ancient and powerful spiritual practice that can help us thrive during challenging and changing times. In our modern-day technological world we have been led to believe that what we see, touch, hear, smell, and taste with our ordinary senses connects us only to the world that is visible around us. Conversely, shamanism teaches that there are doorways into other realms of reality where helping spirits reside who can share guidance, insight, and healing not just for ourselves but also for the world in which we live.

Shamanism reveals that we are part of Nature and one with all of life. It is understood that in the shaman's worlds everything in existence has a spirit and is alive, and that the spiritual aspects of all of life are interconnected through what is often called the web of life. Since we are part of Nature, Nature itself becomes a helping spirit that has much to share with us about how to bring our lives back into harmony and balance.

At the experiential center of shamanism lies the potent path of direct revelation, revealing that in this spiritual discipline, there are no intermediaries standing between the helping spirits and ourselves. We all can have access to the wisdom, guidance, and healing that the helping spirits and Nature have to share with us.

There are ways to achieve connection with these helping spirits as well as with the transpersonal aspects of Nature itself. Together with four other contributors, Hank Wesselman and I will introduce you to some well-traveled trails on which you may walk, giving you immediate and authentic access to the shaman's path of direct revelation.

There are multiple reasons why I was led to write this book and bring in other contributors to share their teachings. We have been seeing a spiritual awakening on the planet as more and more people are reading about and exploring different spiritual practices that lead to self-realization, personal development, and much-needed evolution of consciousness in humanity as a whole.

During this time of spiritual awakening, the term "shaman" has become part of popular culture. In the grocery store I see soaps and shampoos that have the word "shaman" on them. I see advertisements in newspapers and magazines that combine the title "shaman" with a host of professions. And even though I have been engaged in the practice of shamanism for thirty years, I seldom know to what these advertising references to shamanism refer. I can only imagine that you might be wondering too.

As the terms "shaman" and "shamanism" have become watered down by such marketing endeavors, there has been a reaction by some who have tried to create rules about what shamanism is and what it is not. Despite good intentions, this has often tended to add to the confusion, and in many cases it has created misunderstanding and an injustice to the practice.

There is a paradox here, for first and foremost, shamanism has always been a practice in which each practitioner gets unique directions and guidance from their helping spirits—those same transpersonal beings that are often referred to as spirit guides and angels. At the same time there exist time-tested guiding principles for the practice of shamanism, and so we have created this book together to share with you some of these principles so that you will be able to determine what shamanism is without giving you hard-line definitions and directions.

In times of great change such as we are experiencing today, many people react by turning within and becoming spiritual seekers, and often this includes searching for more personally sustaining ways of living and working, both individually and in groups.

Among these seekers, some tend to be drawn to systems that create rules and regulations that tell them what to do, thinking that this will bring them safety and reassurance. In much the same way, there are people who turn toward the practice of shamanism who want to be given rules for contacting the helping spirits and wish to be told that there is a right way and a wrong way to do the work.

There is also a pervasive tendency for people to give their power away to others. Such seekers often desire to find a teacher who will act as an intermediary between themselves and the helping spirits—a trait that is more characteristic of our organized religions in which bureaucratized priesthoods stand between us and the sacred realms. This is not typical of the path of shamanism and it is not a path of direct revelation.

In my workshops on shamanism I lead people into connection with their helping spirits, and I convey to them that once in connection, they can rely on their spirit helpers to teach them and advise them. When I offer workshops on powerful and effective healing methods, I advise my students that the best healers are inevitably those who abandon their workshop notes and rely instead on the guidance provided directly by their helping spirits.

In the discordant times in which we live today, new diseases of the mind and body have appeared, and the problems that are occurring on the planet all demand our creation of new solutions, encouraging us to tap into our own unique creative genius to help with the change. These times call for us to be willing to seek out the guidance of the helping spirits who can help us grow and progress through our life stages and life transitions with grace and power.

This also means that we must own our power and find new and unique ways of working with each other.

As I train some of my advanced practitioners to become teachers themselves so that they may carry on the shamanic tradition in our own time, I explain how I was guided by my helping spirits to teach as well as why I use certain exercises in my shamanic workshops. I then ask those in my Teacher Training Programs not to teach as I do but rather to follow the lead of their own helping spirits because it is in this way that the ancient shamanic tradition has come down to us across tens of millennia—and this is how it continues to stay filled with spirit, power, and meaning for those who practice it.

The goal of any spiritual path is to bring us into connection with our own divinity and into awareness of our own creative genius. All of us have great creative potential. To believe that only some people have the answers will not necessarily move us toward creating a harmonious life on a healthy planet.

We can all share different answers on different levels as we express our unique talents and gifts. We can all express different aspects of divinity in the same way that a diamond has different facets that shine together to create our own brilliant and dazzling light. By engaging in the shamanic path of direct revelation, our inner light is ignited, and when it is combined with the sparks of others around the world, I believe it will create the light needed to manifest a planet filled with harmony, love, light, peace, and abundance for all.

I have been writing books on shamanism since the early 1990s—books in which I have expressed my passion about bridging this ancient practice into our modern-day culture in a way that addresses the issues and needs of our times. One book led to another and then to another, and what I have found is that as the times have changed, my helping spirits have shared new forms of guidance and new ways of facilitating healing with me in order to help others as well as myself. My professional background as a psychotherapist has also encouraged my process of working with shamanism to be an organic one that has been, and is, ever-changing.

Across the years, I have come to understand that it is our responsibility to upgrade this ancient tradition into a new form that is meaningful to modern spiritual seekers and visionaries today. The challenging times in which we live are calling us to work together as a community to create positive and enduring changes that will benefit us all. In this regard, I was guided to invite some other shamanic teachers to contribute to this book, for in doing so I wanted to introduce you, the reader, to different ways of working as you too are called to the path of direct revelation.

In 2005 I became a founding board member of the Society of Shamanic Practitioners, whose purpose is to bring together a global shamanic community in which we might share what we have learned about bridging the ancient and time-tested visionary practices of the shaman into our modern-day cultures—an impulse that underscores the importance of this book.

In 2008 I asked those board members of the Society who are accomplished teachers, practitioners, and writers to come together to share some of their wisdom in this book so that together we may be of service to countless others in society at large. All six of us who have contributed to this project have a great deal of personal history and experience with the shaman's path.

As I reorganized the book accordingly, I invited anthropologist and author Hank Wesselman to be one such contributor. As we talked about this project with growing enthusiasm, I was guided to invite him to co-author the book with me and to help create the main fabric of the narrative text. As this project progressed, he also assisted in the weaving together of the teachings of all the contributors. I really enjoyed co-writing this book with Hank, a practitioner and shamanic teacher whom I have known as a friend and colleague for almost thirty years.

Among the other contributors, Tom Cowan is a wonderful writer and teacher about the Celtic ways, and you will notice how Tom writes in a poetic fashion. Carol Proudfoot-Edgar and I have co-taught workshops together across many years and became spiritual sisters and good friends the day we met. Like Tom, Carol is an amazing poet. I have known José Stevens since the early 1980s when I first started my formal shamanic training and we were in a journey group together in the Bay Area for three years. I have deep respect for the integrity that José brings to the work and appreciate his devotion to living what he teaches. And for many years now, I have known Alberto Villoldo, whose commitment to being in service has touched so many on the shamanic path. I am delighted that all of these people have contributed to this book.

After reorganizing the chapters for the book, I asked all the contributors to share their teachings in those chapters to which they felt called. In this regard, not every contributor wrote something for every chapter.

Hank and I have a dual role in these pages. Throughout most of the book, our voices are merged, reflecting the unity as well as the flow of our shared wisdom and friendship across many years. As such, the narrative that forms the fabric of the book will be our collective voice. And yet we are also contributing members of the group of six and we teach in our own way. So in those passages where we share our own unique ways of working, we will use our individual names to present our teachings.

Here I would like to introduce you to Hank Wesselman, and then together in the Introduction we will share the format of the book and how to work with it.

Preface from Hank Wesselman

In accepting Sandra Ingerman's gracious invitation to co-author this book, I was immediately aware as an anthropologist that an opportunity has been created to explore the dimensions and boundaries of an extraordinary subculture that has taken root in the Western world in our time, a community to which you, the reader, most likely belong.

We could think of it as the Transformational Community, and since the word "transformational" has become a buzzword in this time of change, there is something quite mysterious we should mention right at the onset.

A new spiritual complex is quietly, yet definitively, taking form within the heart of this community, one that brings us to the subject that lies at the epicenter of this book—the path of direct revelation.

This is the path on which each of us, as individuals, may directly engage with the Great Mystery of existence, however we may think of it, bringing it into our everyday lives and, by association, into our relationships and our work in the world.

This is the ancient, time-tested way of the shaman, the mystic, the visionary—the spiritual path that may take each of us straight into the experience of authentic initiation—a way that may guide us into the irreversible vortex of personal awakening that is referred to in the East as "enlightenment" and in the West as becoming "God-aware."

This is the path on which each of us may discover who and what we really are, gaining insights that may be quite in contrast to the scripts that society at large has handed to each of us to act out. In the process, we may discover that these scripts have suddenly become completely and utterly outdated.

As Sandra and I begin to share our thoughts about this extraordinary social transition with you, the reader, my attention inevitably turns toward those parts of my life spent working as an anthropologist among the tribal peoples of Africa, for it was there in the bush, among the indigenous traditionals hundreds of miles from the nearest road, hot bath, or cold beer, that I first stumbled upon this path more than thirty-five years ago. It happened through a series of spontaneous dreamlike visionary experiences that were intensely real and that became utterly life-changing.[1]

I was thirty years old then, a member of a scientific research expedition exploring the arid, eroded landscapes of eastern Africa's Great Rift Valley in search of answers to the mystery of human origins. In those days, I suspected that my fellow scientists were unlikely to be receptive to talking about these anomalous experiences, so I turned toward some of the African tribal men who were working with me. We had become friends across the years, living in a tented safari camp in remote areas of southwestern Ethiopia far from the tourists' tracks. In my discussions with these men, I slowly discovered that they held a perspective that was quite foreign to my scientist's way of thinking about the world.

Right at the core of their worldview lay the perception that the multi-leveled field of the dream is the real world, that we human beings are actually dreaming twenty-four hours a day, and that the everyday physical world came into being in response to the dream, not vice versa. These assertions were always accompanied by a conviction, strongly held, that the dream world is minded, that it is consciousness itself—alive, intelligent, and power-filled—infusing everything that emanates from it with awareness, vitality, and life force.

Of course it took me many months, even years, to fully comprehend and assimilate what these indigenous men were talking about, but I did understand right from the start that this was not a philosophical theory for them, nor was it a concept. It was a percept, an absolute known based upon direct experience—upon direct revelation if you will. It was also among them that I first encountered shamans.

Interestingly, I was also to learn from them that shamanism is not a religion, nor does it conflict with any religious tradition. It's a method, and as I was to discover first-hand it can become a way of life when practiced with humility, reverence, and self-discipline —a way that has enriched my own life beyond measure.

So allow me to take up Sandra's invitation, and in the book that follows she and I will share with you something of what we have learned along the path—something that may have provided us with priceless and quite unique pieces of the puzzle about who we are, how we got this way, and where we are headed.

The shaman's practice of direct revelation is the ancestral precursor of all our religious and philosophical traditions, both ancient and modern. This is a given, and while some may consider this to be an extraordinary claim, the great antiquity of the shaman's path is confirmed by what we know from the archeological evidence of rock art and cave art from Ice Age Europe and elsewhere in the ancient world.

For example, a paper published in the American journal *Science* in January 2002 reveals that the shaman's path may date back to at least 77,000 years ago. The evidence for this includes slabs of red ochre excavated at Blombos Cave in southern Africa along the Indian Ocean, several of which were deliberately inscribed with curious designs that seem to represent a matrix or web or grid-like net.

What these cryptic symbols meant to those distant peoples cannot be interpreted with accuracy by us today, but the symbol itself, once created, is repeated endlessly in rock art from that time forward in Africa, Europe, Asia, Australia, and in North, Central, and South America as well. Cross-cultural studies carried out with the last makers of traditional rock art, the !Kung San Bushmen of the Kalahari, reveal that this grid or net or web is a visual phenomenon seen by entranced shamans on their journeys to the "other world."[2]

In the Western world, when we hear the word "shaman," most of us tend to conjure up an image of a masked and costumed tribal person dancing around a fire in the dark, involved in some sort of mysterious ritual accompanied by drum beats. But inside that cultural shell of mask, costume, and ritual, there is a woman or a man with a set of very real skills.

All true shamans are gifted visionaries—masters of the trance experience who are able to achieve expanded states of consciousness in which they can dissociate their focused awareness away from their physical body and enter into an alternate reality in which they typically encounter numerous archetypal and transpersonal forces who are waiting just offstage of the human drama, yet willing to help us in various ways. Indigenous peoples and modern mystics alike usually refer to these forces as spirits, and specifically as "helping spirits."

Among those forces frequently met are the spirits of nature, including the spirits of animals and plants and elementals, many of whom have been in service to humanity as helpers and guardians for tens of thousands of years. But visionaries of all traditions and religious faiths also encounter the spirits of their ancestors and the higher, compassionate angelic forces, many of whom serve us as spirit teachers and guides. Among them can be found our own transpersonal spiritual aspect—our higher self or oversoul of which we shall make mention.

Perhaps the most fundamental shamanic principle from which everyone may benefit is that in the shaman's practice, there is no hierarchy or set of dogmas handed down to supplicants from some higher religious authority complex. Shamanism is the path of immediate and direct personal contact with Spirit, deeply intuitive, and not subject to definition, censorship, or judgment by others. On this path, each seeker has access to this transcendent connection and all that this provides.

Interestingly, shamans tend to run in families, a fact that has led some investigators to suggest that there may be a genetic foundation recorded in our genetic code—our DNA—for the ability to expand our conscious awareness and achieve trance. It has also been suggested that a substantial portion of the human population may possess this genetic program—a hypothesis supported by some anthropological field observations. Among the traditional !Kung San Bushmen of the Kalahari Desert in southern Africa, for example, up to 50 percent of the typical hunting-gathering band could "shamanize" when the need required it.[3]

This suggests that the ability to engage in the visionary experience of the shaman may be one of the hereditary birthrights of all people everywhere, revealing that one does not have to be a traditional tribal person to engage in this ancient mystical experience.

The shamanic tradition, like all the other mystical traditions, transmits a body of information and techniques that allows novices to re-create and directly experience the abilities of their ancestors, and if we go back far enough, we are all descended from indigenous ancestors, Westerners and non-Westerners alike, and they all had great shamans.

It was through rediscovering and re-experiencing our ancestors' abilities that each new generation took on the responsibility to perpetuate and refresh a continuously recreated tradition, even adding to and changing the accumulating spiritual treasure of wisdom and technique. For it was always in this way that the visionary path remained vital and meaningful to those who chose to walk it across time.

The growing body of cross-cultural ethnographic literature about shamans and their unusual abilities confirms that the path of direct revelation is part of the cultural heritage of all people, although it was largely lost in the West for more than a thousand years due to ruthless and systematic suppression by our organized religions.

Introduction

This book, with its accompanying CD, may provide you with a body of sacred knowledge that contains the key with which to open your own inner, visionary doorway into the sacred realms.

Needless to say, it's not designed to replace the years of disciplined practice engaged in by the mystics of the world's many visionary traditions. But it may serve as a catalyst in helping you embark upon an extraordinary spiritual adventure, assisting you by double-clicking the "visionary program" on your own inner hard drive, your DNA, so that you may find your way into connection with your own inner sources of wisdom, power, and healing.

It is this extraordinary ability to access the transpersonal worlds that sets shamans apart from all other religious practitioners, something we shall examine in greater depth in Chapter 1.

Chapter 2 will explore the experiential centerpiece of the shaman's practice—the shamanic journey. It will also provide us with guidance in how we may utilize techniques such as monotonous, rhythmic percussion (provided by the enclosed CD) combined with our focused intentionality, a safe and time-tested meditative way to access the sacred realms of the spirit world. And as we shall see, this practice is anything but primitive.

The shamans of antiquity were the first brave pioneers to begin to investigate our human body-mind-spirit complex as well as the nature of reality, both outer and inner. Their discoveries, derived from the path of direct revelation, have served as the foundation for who we are and what we have all become today.

In our time, the shaman's path could be equated with the path of the modern visionary—one that is very much available to all who care to walk it. In making this assertion, our thoughts turn inevitably toward our reconnection with Nature, for Nature is, and forever has been, the gateway into the invisible worlds that are all around us, and all the time—something we shall touch on in Chapter 3.

Surprisingly, most are able to do this on the first attempt, and once "there," most are able to establish connection with those inner sources of wisdom and power that the traditional peoples call spirits, returning with accounts that would pass muster at any aboriginal campfire. Accordingly Chapter 4 is focused upon how we may work with Nature, including influencing the weather.

Motivated by the need to more fully understand what happens in these transcendent realms of experience, as well as how to access them, Chapter 5 will explore the nature of ceremony and ritual, allowing us to investigate aspects of the ancient technology of transcendence that was pioneered tens of thousands of years ago by the shamans of the Upper Paleolithic Period—the Late Stone Age.

In Chapter 6 we will focus upon this process with respect to dreams, the nature of dreams, and the experience of dreaming-while-awake. In Chapter 7 we explore other ways of accessing the sacred realms of the transpersonal, specifically through the creative arts that may serve us as another experiential bridge, revealing the various paths on which the participants in our gatherings across the years have been able to find that inner doorway through which they were able to make the journey into the dream worlds while very much awake.

Allow us to add here that our many years of facilitating such groups have left us deeply impressed by the internal consistency of these experiences as well as by the transformative effect that they obviously confer upon the experiencer. We have watched, fascinated, as our inner explorers are led toward an inescapable conclusion shared by the indigenous peoples—that the fabric of reality is composed of a multi-leveled vibrational field that is conscious and intelligent—and when conditions are favorable, this field can and does respond!

In Chapter 8 we will explore how we may work with sound and light, and in this respect, we can observe with confidence that all authentic visionaries speak about the spirits, and the states of consciousness that become available to us through them, as "the light beyond the form, and the formless beyond the light."

In Chapters 9, 10, and 11 we will discuss the death experience as a passage on the one hand and as a necessary and omnipresent force in all the changes that take place throughout our lives on the other. The fact remains that ten out of ten of us are going to go through this experience, and it was always the job of the traditional shaman to scope out the dimensions of the death transit, returning to describe where we will find ourselves and what we will experience at this stage, enabling these gifted visionaries to prepare the living for the experience of dying.

Chapter 12 is dedicated to our children as our connections with our future—bringing us into considering who we are today, who we are becoming, and what our responsibilities toward our communities and our children may be. There is absolutely no question that they, and their descendants, are our future.

In Chapter 13 we will describe ways of working together in community from the shamanic perspective, and Chapter 14 will summarize and reveal who and what we are becoming as members of the transformational community. We will present an overview of those values and beliefs that we all hold dear, allowing all of us to understand more fully what the nature of our path through this life may be—the path on which we most likely chose to walk before we came into this life.

And finally in Chapter 15 each of the contributors, including ourselves, will share our visions for the future of the work, including the challenges that we face as practitioners and teachers and the insights we have gleaned along the trail.

HOW TO WORK WITH THE BOOK

Shamanism is a spiritual practice in which you can have immediate and dramatic access to the wealth of knowledge, as well as the power and protection, of the helping spirits. It is a practice that is difficult to learn by simply reading about it. You must experience it for yourself.

Accordingly, all the contributors have shared different meditative exercises that are seeded throughout the chapters to help you engage in the shamanic path of direct revelation. As some of these exercises involve shamanic journeying, we have included a journeying audio with recordings of drumming, rattling, and different instruments that will allow you to work with the practices in this book. Instructions for shamanic journeying are given in Chapter 2.

HOW TO USE THE AUDIO PROGRAM

The audio that accompanies this book includes four tracks. Track 1 is five minutes of whistling or rattling that will give you time to prepare for your journey by taking some deep breaths, setting your intention, and giving thanks to the helping spirits for the assistance you will receive.

Track 2 is a fifteen-minute session of drumming and rattling with a return beat. Track 3 is a fifteen-minute session of monotonous rhythm involving the *berimbau* (a Brazilian stringed instrument), rattles, and Australian click sticks. This track also has a return beat. And Track 4 is twenty-five minutes including a return beat involving three drummers.

As you practice journeying with this audio component, you might notice that you prefer one track to another. Some people like a longer session for journeying and some a shorter. Just notice what works best for you. All the tracks are played at a steady rhythm, the theta brain wave rate of four to five beats (or shakes) per second.

One very important note: Don't listen to the audio program in your car or while operating machinery. The audio is designed to help you achieve the shamanic trance state, and for obvious reasons this is not appropriate while driving a car or mowing the lawn.

ENTERING THE CIRCLE OF ELDERS

In summation, we are going to explore the path of direct revelation as a personal practice in this book, and we will discover that it is essentially an ancient form of meditation. When practiced with humility, reverence, and discipline, it can give the spiritual seeker virtually instant access to many varieties of experience, including connection with the spirit world if that is his or her intention.

Speaking as highly educated persons who unknowingly stumbled onto this path decades ago, we can affirm with confidence that the ability to achieve the shamanic state of consciousness is a learned skill that improves with practice. We also know with absolute certainty that once the "visionary program" on our DNA is activated, this can enable us to ascend toward the luminous horizon of our personal and collective destiny as we travel across time in a completely new way.

The wise ones among the tribal people would agree with this statement because they know a great secret: any human activity or endeavor can be enormously enhanced through utilizing and eventually mastering this sacred technology. Another secret: if we go back far enough (as Hank has said), we are all descended from indigenous tribal ancestors—Westerners and non-Westerners alike—and they all had great shamans.

The six contributors to this book are all accomplished professionals, writers, and fully initiated shamanic practitioners and teachers who walk the path: Sandra Ingerman, a psychotherapist; Hank Wesselman, a paleoanthropologist; Tom Cowan, a historian; Carol Proudfoot-Edgar, a psychotherapist; José Stevens, a psychologist; and Alberto Villoldo, a medical anthropologist. We all have different voices and we all bring our shared wisdom for you to soak up and work with in the ways that speak to you.

Together, we will shed light on how the shaman's time-tested method may help us awaken from the consensus slumber of culture at large, enabling our life experiences to manifest as a true hero's journey, as an upward quest that may lead us into the direct experience of spirit—a journey that becomes possible for us through the doorway of the heart.

It is through this gateless gate that we can personally experience reunion with unlimited power and a mysterious, godlike mind. Once in connection, we then know with certainty that no holy words or books, no secret ceremonies or rituals, no spiritual leaders or gurus or faiths can do this for us.

Once the higher evolutionary functions are triggered within us, some mysterious predetermined schedule is set into motion, activating a program that cannot be given to us by any outside agency. This is because most of us already have it.

In the chapters that follow, we will explore a path on which we may learn something truly interesting about ourselves, as well as where we are headed.

We are excited about this literary project, for in it we will be sharing different perspectives on how we as modern people may walk the shamanic path. We are also providing you with a book filled with enlivening narratives and spiritual practices that you may incorporate into your life—ways that may help you establish your own bridges into the sacred realms.

To create a readable narrative, we could not represent every shamanic tradition. Rather we are giving you a sprinkling of stories from some traditions, providing you with a foundation that hopefully will lead you onto your own path of direct revelation.

Now imagine yourself sitting in a circle of elders, listening to each share his or her stories and teachings with you. As you listen to and absorb their words and thoughts, you will inevitably cross-reference them with your own experiences and your own dreams ... and this is good medicine indeed.

Chapter 1

What Is Shamanism?

AN INSPIRED VISIONARY

Shamanism is the most ancient spiritual practice known to humankind and is the "ancestor" of all our modern religions. As a method, it is a form of meditation combined with a focused intention to accomplish various things, as will become apparent in this book. As a spiritual practice, shamanism can become a way of life that may utterly transform the one who practices it.

The word "shaman" comes from the language of the Evenki peoples, a Tungusic tribe in Siberia. This is a word whose meaning has to do with esoteric knowledge and extraordinary spiritual abilities and as such a shaman is often defined as an intermediary between the human and the spirit worlds. In shamanic cultures, the word "shaman" has come to mean "the one who sees in the dark" or "the one who knows."

Most of what we know about the ancient practice of shamanism comes from ethnographic fieldwork done among the tribal peoples of

Siberia, Asia, Africa, Australia, Greenland, from North, Central, and South America, and from cultures of northern Europe such as the Saami of Lapland. The existence of technical papers, monographs, and books about shamanism is only expanding, but suffice it to say that we have come to know that the shaman is a universal figure found in virtually all the world's cultures.

There are certain commonalities in a shaman's worldview and practice across the world that allow us to make certain broad generalizations about shamanism. In the majority of indigenous cultures, the universe is viewed as being made up of two distinct realms: a world of things seen and a world of things hidden, yet no distinction is drawn between them. A shaman understands that these two worlds present themselves together as two halves of a whole. The shaman is the inspired visionary, a man or a woman who learns through practice how to enter into this "world of things hidden," and once there, he or she typically encounters extra-mundane personalities or archetypal forces that the indigenous peoples refer to as spirits, ancestors, and even gods.

All true shamans—and by association all authentic modern visionaries—discover, often by accident, that they possess the ability to go into trance very easily, which allows them to make contact with this hidden world. Trance in this sense is not an unconscious state, but rather a state of expanded consciousness in which the individual intentionally dissociates his or her focused awareness away from the everyday world and enters into an alternate or parallel reality that indigenous peoples regard as "the spirit world."

Through practice, shamans develop relationships with these spirits, allowing them to do various things, initially on behalf of themselves, and then increasingly on behalf of others. What sorts of things?

For example, a shaman may help restore power and focus to a person who has experienced a traumatic loss experience. Shamans may extract spiritual blockages from the body that can manifest as a physical or emotional illness. A shaman may engage in healing work at various levels—physical, mental, emotional, and spiritual—and he or she may be able to access information from "the other side" through enhanced powers of intuition, a practice known as divination. Some shamans are also gifted in their ability to guide the souls of the dead to where they are supposed to go in the afterlife through psychopomp work. Some are even accomplished at reweaving and restoring the fabric of a person's damaged soul through the practice of soul retrieval.

Alberto Villoldo, a medical anthropologist of Cuban ancestry who has spent much of his life living with and studying with the indigenous peoples of the Andes, emphasizes the fluidity a shaman has between the human and the spirit worlds. He points out how much of the modern world dismisses the existence of these other realms:

> The shaman is one who mediates between the visible world of form and matter and the invisible world of energy and spirits. For the shaman there is no supernatural world. Only the natural world exists, with its visible and invisible dimensions. In the last century, science has dismissed the mysterious world of the ancients. Scanning electron microscopes allow us to peer deeply into the heart of matter, and invisible "spirits" have been catalogued as merely microbes. Space telescopes show us that beyond the blue sky there is no Heaven, only the vast darkness of space.
>
> The quest for a single explanation that could unite all the observed forces at play in our universe left the arena of religion and spirituality behind and has become the search for the Unified Field Theory. Today, many of us who study shamanism feel compelled to describe our art and practice using the language of quantum physics in an attempt to give the shamanic arts more credibility. I believe that doing so actually devalues the 50,000-plus-year tradition of shamanism.

3

On the contrary, we are noticing that although science is often used to describe certain "otherwordly" phenomena, the practice of shamanism is ever so slowly working its way toward the mainstream. Carol Proudfoot-Edgar, a shamanic practitioner of Native American ancestry who has walked the path for more than two decades, has noticed that shamanism is growing in popularity:

> When I began teaching shamanism in 1989, shamanic practice was a relatively new concept to most of those I encountered in my workshops. Twenty years later, it is rare for me to meet someone who has not heard the term "shamanism." Of course, I tend to encounter only a select group of the population, but this marks quite a change in the collective consciousness.
>
> Shamanism is part of the popular culture. There is a surfeit of material available on the subject. Novels with a shamanic focus have become bestsellers, and television features more and more programs with an altered-reality theme. Medical school programs provide courses on what is called alternative or complementary healing: these courses usually have components on shamanism. This change has happened so fast that it is hard to remember that looking at the universe from an alternative point of view wasn't as popular in recent history.
>
> I find this transformation of shamanism from an esoteric to an accepted source of wisdom to be true no matter where I travel in the world. My dreams inform me that we are gathering wisdom in various forms in order to co-create the next reality, the next stage of planetary evolution. We don't know yet what paradigm or what visions will be decisive in this evolutionary process, but we do know that the practice of shamanism will offer us essential understandings by which to guide our actions.

AN ANCIENT SPIRITUAL PRACTICE

Shamanism is the first spiritual practice of humankind and dates back tens of thousands of years. The fact that this spiritual practice of working in relationship and in partnership with the helping spirits is being widely used today speaks to the potency of the work. Alberto Villoldo, who has long studied the origins of shamanism, says that a lot of what we know comes from human excavation:

> Among the early evidence we have of shamanic practices is an elaborate Neanderthal burial found at a cave at Shanidar, in the Zagros Mountains of Kurdistan in northern Iraq. Here a male in his late thirties was interred in a fetal position more than 60,000 years ago, his body deliberately covered with flowers. Many of these plants, including yarrow, cornflower, St. Barnaby's thistle, grape hyacinth, and woody horsetail, are known to have medicinal properties. So even prior to the appearance of modern humans *(Homo sapiens)* shamanic practices seem to have existed.

Hank Wesselman, who has conducted excavations as a paleoanthropologist in Ethiopia, notes that we have been able to discern a lot of detail about ancient shamanic practices from archeological finds. From his ongoing research within the field of human evolution, he has been able to track shamanic burial traditions:

> There actually exists an even earlier mortuary practice that was revealed in the recovery of a fossilized human skull more than 165,000 years old from the Middle Awash region of northern Ethiopia, a modern *Homo sapiens* cranium (with some residual archaic features from our more primitive forebears) that reveals the distinctive patina and polishing of the bone surface associated with ongoing human care and handling over long periods of time. This

scientific evidence, without doubt, exhibits a reverence for the dead that has obviously been part of human prehistory for a very long time.

Although there must have been a great deal of ritual in ancient shamanism, Alberto Villoldo points out that it is important to note that shamanism is not so much a religion as a spiritual path. There is a difference. He also notes that a shaman is much more than a mystic. He writes:

> Spiritual practices are based on personal, direct experience and are replicable by others who choose to undergo the practices and initiations. Religion, on the other hand, is based on belief. My teacher, an old Indian man from the high Andes, once said to me as we were walking the edge of Lake Titicaca, the Sea on Top of the World: "Religions are simple concepts of spirituality: values, standards, truths, *principles* communicated in the form of a story that uses poetry and metaphor to illustrate its wisdom." These stories have been told and retold until even their embellishments acquire profound meaning and the figurative is taken literally and the lessons are lost. And my friends, the priests, were devoted caretakers of a story that was not their own.
>
> But the shaman is the *author* of the story, the myth-maker. El Viejo's (my teacher's) faith was based on his own experience of the divine in Nature. A shaman stands with one foot in this world and one foot in the world of spirit. With the priests and in the schools, I learned the lessons of others. With El Viejo, I learned my own lessons.
>
> El Viejo showed me that the consciousness that creates our waking reality is a universal consciousness, a vast sea that is navigable. Most people are content to live on the land and they know this sea only as it appears to them

from their own shores. But it is possible to know it fully, to navigate the sea, to cross it, to immerse yourself, to let it wash over you, to discover its depths. The shaman is one who has learned how to swim and how to sail, how to navigate through this sea and return to its shore. And to communicate its wonders to his people.[1]

Shamanic training often follows the path known to the Greeks of old as the "journey of the wounded healer," during which the shaman developed his or her powers and abilities as they self-healed. I believe that it is essential to heal yourself before you start ministering to others. But the shaman is different from the mystic, who can also go through a process of healing and discovery of the invisible world of energy and spirits. The shaman is dedicated to service to his or her community, whereas the mystic is dedicated to dwelling on their experience of the divine.

My teacher believed that the new shamans, the new caretakers of the Earth, would come from the West. "The Indios (indigenous people) do not have the power and stamina to hold the world in their prayers anymore," he once said to me. "Many of our peoples have lost their souls. The hope lies with you and your children."

Shamanism, although it may contain ritual and elements of ritual, is therefore not a religion *per se*. And although both the practice and the study of shamanism is growing in popularity, there also remains a lot of confusion in the Western world between the kind of work done by shamans and the work done by a "medicine man" or "medicine woman." This blurring of terms exists because every shaman is a medicine person but not all medicine people are shamans. In fact, most medicine people are not shamans but fulfill social roles more like those of priests in our stratified religious complexes in that they function primarily as ritual or ceremonial leaders. A Plains Indian medicine woman, for example, may perform ceremonies or healing work through her knowledge of medicinal plants, but she does her main work here in the world of things seen.

The distinguishing feature of shamanism versus other spiritual practices is that shamans do their main work in the spirit world where they may accomplish various things through their relationships with their helping spirits. Shamanism, correctly understood, is about working with those transpersonal forces we call spirits. Sanctified by their initiations and furnished with their guardian spirits, the shaman alone is empowered to venture into the mystical geography of "the world of things hidden."

THE SHADOW SIDE OF SHAMANISM

Even though a shaman is not the same as a sorcerer, the work of a shaman is not always an altruistic practice. José Stevens has studied for more than a decade with the shamans of the Huichol Indians in central Mexico's Sierra Madre mountains. As one who walks the shamanic path and who also works with the corporate world, he has seen the darker or shadow side of shamanism first-hand:

> There are many so-called shamans or their equivalents who engage in sorcery, fight with other shamans, and are rather dangerous individuals who will do harm to others for hire. Shamanism is not all love and light, and anyone who has spent time in indigenous communities where shamanism is practiced knows this fact. They also know that all shamans are not equal in terms of their values or their skills, and these differences are what distinguish a great shaman from a mediocre one.

Sandra Ingerman, who has been working to bridge the ancient healing tradition of shamanism into modern-day culture, stresses how crucial it is to self-reflect and acknowledge the darker side of shamanism:

> It is important to address the shadow side of shamanism, for with any practice that works with the principle of power there will be those who abuse the power. You can see this in many areas of life, not just with shamanism.
>
> To avoid falling into the trap of using shamanism to manipulate others and life, it is important to do your personal work. Many people who engage in spiritual practices think they can avoid looking at how their ego and emotions influence their life.
>
> In my writing and teaching I encourage people to address and work with their emotions and also to take care of their physical body. As we engage in spiritual work we must balance our efforts with all aspects of ourselves—body, mind, and spirit. My desire as a woman and as one who has dedicated her life to being in service to the planet is to communicate shamanic principles to the general population. For one, the feminine principle of the visionary steers us away from seeing the practice as a series of techniques and methods to seeing shamanism as a way of life in which we honor and respect the spirit that lives in all things. This way considers how you live to be more important than what you do. This also embraces a way where you continue to be in awe and wonder for the life-giving power of earth, air, water, sun, and the beauty of who you are as well as the nature of life that surrounds you.
>
> This includes the principle of experiencing "power with" versus "power over." We do have to address the issue of the shadow side of shamanism to be truthful about the work. And at the same time our focus is on how you can use the practice of shamanism to live your life from your highest potential. And that includes how to enjoy yourself.

When we continue to work on our egoic and emotional states, we can stand strong in our integrity and work from a place of love, compassion, and wisdom versus using manipulation to get what we want. In this way we can truly walk the path of a shaman who works with the forces of the universe in order to create positive change on the planet.

THE VALUES OF AUTHENTIC VISIONARIES

José Stevens emphasizes the importance of having the solid personal foundation of an authentically initiated visionary in order to be of service to one's self and one's community. Here he outlines three ingredients, or visionary values, that characterize a true shaman:

> All shamans work with spiritual allies in order to suspend or alter the world of ordinary reality to achieve specific goals. However, a person's motivations are the key to what type of shaman he or she may be—a dangerous one to be avoided or a wonderful enlightened teacher who is a true healer.
>
> A shaman's effectiveness depends on three key ingredients: perception, values, and maturity. Once you understand these three interrelated ingredients, you have the key to understanding visionary shamans and people everywhere.
>
> What a shaman values and is interested in determines what the shaman perceives and vice versa. If the shaman is compassionate and kind, he or she will both perceive and channel the compassion of the universe. If the shaman is suspicious and angry, he or she will perceive enemies and attack everywhere, thus attracting the dark side of the force.
>
> This of course is true of all of us. Similarly, what shamans value and then project into the world, they create. If a shaman is run by a distorted ego, then that shaman will be oriented toward personal fame, fortune, and status and thus will perceive only those methods of achieving these things. Such a person will be aware of all the ways her or

his ambitions are thwarted and will become competitive and ruthless.

Finally, what a shaman values and perceives is based on his or her emotional and mental maturity or the levels of self that can be linked to specific developmental and psychological stages—starting with infancy and ending with elder-hood.

When you observe indigenous cultures where shamanism is practiced, there are different roles the shamans serve in their communities and different behaviors shamans exhibit. José Stevens continues on and explains this:

There may be many varieties of shamans in the communities composing the tribe or nation of that people. The Navajo (Diné), the Inuit, the Huichol in Mexico, and the Shipibo of the Peruvian Amazon are all classic examples of shamanic cultures. They all have medicine men and women who doctor the people, perform ceremony, preside over rites of passage, and so on. And all of these societies have five distinct classes of shamans who perceive the world in dramatically different ways.

First, there are those shamans who are considered dangerous, who perform the dark arts, send curses, make people sick, and cause death and misfortune to come to the people. They do this because in an infantile way they are truly fearful of the environment and strike out against it. They do not operate in a conscientious way, and they are willing to do anything to anyone if it so pleases them. These shamans operate from a survival-oriented value system.

A second class of shaman is one who never innovates but does everything by the book or according to strict tradition. They may be effective in some ways but unable to cope with anything they have not seen before or have not been taught to do. They are often willing to use their shamanic powers for harm or to hire themselves out to place curses on others. They like to be big fish in a small pond and are gratified by intimidating or exercising power over others. We can call these shamans "rule-oriented" because they follow the rules implicitly and condemn those who do things in a more spontaneous or innovative way. This class of shaman is not necessarily motivated by ambition.

A third class of shaman is primarily interested in reputation and in being the most important individual in the clan, tribe, or nation. They like power and are willing to use it competitively to dominate and control. They take an instant dislike to anyone who takes the attention away from them and will seek to ruin or run off another shaman who competes with them. They often have big egos and like the rewards of their work, including sex, money, or power. These success-oriented shamans like to keep their knowledge secret and avoid teaching others so they can be seen as the only ones who know.

The second class of shaman doesn't necessarily have ambition but is focused on following rules and will not innovate. The third class of shaman can be innovative but will do anything to boost their reputation.

There is a fourth class of shaman who is dedicated to service and works hard for the benefit of his or her people. They can be called upon at any time to help those in need even if there is no pay or remuneration involved. These shamans are generous, kind, caring people with considerable skill in their profession. They make good teachers and will go out of their way to educate and teach those who are interested in learning from them. We call these shamans "relationship-oriented" because they care about others more than they do about building a reputation or holding power.

The fifth class of shaman has all the traits of the fourth class, only they are self-realized masters of their trade. They do not necessarily follow the rules because they know how to do things their own way and do not rely on the traditions to bolster them. These individuals are truly powerful and can bend the laws of the universe at will. Instead of performing long rituals or ceremonies appealing to the spirits, they can simply pass their hand over someone and heal them. These shamans are rare, but they do exist in every culture. We call these true spiritual masters or visionaries "philosophically oriented" shamans.

Perhaps this way of looking at shamans can help us to understand their differences and see how they can behave (or misbehave) so differently. These differences do not apply only to shamans but to people in many walks of life: business people, helping professionals, homemakers, and modern visionaries.

EXERCISE: **FIVE TYPES OF SHAMANS**
Consider the various teachers you have encountered through-out your life. See if you can evaluate their approach to their trade and to people according to José Stevens's five different shamanic categories. You may find this rather eye-opening.

DIFFERENCES BETWEEN PRACTICING SHAMANISM AND BECOMING A SHAMAN

All authentic visionaries agree that it is destiny that calls one to be a shaman; shamanism is a calling. This is not a profession that one seeks out.

There are many experiences of initiation that may sculpt a person into a shaman or a visionary. Typically an individual in an indigenous community will have a psychological crisis or near-death experience, or they will be called by a voice from nowhere. Sometimes a person will have a visionary visit from a powerful spirit-being or ancestor in their dreams or endure a life-threatening illness or a psychotic break. With these experiences the initiate often achieves a momentary state of transcendence and experiences oneness and unity with the All. Among both Western and Eastern mystics, such experiences are termed "authentic non-dual mysticism."

Having had such an experience usually profoundly changes the experiencer and how they live thereafter. A direct experience of the true source from which everything originates changes them utterly, and they then achieve a vastly different perception of life. Often, such initiates return from their visionary adventures with healing and clairvoyant abilities. This is especially true of those who have recovered from a life-threatening illness.

It is because of this that the shaman is known in many cultures as the wounded healer. Having been grievously wounded or ill, and then having recovered after being at the point of death, the shamanic healer-to-be typically experiences a profound and enduring sense of compassion for the suffering of others. It is from this heart-centered compassion that he or she may become a great healer and even a world redeemer.

As we've already mentioned, there is a resurgence of interest in shamanism in Western cultures, and increasing numbers of people are rediscovering the ease with which shamanic practices can be learned and practiced, bringing them into their lives for personal healing and problem-solving.

An important point needs to be made here. Bringing simple shamanic practices into your life is not to be confused with being called to be a shaman. We can all bring shamanism into our lives for personal growth and healing, but that does not necessarily mean that we are called to become shamans. Becoming a shaman is a practice that typically develops slowly across months and even years of time—a period during which many difficult initiations can literally sculpt a person into being a great healer and visionary for the community.

In virtually all indigenous traditions one never calls him or herself a shaman. This is seen as bragging about one's power. There are no certificates or diplomas in the shaman's world, and whenever you brag about your power, you tend to lose it. The term "shaman" is a mantle bestowed upon the practitioner by his or her community and is based upon the individual's abilities to stand and deliver the goods as a healer or as a diviner of information on behalf of others. José Stevens points out that although it is difficult to come up with a concrete definition for a true shaman versus a healer of another kind, making these distinctions is not always what is most important:

> The debate about the exact qualities of a shaman, who can be a real shaman, and how one becomes a traditional shaman is an endless one for both academics and those who are interested in splitting hairs. We can leave these discussions for others so that we can focus on what is of greater importance—how to use the ancient art of shamanism for practical visionary purposes in our daily life without actually being a traditional shaman.

Throughout recorded history, on every continent, people have rubbed elbows with shamans. Although not everyone who was guided or healed by a shaman became shamans themselves, they certainly learned enough to apply with great advantage the shamanic knowledge they had gained to influence their societies and cultures everywhere.

Consider, for example, the effect on society at large of the literary works of Lewis Carroll *(Alice's Adventures in Wonderland)*, J. M. Barrie *(Peter Pan)*, and modern writers such as J. R. R. Tolkien *(The Lord of the Rings)*, Carlos Castaneda *(The Teachings of Don Juan)*, and J. K. Rowling *(*the *Harry Potter* series*)*. All these writers are visionaries who understood the dimensions and the frequencies of the shaman's world from direct experience.

People with shamanic knowledge have become healers, hunters, architects, builders, artists, actors, politicians, writers, or great leaders of their people. They are not shamans *per se,* but they certainly are aware of shamanic principles, attitudes, perspectives, and ways of seeing, which enable them to not only survive but to thrive and to extend their knowledge to others.

For these reasons, ongoing generations have been powerfully influenced by the path of direct revelation of the shaman, and this is reflected in all our religious traditions, our philosophies, and our practices—from Taoism to yoga, from sports to religion, from government to business, from intuitive wisdom to healing. It is not an exaggeration to say that without the visionary influence of shamans and shamanic practice, the human race would probably not have survived.

The truth is that humans everywhere share basic traits, abilities, and skills with shamans—visionaries who simply develop these skills to a masterful degree through their initiations and subsequent training. Although shamanic abilities usually remain latent in many people, everyone can make use of the shamanic approach to life because it is natural and basic to all humans everywhere on the planet. All humans have intuitive abilities at some level. All humans are capable of achieving trance states, comforting others, performing simple ceremonies or rituals, influencing others, dreaming, and molding their environments based on their imaginations and their visions.

A TECHNOLOGY OF TRANSCENDENCE

Many who study and practice shamanism consider the ancient methodologies developed and refined by traditional shamans for achieving expanded states of awareness to be a form of technology—a technology of transcendence, or a technology of the sacred—in which each new generation has the responsibility to perpetuate and refresh a continuously recreated tradition, even adding to and changing the ever-accumulating trove of wisdom and technique. For it was in this way that the ancient path of the shaman remained immediately meaningful and vital to those who practiced it.

Indigenous people know everything there is to know about their surrounding environment, and if there are psychotropic plants growing nearby, the ritual use of hallucinogens derived from these "plant teachers" is sometimes utilized for the purpose of expanding awareness and accessing the sacred realms.

Many investigators such as Terence McKenna and Ralph Metzner, the anthropologists Michael Harner and Luis Eduardo Luna, and researchers such as Graham Hancock, Rick Strassman, and others have suggested that the use of plant-derived psyche-delics (the word "psychedelic" means "mind manifesting") may have been responsible for the beginnings of spiritual awareness in human beings. This implies that hallucinogens may have actually served as the genesis of religion in the first place, which explains why these "plant teachers" are often referred to as "entheogens" (meaning they "release the deity within").

The growing literature on hallucinogens reveals striking cross-cultural similarities in the reported effects of these natural substances on human consciousness. These include the capacity to channel the energy of the universe, discover the most profound secrets of Nature, and acquire wisdom that may be used for magi-cal, medical, and religious purposes. But equally powerful and far more widespread are the psychological and physiological technol-ogies developed by traditional shamans for altering consciousness and re-patterning it in specific ways. These highly effective tech-niques include fasting and sleep deprivation, physical exhaustion and hyperventilation, and the experiencing of temperature extremes during rituals of purification such as the sweat lodge and the vision quest.

It is also generally known that the intensely physical stimulus of monotonous drumming and rattling, combined with culturally meaningful ritual and ceremony, prayer and chant, singing and dancing, can be equally effective in shifting consciousness into visionary modes of perception. Not surprisingly, the use of drums and rattles by shamanic practitioners is a universal practice.

Until relatively recently, most Westerners have tended to regard these technologies of transcendence as mysterious, paranormal, even pathological, and so some of us, in ignorance, still respond to the idea of expanded awareness and connection with spirits with fear and rejection.

By contrast, in a traditional indigenous society such technologies are valued and treated with great respect. Each girl and boy grows up in relationship with elder ceremonial leaders and shamans who are able to access expanded states of consciousness intentionally for the benefit of themselves, others, and the entire community. In these societies, everyone knows that virtually anyone can learn how to access sacred states of consciousness to some extent. They also know that some of us are real naturals at it.

Whether the practitioner of shamanism is a traditional shaman or you, it is important to understand that the nature of the visionary experience can be determined, to some extent, by our intentions, by our belief systems, and by the nature of the experience—the set and setting—in which we find ourselves. Taken together, these parameters serve as "patterning forces" that can shape the visionary experience once the initial state of consciousness has been destabilized by the drum, the rattle, or the hallucinogen, if one is used.

Furthermore, as most modern shamans are well aware, the psychedelic is not necessary. The ritual use of hallucinogens is only one facet of the path of direct revelation. Many of us who have never experienced mind-altering substances have had spontaneous visionary experiences that have carried us through some unknown inner window into the realms of things hidden, which are so well-known to tribal peoples.

These technologies—from drumming to hallucinogens, from sleep deprivation to singing and dancing—enhanced by ceremony and ritual, collectively and singularly, are being reworked in our time into something entirely new, something that reflects who we are today and what we are becoming. Hence, there's the need to achieve an upgrade that reflects who we are as modern people in our own time.

THE PATH OF SHAMANISM TODAY

At one time, the way of the shaman was practiced exclusively by hunters and gatherers in order to find food and other resources for their tribal bands. They accomplished this by achieving expanded states of awareness in which they could connect with the spirits of the animals that they needed to kill for meat and hides. Connecting with the spirits was about correct protocol—about getting permission to—and this always fell within the realm of the shaman. In traditional cultures, there were often just a few people in a community who were able to step into the role of the shaman to ask the transpersonal forces with whom they were in relationship for sustenance, support, guidance, and healing on behalf of others.

By comparison, today we see a wide range of people integrating shamanic practices into their lives. More and more people of today's world are beginning to realize that the path of direct revelation brings us into relationship with the worlds of things hidden, through which we may learn that everything that exists is alive and has a spirit (and a voice), and that there is a field of energy that connects us to all of life. This awareness of interconnection is shared by tribal shamans at one end of the human continuum and by quantum physicists and Zen Buddhists at the other.

In today's Western world, our culture is very much defined by a pervading sense of fear, competition, separation, and alienation, and increasing numbers of people are experiencing a deep internal need to feel direct, transpersonal connection to the web of life—and through this web to each other. The visionary practices of the shaman bring us into this connection, awakening us once again to the knowledge that we are more than a body with an ego.

Many have observed that we are actually spiritual beings inhabiting a body. When we engage with the compassionate spirits directly, everything—both healing and the assistance we need in life—becomes available to us. Dealing with these transpersonal others is not about worship. It is about relationship.

THE TOOLS OF THE VISIONARY

Through the experiential centerpiece of the shaman's practice—the shamanic journey—we can tap into our extraordinary nature as well as the nature of everything around us. But, before taking this journey, we must prepare ourselves by making sure we have the things we will need for the road ahead. As such, José Stevens makes it clear that taking the shamanic path requires acquiring those innate "tools" needed to reawaken so that we can successfully navigate that path:

> Shamans the world over understand that humans are born with a toolbox preloaded with three exceptional tools for healing and accelerating freedom. These user-friendly and quite ordinary tools are often overlooked as being simplistic and not respectable, especially in the fields of science and Western psychology. Even those who know about the tools tend to misinterpret them and fail to understand their true significance. Shamans, however, make a point of developing and mastering these tools because they know that they are the keys to a shaman's power.
>
> Like wrenches or drills, these shamanic tools do not work all by themselves; they simply sit in the toolbox patiently waiting to be picked up. In other words, these tools only work if backed by intent and used with deliberate focus and willingness. Shamans know that if there are other agendas—if the mind is preoccupied with hostility, martyrdom, competitiveness, and the like—the tools will be difficult to use effectively. Nevertheless the tools are so powerful that just by one's willingness to pick them up, they will begin their extraordinary work.

Gratitude

The first shamanic tool in your toolbox is gratitude, an attitude and an orientation designed to open the heart. Gratitude is a high-level amplitude that is designed to open portals, windows, and doorways into the spirit world.

Shamanically speaking, in everyday reality (what a shaman considers a consensus dream), Spirit is not apparent to the naked eye. In fact this ordinary world of stone, flesh, and fiber is often quite depressing because it involves frustration, pain, and frightening circumstances and events. The pleasures are more often than not offset by the stress of everyday survival and the constant mind chatter that is enough to drive even the most stable person crazy.

Yet a shaman knows that just behind the movie set that makes up the world, Spirit lies camouflaged, bursting with light and freedom, waiting to be recognized and resourced. Spirit has cleverly arranged portals in strategic places that if opened, lead directly past the everyday outer world into the power of the inner reality where all answers lie and where all problems are revealed to be the illusions that they are.

These portals are literally everywhere, but there are primary ones that are so close to us that they are practically impossible to miss. The one most accessible is the heart, which lies smack in the middle of your chest just below your chin, and it is so accessible that you can easily reach your heart with your hands. When you speak it vibrates, and when you breathe it is massaged all around. It is hard to comprehend how you would miss it, yet we do ignore it every day unless we should have the misfortune of a heart attack.

Shamans "see" through their hearts. Shamanic tribes like the Maori of New Zealand believe that the physical world we experience is actually a projection coming from each individual heart. The Mayans and the Q'ero tribe in the Peruvian Andes have their own versions of this basic understanding. Their shamans know that self-importance, created by the ego, is dedicated to keeping the powerful heart portal closed off enough to prevent Spirit from shining through.

The ego accomplishes this by shutting down the heart to the point where the portal remains closed to the spirit world. The portals pop open only when a certain amplitude is reached, so keeping it below a certain level prevents opening. What keeps amplitude low are all the familiar maladies: fear, hostility, self-importance, depression, self-doubt, cynicism, and frustration. Because of these, most people's hearts are shut down most of the time, which feels bad in the chest and cuts off the main avenue of escape from pain and suffering—an open heart.

Gratitude counters these ploys by the parasitical false personality and raises the amplitude high enough to begin the heart-opening process.

EXERCISE: FOR GRATITUDE

When you feel down in the dumps, it is difficult to spring into complete gratitude for anything, so you have to work up to feeling grateful little by little. Turn your thoughts toward something you love, something that is innocent and deserving of gratitude such as your cat, dog, or parakeet. Allow yourself to feel a little bit of gratitude for this creature in your life. Then begin extending this feeling to other beings or things to which your false personality (usually created by your ego to deal with life at large) has a hard time objecting—sunlight on a cold morning, hot chocolate, or shade in the hot sun. Now remember that the ego has no effect whatsoever on Spirit. Our false sense of self can only affect our spiritual side temporarily, so the advantage of gratitude is that it engages Spirit by coopting the personality, thus separating it from the clutches of self-importance.

The gifts of gratitude are plentiful. Here are just some of the things gratitude will do for you:

1. Gratitude reframes experiences so that what seemed like a problem or something that hardly mattered becomes a good thing instead. For example, when you are grateful for the tree in front of your house, you stop ignoring it and focus instead on its gifts and benefits to you. The world instantly becomes a better place because you are grateful.

2. When you are grateful, you connect to something outside of yourself and recognize that you depend on others or on Spirit. In other words, having gratitude instantly switches your orientation away from self-importance and self-referencing and reminds you that we are all interconnected.

3. Gratitude reinforces what is benefiting you because Spirit is always inclined to give you more of what you recognize and acknowledge. The greater your gratitude, the more you will receive that for which you are grateful.

Seeing

The second great shamanic tool in your toolbox is seeing. For a shaman, "to see" is to cut through the veils of ignorance, the false appearance of the world, in order to see clearly into the true nature of Spirit as it manifests through all of reality. In other traditions, it is known as forgiveness or compassion. Seeing is the most powerful method of releasing blame, guilt, and shame.

Seeing ends the war within us just as it resolves conflicts with externals and paves the way for our cooperation and extension. The false personality tries to convince you that forgiving or having compassion is a weakness, that you are setting yourself up to be taken advantage of again. It also tries to get you to believe that you and others have no value and therefore deserve ill treatment or self-loathing. Seeing makes these terrible perceptions impossible. Seeing the truth provides relief from the terrible stress of guilt, and this results in shifting our energy in a way that allows us to open the heart and other portals to the world of spirit.

When shamans speak of "seeing," they are actually talking about clearing away the projections and distorted thoughts of the conscious mind onto the world at large and all its forms.

Shamans and visionaries know that these projections are blinding and the source of endless misunderstandings and assumptions based on fear of the unknown.

Seeing means that we are perceiving the truth, and therefore there is no room for hostility, blame, fear, or set decrees. How does this take place? When we really see in the shamanic or visionary way, we know that we are Spirit and that we have simply become confused and are lost in appearances for awhile. The false personality is only a delusional construct created by the egoic self; in dealing with the world, it tends to create lies in which we and others take refuge.

Shamans say that when people learn to see they are able to access almost limitless power because they realize they are intimately connected to the vast web of life. For the shaman, seeing into the true nature of reality and the self is a great power; it is a required skill for self-realization and ultimately enlightenment.

In order to reconnect with the tool of seeing, you might integrate these seeing practices into your daily life:

EXERCISE: FOR SEEING

1. First, we must prepare for our exercise on seeing. Think of something you did as a child for which you were punished or that you felt bad about at the time. Maybe you took some money from your parents or stole some candy. Maybe you tortured an insect or beat on your brother or sister. From your perspective now, you can see that this was simply an error of an ignorant child and most likely you have long since let go of feeling guilty over this. Often the memory simply elicits compassion or a little chuckle as time has healed it. If there is any sense of guilt left over, don't use this event in the exercise. Find something that was very minor.

2. Take a moment to envision a time in the future when you have grown in compassion and wisdom, perhaps a time when you are a self-realized being. From that point of view, look upon yourself today with the same kind of compassion that you now look upon yourself when you were three years old. You will no longer blame yourself or feel guilt over whatever you now hold over your head. Since your essence exists

outside of time, it is already capable of that kind of neutrality. See if you can tap into that perspective for a few moments. This is seeing.

You can also try this exercise using the image of someone you blame or someone from whom you feel very separate. Try to see this person from a future reference point, looking back at the now as if it were the distant past. Realize that at some point in your evolution you will let this blame and separation go because it only prevents you from achieving limitless power.

Blessing

Now we come to the third great power tool in that shamanic toolbox that everyone has from birth—the ability to bless.

In general, people do not know their function as human beings, and it never occurs to them that their job is actually to bless the world. Many people have been taught to bless their food; they consider a blessing to be a few words mumbled over the meal that lack heart and meaning. This is hardly what shamans mean by blessing.

Blessing is the act of recognizing that Spirit is coming through what we are witnessing or experiencing. It is recognizing and acknowledging the grand flow of Beingness that is present as what we eat or what we see as the landscape, or what we experience in making love, cleaning, or creating with tools. That Beingness flows through the landscape, through our bodies, through each moment of now and gives it indescribable vitality and life force. Yet the physical plane appears to most as a camouflage universe where Spirit does not appear to exist.

Shamanically speaking, many of us respond to the physical world by assuming a deep hypnosis, a deep sleep where we no longer recognize that Spirit is present. Not only do we go to sleep, but large parts of the world may temporarily go to sleep as well. So it is our job to wake up and to awaken all that is around us.

This act of waking up could be called "blessing the world."

Many of us have been taught to believe that only people who have gone to seminary or special training programs to become ministers, rabbis, priests, imams, or shamans have the right to bless. We invite the ordained individuals to come before us and bless ceremonies, fields, businesses, projects, meetings, and banquets, and we bow our heads while they talk to Spirit for us.

This is not a bad practice, but it is extraordinarily limiting. Many of those we invite to do the blessing for us are the most asleep of all, revealing that no one can do the work of blessing for us. Each human comes with that capacity, with that ability, and with the responsibility to bless.

So what happens when we bless, and how do we go about blessing in an effective way?

To bless means that you become conscious that you are alive and that Spirit is flowing through you. This realization allows you to see that Spirit is flowing all around and that what is coming through you is coming through everything and that it is all the same. When you see or sense or feel this you merely say something like, "I am Spirit. Let us awake. Let us awake Spirit in everything I see."

While saying this you can look around and bless with your hands and arms outstretched, waking everything up to the incredible power of Spirit that flows through everything with great passion and peace. In response, everything receives a boost, everything celebrates, everything is grateful, and everything forgives its slumber. There are few practices as powerful as this awakening. If you want to add a little something else to your blessing, you may bestow upon everything that you are experiencing or witnessing the gift of well-being from the bottom of your heart.

You might say, "I give you great happiness and love. May all who come here or pass this way be blessed with joy, abundance, and wellness." What you give is what you get, so make sure you give the best you can imagine.

Blessing is incomprehensibly powerful and is perhaps the greatest tool of all because it is the pathway back to Spirit. Yet it is hard to bless if you have no gratitude and you have not *seen* the need to forgive. These three tools work together as a powerhouse trio. They are all important characteristics of the physical universe: Truth, Love, and Energy—or Yachay, Munay, and Llankay, the three Andean shamanic principles of living. Each tool works with all three components. Gratitude recognizes truth, transmits love, and enhances energy. Seeing tells the truth, generates love, and liberates energy. Blessing acknowledges the truth, radiates love, and releases phenomenal energy.

Always remember that you have shamanic tools resting in your toolbox. They require deliberate use to become effective. These three tools, when used regularly, are all that is needed to become liberated and self-realized and to gain mastery over life. Why wait?

EXERCISE: **FOR BLESSING**

First thing in the morning, go outside and practice blessing the sky, the Earth, the trees, or whatever elements are most visible. Then go on to bless your family, your colleagues, your students, your teachers, and all of their communities as well. Bless all their relations and on and on until everything and everyone has been included. Bless Spirit and don't forget to bless yourself. Now experience how you feel. Do you feel more expansive, more powerful, more happy, more on the right path? This is the true shamanic way—and the way of the visionary.

Chapter 2

The Shamanic Journey

One of the most common ceremonies in the practice of shamanism is the shamanic journey. Shamanic journeying is a method of direct revelation and it is the experiential centerpiece through which shamans make contact with their helping spirits to access empowerment, personal guidance, and healing help.

Shamans and visionaries know that the nonordinary reality of the "world of things hidden" is really a kind of a parallel universe to the one in which we live. The Australian aborigines call the nonordinary realms the "Dreamtime." It is also referred to as the "Other World" in Celtic traditions, or as the "Spirit Worlds" by many indigenous peoples. As we have mentioned, these hidden realities are inhabited by compassionate, helping spirits, who may offer guidance and healing on behalf of all life on Earth.

ACHIEVING A SHAMANIC STATE OF CONSCIOUSNESS
Modern shamans will often use some form of monotonous, driving

percussion, such as drumming or rattling, to achieve an altered state in which visionary experience becomes easily accessible. In Australia, shamans play the didgeridoo and/or click sticks, and some traditions, like the Bön Po shamans of central Asia, ring bells. The Saami people of Lapland and Norway use monotonous chanting called *joiking*.

Research has revealed how the steady beat of the drum affects the brain to achieve visionary experience.

When we are asleep and dreaming, our brain typically fires nerve impulses in the delta wave state at 1 to 3 cycles per second, or hertz (Hz). When we awaken, the brain typically moves rapidly toward alpha brain waves that fire at 8 to 13 Hz. This is a resting state in which we are awake and aware, but we're not doing anything in particular. When we have our first espresso of the day, our brain waves move into beta-wave states that fire at roughly 13 to 20 hz. These are high-frequency brain waves in which we concentrate, do our main work, and in which we function for much of our waking reality.

During a typical day, the left hemisphere of our cerebrum, the higher brain that is the seat of our intellect, functions mainly in these beta waves. The right brain, which includes much of our emotional and intuitive functions, remains in alpha waves. We typically shift back and forth between these two halves of our brain, so we experience surges that involve our work in the world (beta) and rest breaks for creative reflection (alpha).

Below the alpha state and above the delta state of sleep is an in-between zone commonly called the theta-wave state in which the brain typically fires nerve impulses between 4 and 7 Hz. This is a deep, reflective, dreamlike state that has been recorded in Zen masters and transcendental meditators, in psychics and trance mediums, and in shamans in altered states of consciousness.

In the theta state, the visionary experience is easily accessed, a fact that has been confirmed by investigators of higher states of consciousness. The drum or rattle is of great service in accessing this visionary state of consciousness. As we listen to the monotonous percussion of the drum or the dry whisper of the rattle, beaten or shaken at four to seven beats or shakes per second, both halves of the cerebrum entrain to this rhythm, essentially following the sonic driving of the drum or rattle. In response, both halves of the brain synchronize, slow down, and start firing impulses at 4 to 6 Hz, thus allowing an individual to enter the theta state of light trance. It is precisely here that we may find that numinous space between the worlds.

THE SPIRITUAL WORLDS

The shaman is a universal figure found in all the world's cultures, and all shamanic traditions agree that the spiritual worlds are organized into three primary levels: the Lower World(s), the Middle World(s), and the Upper World(s). There are also numerous levels within each world. Although descriptions of these nonordinary worlds are subject to cultural interpretation, we will describe some of the more common shamanic experiences of them.

The Lower World is usually reached in the visionary trance state by journeying through a tunnel or some other kind of cylinder-portal that leads into the earth. This world is very tangible to the shaman and is characterized by caves, seas, dense jungles, forests, and deserts. The beings inhabiting the Lower World are the spirits of animals, trees, plants, and rocks as well as humanlike spirits who are connected with the mysteries of the earth. The Lower World is formed by the dreaming of everything that makes up the mosaic of what we call Nature.

The Upper World is experienced as above where we are now, and it is more ethereal than the Lower World. The lighting is bright and can go from pastels, to gray, to complete darkness. In these regions, many encounter crystal cities, cloudlike realities, and a variety of higher spirits. The Upper Worlds are formed by the dreaming of the higher gods and goddesses, the ancestors, the ascended masters, and the compassionate angelic forces that are willing to be of service to us—most often as teachers and guides.

The Middle World is the hidden reality, or the dream aspect, of the everyday world in which we live. This means that the Middle World has an ordinary and a nonordinary aspect to it. In the Middle Worlds the shaman can travel back and forth in time. It is also a place where the shaman can journey to look for lost and stolen objects, to perform long-distance healing work, and to find the souls of the recently deceased in order to help them across to where they are supposed to go in the afterlife.

It is also the level where the shaman can speak to the spirits of the rocks, trees, plants, wind, water, fire, and earth, because everything that exists in our physical world has its corresponding dream aspect in the Middle World of dream. Here, the shaman can also communicate with "the spirit that lives in all things." We should add that the Middle World is also inhabited by a variety of spirits some refer to as "the hidden folk"—the faeries and elves, the trolls and forest guardians who are present in so many myths and stories. The hidden folk remind us of a magical time in our lives before the veils between the worlds were closed to us through cultural conditioning.

HELPING SPIRITS

The Lower and Upper Worlds are transcendent realities where there are a variety of helping spirits who can assist the shaman in facilitating the healing of individuals, the community, and the planet. There are also helping spirits in the Middle World that are the nature spirits we described above. Who are the helping spirits in the Lower and Upper Worlds? The most common types of spirits who work in partnership with the shaman are animals, plants, or spirits who appear as teachers in human form.

The ones who appear as animals, or as combinations of animal and human form (therianthropes), are commonly known as "power animals." These spirit guardians provide us with power, protection, and support. Shamanic cultures believe that when we are born, the spirits of at least two power animals volunteer to remain with us to keep us emotionally and physically healthy and to protect us from harm. These animal spirits are akin to Christianity's guardian angels, and to the teddy bears and stuffed animals children bond with—they are much more than toys.

According to the shaman, the power animal is not the spiritual essence of one animal but rather the essence of the group oversoul of the whole species. So we don't have the spirit of a bear, a kangaroo, a snake, or an elephant as a power animal. Rather, the spirit of all lions, all owls, all eagles, provides us with protection and power.

It is also understood that one power animal does not have more power than another. The spirit of mouse has just as much power as the spirit of tiger, but mouse does have different qualities and abilities as well as different *lessons* to teach from those of tiger. Once in relationship with a human, each power animal serves as a teacher in the initial stages of a fellowship in which it reveals to its human friend the qualities and abilities—or as some would say "the medicine" that it carries.

Trees are also seen as guardian spirits so we often use "power animals" and "guardian spirits" synonymously. Plants seem to provide help for very specific issues, so shamans often work with hundreds of plant helpers in their healing work.

It is not uncommon for people to have a guardian spirit or power animal such as Pegasus or a griffin, dragon, or unicorn. Although these creatures are mythical in our everyday reality, in the Lower Worlds they are real, and this is where they come into our conscious, mythic awareness. The same holds true for species that lived in the past and that are now extinct. The group oversouls of these creatures still exist in the Lower Worlds, so some people may have a dinosaur, mammoth, or saber-tooth tiger as a power animal.

The practice of shamanism is one of direct revelation and therefore there are no rules as to how many power animals or guardian spirits a person may have. We have as many animal spirits as volunteer themselves. We also discover through relationship with them that the animal and tree spirits may have very individual and specific teachings for each person.

Instead of pulling a power animal card or an angel card from an oracle deck and then reading in a book (or on the card) someone's opinion of what that being's message is for you, you can journey into relationship with that animal power or angelic symbol and then ask it directly why it has come to you and what its guidance for you may be.

The other type of helping spirits that shamans work with are teachers who appear in human form. In the cultures of the past, these typically were the gods and goddesses of the Upper Worlds; religious figures such as Apollo or Athena, Jesus of Nazareth, Gautama the Buddha, or Yogananda; or one of our own ancestors who wishes to be of service to us.

These helping spirits act as intermediaries between us and the power of the universe. They have compassion for our pain, suffering, and confusion, and therefore they volunteer their help. These spirits could be called archetypal forces or even transpersonal forces that are ancient human experiences, and as the shaman/visionary journeys back and forth between this world and these numinous realms, he or she gains access to different helping spirits on the different levels of the Lower and Upper Worlds. Through direct experience, the visionary learns where and to whom to go to for different types of help, yet, as José Stevens points out, it may be that the various helping spirits are all part of one source:

> Perhaps not all shamans would agree, especially those of a more traditional perspective, but the main shamanic consensus is that all helping spirits are extensions of the One Spirit, whom we could call the Great God, Atman, Allah, the Tao, All That Is, or whatever you like to call the almighty. What this means is that all the helping spirits are literally aspects of the One, and as such, they are everywhere and available to support, inform, and assist us in myriad ways.
>
> Helping spirits come in two primary categories, those who have a physical form and those who do not or no

longer do. Those that have a physical form are called "elementals" and may include representatives from the plant, animal, or mineral kingdoms, or an element such as the wind, fire, water, a mountain, a canyon, a cave, a star, the moon, and so on. Those helping spirits that do not have a physical form may include what have popularly been called angels and beings who can take on a physical appearance temporarily but do not operate out of the physical universe. They may include great teachers such as Buddha, Jesus, Mary, Quan Yin, Yogananda, St. Germaine, and Babaji.

It is important to understand that allies from both categories often work in tandem—so that it may be that if a shaman works with an eagle ally he is also working with Christ-force energy. Yogananda likes to work with hummingbird, Mother Mary with condor, Quan Yin with pelican, and so on. Of course these partnerships may vary shaman to shaman, person to person, culture to culture.

INSTRUCTIONS FOR THE SHAMANIC JOURNEY

In this section we will provide step-by-step instructions for how to perform a shamanic journey, including how to prepare for such a journey, setting the intention, traveling to the Lower World, Middle World, or Upper World, and how to return and interpret your journeys.

Before you begin your journey, disconnect your phone or turn off your cell phone. It is best to do journeywork in a place where you won't be disturbed by loud noises or others around you. Find a comfortable location. You can journey lying down or sitting up. Remember you will have a clearer journey if you are alert.

The rhythm for journeying can be quite relaxing. If you fall asleep, that's fine. You just went too deep. You need to find times of the day that are best for you to journey when you are not too tired and when your conscious mind is not as active.

It is good to put something over your eyes to block out the light. Shamans learn to see in the dark. This is because it's a lot easier to perceive subtle imagery on a dark visual field. In this vein, some people close their shades and curtains. Do what is comfortable for you.

Some people light a candle in the room they are journeying in. The fire of the candle represents the light of Spirit. Some like to burn incense, which helps to create sacred space.

Once you have prepared the room, you might want to dance, sing, chant, or do some movement to get the oxygen moving through your system. This helps to quiet the mind filled with thoughts that prevent you from sinking deep into your journey. Taking the time to dance and sing will allow your heart to open. The spirits communicate with us through our hearts, and we "see" in our journeys through our hearts.

You might choose to use the CD with headphones or you might feel the rattling or drumming more in your body by using external speakers. It is important to remember that you are in full control of yourself in the journey. You can go up or you can go down; you can talk to the animal spirit who comes to you or you may back away from it. You cannot control what spirits come to meet you or what they may say to you, but you can choose how to react, or even whether to stay in the journey. In this sense, shamanic journeying is different from daydreaming, in which you make up who the characters are and all the conversation that follows.

As you begin the journey, listen to the drums, rattles, and other instruments on the track and intentionally breathe into your heart. Imagine your energy moving from your head into your heart. Place your hands on your heart, and as you breathe feel your hands moving up and down with your breath.[1]

Setting an Intention

In a typical shamanic journey, we set our intentions in advance, and these goals set up a resonance, a drawing power, that will bring us toward that which we are seeking. For example, you might ask for guidance in your life, in your relationships, your health, or your work in the world. Or you could ask a question that will help you grow and evolve, such as "What do I need to focus on in my life right now so that I may maximize my potential at all levels—to make a living on the one hand as well as work on my life lessons on the other?"

Other questions might be "How might I resolve the issues around (this) relationship?" or "What do I need to do in order to achieve a successful outcome in my business?" You will note that we are not using the word "should" as in "should I do this?" or "should I do that?" in an intention-setting question. According to Hank Wesselman, it is important to stay away from "should" when asking a question of your helping spirits:

> The word "should" will not bring you into connection with that which you are seeking—intuitive guidance. This is because it's the job of your conscious self, your intellect—or as the Hawaiian *kahunas* would put it, your mental soul—to make decisions. Spirit (your higher self or oversoul) will not do that for you because it is not its function to tell you what to do. But Spirit will provide you with an expanded perspective of the issue at hand, whatever it may be—and in my experience, my spirit teacher/ oversoul inevitably provides me with "the spread." For example, Spirit might tell me, "Well, you could choose this option ... or that possibility ... and if you do, this (or that) might happen."

Your intention for a shamanic journey can also involve questions for friends, clients, and for the communities that you live in. In doing so, be aware that there are ethical issues in the practice of shamanic journeying. It is important to make sure that you have permission to journey on behalf of someone else. If that person has not given you permission to work for them, do not proceed with the journey, because this could be considered a violation of that person's boundaries. Correct protocol involves the person in question asking for you to work on their behalf, because the simple act of their asking is the beginning of their healing process.

Sandra Ingerman shares the ethics of journeying on behalf of someone else. As she points out, there are ways to ask for help from spirit guides when you feel compelled to journey for someone but that person has not given you permission:

> If you are having a problem with someone, don't journey on what *their* problem is. Instead, you might journey on what you need to know for yourself in order to heal the relationship or the issue in question. Don't ask your helping spirits to send help to those who haven't asked for it. Asking for help is a key part of any person's healing process, and so it is they, not you, who must set the process of their own healing into motion.

Another way to entreat the help of your spirit guides is by asking them to perform a healing to alleviate the pain of a physical or emotional issue with which you are dealing. In traditional cultures, a person in need of help went to the community shaman and asked for healing, and the shaman intervened in the spiritual realms on this person's behalf—and this was where the healing happened. In other words, you do not always need to journey for yourself. At the same time, many people report profound healings when they ask a helping spirit to perform a healing on them. It is definitely a journey worth trying.

Entering the Trance State

There are many ways you can use the CD for journeying. To begin, select one of the tracks, then lie down on a blanket on the floor, or sit in an armchair in which your entire body is supported comfortably. Close or cover your eyes with a bandanna or eye pillow, then listen to the sound and focus your attention fully on your goals for the journey. Then you can open the portal by intentionally shifting your conscious aware-ness from "here" to "there," wherever "there" may happen to be.

Keep in mind that the shaman/visionary is always aware, to some degree, of what is going on around their physical body while journeying. You will be able to hear the sound of the drum, rattle, or other instruments throughout your journey—as well as the heater going on, the aircraft flying over your house, or the dog barking next door.

Allow the rhythm to carry you into the spiritual worlds and later to call you back. Each track ends with a short period of rapid drumming, rattling, or use of click sticks and will assist you in refocusing your awareness back to your physical body and in directing your brain waves back from theta toward alpha.

You could also drum or rattle for yourself while journeying. In this way you can choose the speed of the beat that works best for you.

Journeying

In response to the constant barrage of movies, television, books, and computers, we've become a visual culture. Life becomes richer when we can see, touch, taste, and smell, and when we can listen to the sounds of music and nature. As we learn how to use all our senses in this world, as well as in the inner worlds of things hidden, our intuitive abilities strengthen. The same holds true when we use all of our senses in a journey. This allows us to enter fully into the journey.

In shamanic literature, the words "shamanic seeing" refer to seeing with our hearts rather than with our eyes. The shamans and visionaries of all the world's traditions know that the spirits make contact with us through the doorway in our hearts, and what we receive through that channel is sent to our higher mind, our intel-lect, our egoic soul or self, which then thinks about it, analyzes and integrates it, and makes decisions about it.

Thus, our minds interpret and assign meaning to what is "seen" through the heart, and rather than being the villain to be demonized and dismissed, our egoic self is to be trained, uplifted, and brought into a new level of awareness.

Everything that happens or is perceived in a shamanic journey is part of the answer to the question we have asked, and the intellect's job is to assign meaning to the symbols that we have perceived and to figure them out. The heart and the mind are thus in relationship. In fact, your ego/intellect/higher mind is the source of your intentionality as well as your creative imagination. It is your inner chief, your inner director, who, influenced by beliefs and convictions, steers you successfully (or unsuccessfully) through life.

Even if you open all of your senses in your journey, you are still bound to face certain challenges as you begin journeying. Furthermore, we all have our own way of receiving information in our journeys. We live in a visual culture, and so people expect to see images in their journeys. Some people do see images, but others hear their spirits talking to them or experience their journey as sensations in their bodies. If you are not seeing images in your journeys, then notice what you are hearing or feeling. You may be more "somatic" in how you access information rather than visual.

Another common challenge is that you may experience mind chatter that gets in the way of being able to enter into the shamanic state of consciousness. Shamans typically prepare to enter into trance (nonordinary states) by singing and dancing to create a sense of separation between what is "now here," and what is "in there." In this sense, it is good for each of us to find ways to quiet the mind. Perhaps begin your journey by taking a walk, singing, or dancing in order to move your energy away from your mind and into your heart.

It is easy for us to get lost in the challenges of our analytical thinking, a product of our egoic self that creates doubt. The higher mind often proclaims (at times with considerable authority) that we are making up our journeys.

When doubt happens, we must have compassion and patience with ourselves and think about the nature of the culture in which

we were raised. Most of our parents did not talk to us about helping spirits, and in fact, the presence of spirits was not part of our
experienced reality in daily life. We were socialized in a manner
that excluded the presence of helping spirits or the existence of the
invisible realms. Think of how many years you have lived closed off
to these worlds—and of how it is only now that you are discover-
ing that the precious worlds that we visited often as children do in
fact exist.

When your analytical mind interferes during a journey and
tells you that you are inventing all of your visions, Sandra suggests
that you agree with your mind and keep on journeying. If you try
to battle your mind, you will spend the whole journey in internal
dialogue.

According to Hank, it is also important to note that it is not
the analytical mind that is doing the journeying, but another part
of the self:

> The aspect of the soul that journeys is not the higher mind
> or intellect. It is the "body mind" or the "physical soul" or
> what some call the "subconscious" of which we shall say more
> shortly. Enough to say here that this physical soul observes,
> and it sends what it perceives to the mental higher intellect
> that judges and "assigns meaning to." Yet this physical soul/self
> is not creative; it cannot make anything up. It simply observes
> and remembers what it has experienced for later reflection and
> analysis by the higher mind as they are forever in relationship.

As we journey and observe the results of our journeywork
over time, patterns become apparent to us—life lessons that may
have extraordinary, even vital, meaning to us. This is why the shamanic method of direct revelation has been passed down across
the millennia as a time-tested system. For example, in traditional
societies, if the shaman could not divine the location of potential
food sources or perform successful healings, the community did

not thrive, and if the individual could not divine the sources, as well as the nature, of their personal obstacles, he or she did not survive.

In addition to learning how to shut off the intellect, there are several other things you can do to ease into your journey.

EXERCISE: JOURNEYWORK

1. As mentioned before, always set an intention. This helps maintain focus and concentration so that you don't get distracted by mind chatter and the ever-present concerns of ordinary life.

2. Get in touch with the best times for you to journey—i.e., when you are fresh, awake, and rested and when your mind is clear and uncluttered by details.

3. Nourish yourself prior to journeying. What you eat and drink affects your concentration and your ability to stay alert. Discover what kind of diet supports your adventures into the invisible worlds. If you eat a heavy meal before you journey, it might be difficult to concentrate and stay alert. It is also best to avoid drinking alcohol before journeying for the same reason. It tends to cloud the mind.

4. Intentionally breathe into your heart to help shift your awareness from a mental state to a heart space. The spirits communicate with us best through the doorway in our hearts, so at the onset of a journey set your intention to see through your heart into the inner realms of spirits and visions.

5. Find someone else to journey for you. Sometimes you may be too emotionally attached to the outcome of a decision or issue, or you may be in an emotional state about something in your own life or the life of a loved one. In such a case, you might not be able to move yourself (i.e., your higher mind) out of the way in order to access the spiritual guidance accessible to us through the heart. At these times, it might be better to find an accomplished journeyworker who could journey for you.

6. Be innovative and try different ways of journeying. You might be surprised by how much using your body can strengthen your shamanic practice. As Sandra has noticed, there might be a way to go about your journey that will help release the higher mind.

Lying down and journeying is actually not a traditional way of working.

I find that many people cannot journey while lying down as this way does not promote full disengagement from mind chatter and full engagement in the spirit realms. Many people need to move and dance their journeys or sing/chant their journeys.

Many people find that standing or sitting while drumming or rattling for themselves helps them engage more in the spirit realms. I have stronger journeys when I drum for myself, and I often like to sing my journeys while chanting about what is occurring.

There is no right or wrong way to journey. Shamanic journeywork is a learned skill that improves with practice. Allow your journeys to the different worlds to be fluid and organic, and try to pay attention to what you perceive. Explore different levels of the other worlds, both up and down. You will meet new helping spirits along the way who will be willing to guide your path of discovery in your life. In fact, they will be honored to be of service to you in this way. Be an adventurer and accept the love, wisdom, and healing that the spirits and the universe are trying to share with you.

Think of your shamanic journeying practice as a work in progress. It will deepen and grow as you continue the practice. The key is to practice, practice, practice and to establish a long-term relationship with your helping spirits with whom you develop trust and good communication skills over time.

***

You might want to experiment with a longer drumming session or even drum for yourself, dance, or sing, as this can help a person move more out of their higher mind space into the inner realms. Have some patience, and don't give up. We live in a culture of instant gratification, but the shamanic journey requires a patient disposition. It is a learned skill that improves with practice.

If you lose your concentration during your journey, make sure you are breathing into your heart and keep repeating the intention for your journey until you are back on track.

The First Journey to the Lower World

For your first shamanic journey, you might wish to visit the Lower World to meet up with a helping spirit—one who will provide you with power, protection, and support. Often this spirit will appear as a power animal.

Before you begin your journey to the Lower World, think about a place in Nature that you can use as your entrance. Traditional ways of going to the Lower World are through an opening in the earth such as a cave; a body of water such as a lake, river, stream, or waterfall; a tree trunk; a volcano; or a hole in the ground. Any way you can get into the earth is fine. You don't need to have been in this opening before. Just know that it exists in ordinary reality. Hank notes that wherever this place may be, reflecting on it should conjure a feeling of serenity:

> In my training workshops, we call this place the Sacred Garden, the memory of a place in Nature with which we have formed a connection during life, a place where we feel a sense of peace and tranquility. At the beginning of our journey, we simply refocus our awareness into our memory of this place so that it can become a kind of Grand Central Station for our shamanic journeywork into the Lower or Upper Worlds from then on. It can also become our personal place of power and healing in the dreaming of the Middle World.

When the drumming or other instruments on the accompanying CD begins, visualize yourself as you enter into the earth's opening in your place in Nature. You will find yourself in a transition that might appear as a tunnel or cylindrical portal of some kind that leads you into the Lower World. Follow the tunnel down and then out into the light while you keep repeating your intention to yourself, i.e., "I wish to meet a spirit helper in the Lower World."

As you emerge into the Lower World, look around you. Ninety-nine times out of a hundred, someone or something will be waiting there for you.

If it is an animal spirit, ask it, "Are you my power animal?" This will give you information on how your power animal communicates with you. It might answer you telepathically, or it might lead you somewhere or show you something. Once you have an answer from your animal, start to build a relationship, ask it a question, or ask it for healing help.

You might also ask the animal if there is anything you need to know at this time in your life. This is why it may have come to you—to convey that information. If it indicates that it is *not* there as a helping spirit for you, ask it to take you to your spirit helper, and it will. This is probably why it has come to you.

If you want to visit other levels of the Lower World, you can keep looking for openings into the earth. Ask your new friend to accompany you—to guide you into other levels of experience— and it will. Stay in the journey until you hear the call to return: the period of rapid drumming, rattling, or click sticks on the CD. If for any reason you want to come back sooner, just retrace your steps, turn off the CD, and you will be back.

The Upper-World Journey to Find a Teacher
For another one of your first journeys, you might choose to visit the Upper World. To journey to the Upper World, you also want to begin at some location in Nature, but this time you will need

to access the world above. Some shamans use the tree of life and journey down the roots into the Lower World or up the trunk and into the branches to travel into the Upper World.

Other traditional ways of entering the Upper World are by climbing a rope or a ladder, jumping off a mountain, going up on a tornado or whirlwind, climbing over a rainbow, ascending the smoke of a fire or chimney, or finding a bird or something that flies to take you up. Any way you can get up is fine. Some people have even used a hot air balloon to access the Upper World.

Before the music for journeying begins, find a place in Nature in which you can experience yourself standing. Once the drumming or other instruments begins, notice what appears as a way to transport you up. You can ask the power animal friend you met in the Lower World to accompany you, and it will.

If you are seeing planets and stars as you journey upward, you are still in the Middle World. Keep focusing on your intention—to meet a teacher in human form in the Upper World. There will be some sort of transition that you go through that will let you know you have entered the Upper World. For some people it is a layer of clouds or fog. It is not a barrier; it is just a transition. Remember the story of Jack and the Beanstalk—where Jack climbs up the beanstalk and encounters a cloud layer before he enters a new world? That's the transition space.

Allow yourself to go through the transition into the first level of the Upper World. Notice if there is a teacher waiting there for you. If so, you might ask this being if it is your teacher. If you get an affirmative answer, ask your teacher a question that is important to you right now, or ask for healing help.

If your teacher is not waiting for you at the first level, keep searching through the different levels of the Upper World until you find someone. Once again, stay in the journey until you are called back.

In meeting your teacher, Hank teaches that we can reconnect with our higher self in the Upper World:

We may reconnect with our transpersonal aspect, our higher self, or what some call our oversoul in the Upper World. This meeting can be extraordinarily life-changing as we may find that our "spirit teacher" is actually ourself—but ourself in the Upper World rather than ourself in ordinary reality.

Many understand the oversoul to be our immortal-self aspect—the source of our intuition and our inspiration, the higher self that may communicate with us through dreams and visions, ideas that appear in our minds in response to need, those hunches and slips of the tongue. It is the "god-self" or "angelic self" or "transpersonal witness" who loves us unconditionally, who listens to our prayers and works in mysterious ways.

In the Hawaiian kahuna tradition, this oversoul is called 'Aumakua. *Makua* means "parent," and *'au* means "time," making this transpersonal being our "parent in time." The Hawaiians often refer to their 'Aumakua as plural—as "the ancestors," and through journeywork we usually discover it to be a mosaic composed of many personalities. Through relationship, we often discover these personalities to be our past selves in former lives, revealing our oversoul to be our immortal aspect traveling across time, growing, increasing, and becoming more in response to what we do and become in the Middle World of physical existence.

In this sense, the oversoul field that resides in the Upper World could be thought of as one of our ancestral lineages, revealing that we have three ancestral lines: our mother's lineage, our father's lineage, and our own personal ancestral field.

The Middle World

The Middle World is the nonordinary realm of the world we live in. As is explained in this section, you can journey in the Middle

World to communicate with Nature. Middle World journeying was traditionally used for finding lost or stolen objects. To do this, instead of journeying to the Lower or Upper World, you would experience yourself within the journey moving outside of time and searching your house or outside for something that is missing. You will be able to travel very quickly through space, rather than being limited by your physical body.

You can also journey to the sun, the stars, and other planets in our solar system. In the Middle World we also have access to the faeries, devas, and elves, who are collectively known as the spirit people.

For a journey in the Middle World, you can visualize yourself walking out your front door and traveling to some aspect of Nature with which you would like to communicate—a place that you know or have visited during your life—a place where you feel connected, at peace, and in tranquility. Sandra, who emphasizes the connection to Nature in her shamanic practice, stresses the importance of communicating with the natural world as part of your journey:

> In shamanism everything is alive and has a spirit. In our time many of us no longer remember how to communicate with plants, trees, rocks, or weather spirits, yet we can talk to them in their nonordinary aspect. In this way we can speak to the divine in all creation.
>
> Pick something in Nature you would like to communicate with such as a favorite tree or plant, the moon, a rock, or a cloud. When you begin your journey, experience yourself walking out your front door and meeting the spirit you wish you to speak with. Once you finish with your conversation you can return to ordinary reality.

Another way to reconnect to the natural world is by focusing on the image of the Sacred Garden, in other words, a natural place that holds great resonance for you, which Hank teaches about. According to Hank, this Sacred Garden operates by four primary rules:

1. Everything in your Sacred Garden is symbolic of some aspect of yourself or your life experience.

2. You can communicate with all the elements in your garden for personal divination and greater understanding.

3. You can change your garden. This means you can use your creative imagination to add things that you wish to have there—a waterfall, a great tree, a standing stone, or a bed of flowers. Conversely, you can delete elements that you do not wish to be there. You can drain that swamp or clear a beach of rocks to allow you to enter your turquoise lagoon more easily.

4. When you change your garden, some aspect of you or your life experience will change in response. This is how true magic works.[2]

Shamanism is a life-long spiritual practice where you can journey into the hidden worlds time and time again. At yet another time, you can reverse these journeys and ask to meet a teacher in human form in the Lower World and a power animal in the Upper World. You can also continue journeying to visit the spirit of a tree or plant or an elemental spirit in Nature with which you wish to communicate in the Middle World. Or you might choose to do a Middle World journey to find a lost object.

The Return
When it is time to return from a journey, there will be a change in the monotonous beat recorded on the CD. The signal to return begins with four sets of seven beats. At this point say "thank you"

and "goodbye" to whomever you are talking to. Even if you are not with a helping spirit, say "thank you" and "goodbye." The reason for this is that "goodbye" signals to your psyche that something has ended. Saying goodbye will help you feel more grounded when you return from your journey.

Next there will be a shift in the beat to a more rapid percussion for a minute of so. During the rapid return beat, slowly retrace your steps back to your starting place. When you hear the last change in beats, you may take off any eye cover you were using and open your eyes. Then reflect on your experience and take notes.

Coming back from a journey has to do with your intention and making a choice to do so. You can always take another journey at another time if you didn't finish getting all the information you need or if you want to visit another realm of the inner worlds.

Take notes after you return so that you have a record of your experiences. When we reflect on what we perceived during the journey, we receive a whole new level of information. It is almost as though our so-called subconscious or physical soul was aware of all sorts of things that our conscious/egoic soul aspect was not aware of during the journey. By remembering what was perceived or seen, our body-soul gives us even more insight into what the journey holds. Use the information that follows to help you reflect on and interpret your journey.

Interpreting Your Journey
It is most important not to ask others to interpret your journeys for you. Remember shamanic journeying is a practice of direct revelation, and the only one who can interpret your journeys is you. Messages from your journey may come in the form of symbolic communications or mythic narrative, in which there is an inherent truth. Spirits give us these stories/myths/impressions for a reason. The teaching is for you, and you alone. No highly respected psychoanalyst, therapist, or well-intentioned friend can interpret them for you.

The rich legacy of archeology reveals that the spirits have been in service to us for tens of thousands of years. Our journeys are literally ancient human experiences that are helping us to grow and evolve—to change and become more than we are in response to our life lessons. In doing so, the spirits often convey to us metaphorical stories that have deep meanings on many different levels. It is important not to get stuck on trying to interpret your journeys literally. Yet if you look at the story, you may see the deeper truth within the myth that was and is eternal.

To interpret your journey, ask yourself open-ended questions. You could ask, for example, "How did the scene of the sun rising and filling me with warmth answer my question?" Let yourself speak or write in a flowing manner about your journey until the answer comes to you.

You might find that you need to sit with your journeys for a while and allow clarity to come through at its own pace. Some images and visions are given to us to experience first and understand later, sometimes years later.

If you are struggling to uncover your journey's meaning, you can always make a follow-up journey and inform your helping spirits that you did not understand the answer or the information they gave you. You can ask that they give it to you in another way, one that makes sense to you. The spirits often communicate best through metaphor, so be careful about being too literal in your interpretation.

ALTERNATIVE TO JOURNEYING

As Sandra has noted, there seems to be a change in recent history, an awakening, that is allowing for more and more people to connect to the other worlds with more ease:

Many of us who teach shamanism today have found that people are having an easier time accessing guidance from the spirits than they were in the past. And some people find they do not always have to take a formal journey to receive direct revelation. For example, many of my students, especially those in their twenties, tell me they don't travel to the Lower Worlds or Upper Worlds. Rather their helping spirits travel directly to them in a journey.

Carol Proudfoot-Edgar is one teacher who has found that a formal journey is not always necessary, and she has changed her teachings to reflect this change in consciousness:

> In past years, I required participants to have some shamanic training before taking my advanced courses. It seemed especially important that individuals be trained in the shamanic journey method.
>
> In the past four to five years, however, I have loosened this requirement, and I simply ask potential participants to share their method for connecting with seemingly invisible beings or entering realities other than the ordinary. I came to realize that the Ancestors, the Guardian Spirits, and the entire invisible web surrounding and holding us were behaving differently. It is almost as though the spiritual work done in the last three decades has opened doorways through which helping spirits are now moving with ease; we only have to quiet our minds, open our hearts, and make known our compassionate intentions in order to make contact with them.

EXERCISE: WORKING WITH YOUR ANIMAL COMPANIONS

One way we can experience these spirits moving to and fro is by working with one of our animal companions, who are always aware of altered realities, says Carol Proudfoot-Edgar. Perhaps the increased presence of our animal companions in our lives is one signal that we, too, are drawing closer to our spiritual interconnectedness across all dimensions.

If you do not have an animal companion, then work with a friend's pet. It is important that you and the animal are comfortable in each other's presence.

Most animals are happy to hear either quiet drumming or the sound of the rattle shaking gently. Sit beside the animal and spend some time speaking with and assuring the animal you wish to connect with his or her helpers. Once quietude is present, very gently drum or rattle and perhaps hum softly; the air around you will change and you will experience even more of the alert relaxation of the animal companion. Soften your eyes behind your lids and ask to see the spirit beings that are the allies of this animal. Once they reveal themselves to you (through sight, smell, or touch) you might ask them how they help this animal and if there is anything that you need to know about this animal companion. The primary purpose of doing this is to discover just how close and available to us the myriad spiritual beings who are the guardians for our animal companions are. This is one form of direct revelation. However, we must be prepared when doing such activities to honor everything shown to us and to thank those beings who present themselves to us.

Shamanic journeying is a wonderful and potent way of accessing spiritual wisdom. In the next chapter we will learn the importance of reconnecting to nature and how we can use the shamanic journey to assist in this.

Chapter 3

Reconnecting with Nature

The path of direct revelation walked by the modern visionary finds its origin, as well as much of its meaning, in the way of the traditional shaman, yet when we examine the traditional practice from our Western perspective, we find that it is much more than just a methodology or a set of rituals and ceremonies. When followed with humility, reverence and self-discipline, the shamanic path of direct revelation becomes a way of life.

We have revealed that the shaman is a man or woman who is able to see with "the strong eye" through the heart. Through this way of seeing they discover an inner visionary doorway through which they can journey into hidden worlds where they may enter into relationship with the spirits, gods, and ancestors who reside there.

Our discovery of this path often begins with a spontaneous, yet profound, awareness of our direct connection with Nature. Usually this happens in childhood, and yet it can occur and reoccur at any time of life. It is through this awareness that modern mystics may find themselves drawn into an intimate and compelling connection with the overarching web of life.

All shamans speak of this web or net that connects us to everything, everywhere, as well as to the spirits that live in all things. The idea that we are separate from other life forms is simply an illusion. This is the initial underlying mystical insight of direct revelation, and it provides us with a profound sense of oneness—of unity. Acknowledging this idea that we are all connected, says Sandra Ingerman, is important for our well-being:

> The metaphor I use in my teachings is that we are like fingers of a hand that have dropped to the floor and who think they have a life of our own. For our health and for that of the planet, we must once again remember that we are part of a collective energy field, not separate from it.

Anthropologist Alberto Villoldo, who also stresses the importance of remaining connected to Nature in his work, has noticed this value system in many cultures, including the Andean culture:

> It is important that we become conscious of how connected we truly are with Nature. Every breath we take, every gulp of water we swallow, everything we eat, comes from Nature. It is easy to forget this. I have endeavored to take my children out of the city and into the country (and with me to the Andes in Peru and Chile) so they can see that chicken does not come from a plastic-wrapped package in the supermarket and that there are edible greens all around us in the fields.
>
> For the shaman, the *quality* of your relationship with Nature is of the utmost importance. In the Andes they call this *ayni,* which roughly translates as "right relationship," or reciprocity. You make ayni to Mother Earth, and

she returns your prayers with fertility and abundance. You make ayni to the Sun, and he returns gifts to you of warmth and sunlight. You make ayni to the mountains, and they give you strength and endurance. There is a saying that the shaman lives in perfect ayni. My teacher once said to me, "The universe reciprocates the shaman's every action and mirrors his intent back to him as the shaman is a mirror to others." The shaman lives in synchronicity with Nature, because the shamanic world mirrors the shaman's will, intent, and actions.

We begin by making ayni out of primitive superstition: to please the gods. Later we make ayni out of habit, as part of a ceremony. These forms of ayni are performed out of fear or convention, not out of love. Eventually we make ayni because we *must,* because we feel it in our hearts. They say that only then is ayni perfect, but I believe that ayni is always perfect, that our world is always a true reflection of our intent, our love, and our actions. The condition of our world depends upon the condition of our consciousness and of our souls.

Shamanism is an animist tradition. Animists believe that everything has a spiritual aspect or soul and thus everything is alive and aware to some degree. The Middle World is the place where the shaman communicates with the spiritual aspect of the land, the trees, the plants, the rocks, and the animals that exist on the Earth. As we have mentioned, the Middle World is also filled with hidden folk who are caretakers of the Earth and who help the shaman maintain the balance with natural forces. You might wish to perform some journeys to trees, plants, rocks, and animals as described in the previous chapter, in order to speak to and learn from what José Stevens calls "the elementals with whom we share this Earth."

There are also other helping ancestral spirits with whom the shaman may work, especially those that serve as guardians of specific natural places and localities. You might discover that you need to ask permission from a spirit guardian before you can access its wisdom, which is what Hank Wesselman discovered when he returned to live in Hawai'i in 2007:

> When my wife, Jill, and I moved back to Hawai'i's Big Island, we discovered in our journeywork that each land division, or *ahupua'a*, that runs down from the mountain to the ocean has a spiritual caretaker or landlord. As we engaged in journeywork on different parts of the island, it was revealed to us that correct protocol involved inviting the guardian of that district to approach so that we could announce who we are and what our intentions were for being there.
>
> It was about asking permission, and once that protocol was established, it brought our visionary fieldwork to a whole new level. Asking permission also brought us into alignment with the power and support of the spiritual guardians who live in the dreaming of the island and the ocean.

Whenever you move or travel to a new place and find it difficult to feel at home there, you might need to connect to the spirit of that place, teaches Sandra:

> When I first moved to Santa Fe in the early 1980s I had a very hard time adjusting to living here. Everyone kept talking about "the magic of Santa Fe" yet I could not experience any magic here. Nothing I seemed to do to make life better worked, and I was going on a deep downward spiral.
>
> Finally I decided to try to meet the spirit of Santa Fe in a journey. I journeyed and met a female spirit who shared with me a list of five changes I needed to make to improve the quality of my life here. Once I followed the spirit of Santa Fe's directions, my life changed for the

better. After this journey I could fully embrace and feel the magic of this land.

Since then, whenever I travel, I journey to meet the spirit of where I am teaching. I introduce myself and explain I am bringing a wonderful group of people to the land who want to improve their lives and be in service to the planet. I ask permission to enter the land along with my group.

I know I will be given permission. I have found that this is common courtesy and that the land always embraces my groups with love.

EXERCISE: TO MEET THE SPIRIT OF THE LAND

Try to journey to meet the spirit of where you live and also try this journey before you travel. From Sandra's experience, you will then notice yourself moving into a place of deeper harmony with these places.

SPIRITUALITY OF PLACE

People around the world have always recognized that the place they live has a spirit. The spirit of this place was honored and called on in healing ceremonies and for celebrations. Once again, to live in harmony, the spirit of all things must be recognized on all levels.

According to Carol Proudfoot-Edgar, the "indigenous spirituality of place" includes every aspect of a landscape:

I have come to think of the indigenous spirituality of place when focusing on our relationship with Nature. "Place" refers to much more than the individual spirits; it includes the entire ecology of being and Beingness that occurs within some landscape of the world.

Every place or landscape can be considered as a web within the Great Web of Being and Becoming. Within this Great Web, each of these smaller webs has its own purpose, its own intention, and beings living within each web participate in the unfolding of a larger purpose. This is true whether the being is an elemental force, fauna, flora, or a seemingly invisible spirit.

I refer to the larger purpose as the "indigenous spirituality of place." My task is to teach ways for participants to consciously engage with the spirituality of place and thus become partners in each place. We can help "place" fulfill its destiny and thus contribute to the health of the Great Web.

By practicing the indigenous spirituality of place, people sometimes become aware that what they are doing resonates with what people did in that same place for decades if not centuries. That's because shamanism *arises* from place, and spiritual practices are profoundly influenced by what is allowed within the environment. For example, certain winter ceremonies will only occur where winter is a distinct season, and this is true of all seasonal ceremonies.

It is through such ceremonies that we are able to build a bridge between ancestors and place and ourselves.

EXERCISE: FOR CONNECTING WITH PLACE

Go to some place in Nature—preferably a locale you have not visited before, suggests Carol Proudfoot-Edgar. Do whatever activities assist you in entering a deep meditative or trance state; drumming, singing, or rattling with your eyes closed are some suggested ways. Once you have entered this altered state, ask the place to show you its spirit and some of the beings living in it.

Accept whatever you are shown and make a note of what you experience. If possible, return to the same place four different times in four different seasons. This allows you to have direct experience of how place responds to the greater weather patterns that sweep across the globe. After you have done this—whether once or four times—sing a song of thanks to the place, and if possible, sing this song into a stone or some mineral in the place. Minerals are wonderful holders of sound energy; by singing thanks to place into a stone, you leave notes of gratitude. By its nature, gratitude amplifies health.

You can also try Proudfoot-Edgar's ritual for honoring the spirit of the land where you live. Find a place and time when you can acknowledge the spirit of your locality, and request in the process that your life will become more harmonious. Every day when you leave your house you can simply leave a small offering outside in your surroundings—a shell, a bead, a pebble—or you may simply say words of thanks.

You might say something like: I give thanks to the spirit of this place, this house, this land, for all that I receive. I give thanks to the spirit of the earth, the air, the water, and the sun for the life you give me so I may thrive. I give thanks to my ancestors for my life.

Through building relationships with the natural world and connecting to place, shamans may also be given omens as messages from Nature—communications that help us choose auspicious times to undertake activities such as hunting for food or planting our gardens. Shamans usually respond to such omens with ceremonies to celebrate and honor the ancient spirits of Nature.

These observations reveal that it is the shaman's role to mediate between the community and the forces of Nature. In this sense, a shaman is the harmonizer between humankind and the natural world.

Many of us today sense a deep need to reconnect with Nature and its cycles and rhythms. Living as we do in a technological urbanized society, many of us experience the natural world only through television or the golf course. Yet there is within each of us a deep aspect of our soul that knows that we are part of Nature, and in response, increasing numbers of us yearn to see the stars once again, to hear the calls of migrating birds, and to feel the wind on our skin. We yearn to flow once more with the river of life, and it is precisely this that the shaman's practice of direct revelation and the spirituality of place enables us to do.

WORKING WITH THE DIRECTIONS

Part of working with the spirit of the land and the spirit of Nature is honoring the directions. Most shamans honor the east, north, west, and south, the earth below, and the sky above as they begin any ceremony. Each direction has a different meaning in different shamanic cultures. For example, shamans usually begin by honoring the east, the direction where the sun comes up. In indigenous cultures it has never been assumed that the sun will rise every day. For this reason, indigenous people welcome the sun each day and give thanks for the life the sun will bring. In that sense ceremonies begin by honoring the direction of east.

Some shamanic traditions honor the north for the power of wisdom and the south for the power of protection. And the west is honored as the place of the setting sun. In other traditions different qualities of life are assigned to the directions. There is no cross-cultural agreement to the qualities that each direction represents.

The earth is honored for its abundant life and the sky for the sun, the stars, the moon, the planets, and the spirits that live in the earth and sky that shamans call on for assistance.

Sandra teaches the importance of finding personal significance in what each direction brings.

> When we honor the directions in our work, it is important to do this with heart and meaning. If you copy another teacher's or tradition's way of working, your work will not be as potent as when you understand for yourself why you are honoring a direction and how to do this.
>
> On the CD with this book the first track includes

five minutes where I use whistling and rattling to give people time to honor the directions and the helping spirits by giving thanks for the help you will receive in your journeys.

EXERCISE: LEARNING ABOUT THE DIRECTIONS

Pick a track on the CD and journey with the intention of learning about the directions of east, north, south, west, the earth below, and the sky above. You can ask a helping spirit that you work with to teach you the qualities of each direction.

Then when you do your journeywork or when performing a ceremony (as we will teach you to do in chapter 5) you can add honoring the directions to your preparation work. When you understand for yourself the qualities associated with each direction then you will be able to bring heart into your work rather than memorizing what someone else does without understanding the meaning of how they work.

NATURE'S CYCLES

We are all affected by the change in seasons and by the cycles of the moon. As indigenous peoples know, the earth has a heartbeat and we are one with it.

As we have become dependent on modern technology, we have become hypnotized by the glitter of our new gadgets, and in response we have separated ourselves from Nature's rhythms. We have alarm clocks to tell us when we should wake up instead of relying on the cycles of the sun and our dreaming to tell us when it is time to rise. The homes we live in isolate us and keep us from living in accordance with the change of seasons. Many of us no longer watch Nature's signs so that we know when the seasons are changing. We rely on calendars to do the work for us. Our cycles of activity and rest do not always flow with Nature's cycles.

Think of the flow of a river. If you are wading against its current, this may create a very stressful journey marked by ever-increasing

effort. This is what we see in the world today. As we separate ourselves from the cycles of Nature, we move against the river of life, and
this may cause a wide variety of emotional and physical illnesses.

One way to align with Nature is to observe how you feel with
the change of seasons and cycles of the moon. Today people rely
on books to tell us how we should feel during these changes, but
the truth is that we are all unique individuals who react differently.
According to Sandra, for example, we all have different times of
power in relation to the seasons:

> I have written in some of my previous books that I am
> happiest and in my full power during fall and winter. I
> tend to want to hibernate like a bear during summer.
> Summer is not a time for me to be social. I was surprised
> by the hundreds of letters I received from readers saying
> they felt the same way. We can't put everyone in a box and
> say that winter is a time to go within, for not everyone
> feels that way.

We also cannot proclaim that everyone should feel a particular
way at the new moon and full moon. We know the moon affects
the ocean's tides, and the human body is mostly water, so we can
say that we are affected by the moon's phases in a most dynamic
way. As Hank has discovered, the moon has a deep and profound
effect on everything on Earth:

> In Hawai'i, a revered kahuna elder once told me that the
> moon is the foundation for the Earth. He didn't explain; he
> just left me to ponder this. Another time, when I observed
> that at the physical level we are mostly water, he informed
> me that the spirit of the ocean is called Kanaloa, a name that
> means "the great peace" or alternately, "unconquerable." And
> he said to me on that day, "There is only one thing in the uni-
> verse that is unconquerable, and that is Aloha—love."

Kanaloa, called Tangaroa in the southern ocean, is also regarded as the great progenitor and sustainer of life. This transpersonal force or spirit is dual-natured, both male and female. And as the spirit of the salt water, Kanaloa is the essence within everything everywhere. Both Kanaloa and Hina, the spirit of the moon, were highly revered as household gods by some traditional Hawaiian families and were often invoked for healing.

That same Hawaiian elder once took me to a cinder crater far up on the side of the great mountain, Mauna Kea. There was a simple shrine dedicated to Hina, the moon goddess, on the crater's floor, and there I received an extraordinary healing by praying to that spirit and listening to what she said.

Sandra notes that the phases of the moon, like the seasons, can affect people in a variety of ways:

I used to live with a friend who was very sensitive to the change in phases of the moon. During the full moon he would get depressed and lose his energy. And then at the new moon he felt regenerated and refreshed. I am the opposite. I thrive during the full moon and I am less energetic during the new moon.

When we rely on others to tell us how to feel at different seasons and phases of the moon, we further separate ourselves from our connection with the cycles of Nature. Again, simply observe how you feel at different times. It is understood that you cannot call in sick every time the moon is at a phase where you do not feel energetic. But you can start to organize your life in a way that allows you to rest more during the seasons and the phases of the moon that require you to go inward. You can choose to take more time for yourself when you need it and schedule social times with the cycles that support you in being out in the world.

One way to harmonize with Nature, suggests Sandra, is to gear your journeys toward looking at your own cycles:

> Journey to a helping spirit to help you look at how you can harmonize with the cycles of nature. When I journeyed to the moon, the moon showed me how I flow with her cycles, and she gave me wonderful advice about changes I could make in scheduling my life in order to create harmony with her different phases.
>
> A "merging journey" is another wonderful option. To do such a journey you simply hold the intention that you want to merge or become one with the earth where you live. In this way you learn about earth by becoming earth. Merging with the earth where you live at the change of each season can reveal a great deal about the effects the seasons have on you.
>
> In returning from a merging journey, remember to disconnect from the earth quality with which you are merged.

MERGING WITH THE ELEMENTS

As we start to honor and respect the earth, air, water, and sun for the life they give us, the elements will enter into relationship with us and reflect back to us a state of balance. Right now pollutants are dumped into that which gives us life, and we no longer honor these incredible elements for their life-giving energies. We receive so much beauty and nurturance from earth. We depend on water for our life. We are bonded with air from the very first breath we take, and air is the last element we say goodbye to at the end of our lives as we release our last breath. The sun is a great teacher of unconditional giving as it continues to give the energy we need to thrive. There would be no life without our connection with these wonderful beings that nurture and sustain us unconditionally.

According to Sandra, one way to reconnect with Nature is to merge with an element when we journey:

EXERCISE: MERGING WITH AN ELEMENT

The best way to learn about the elements is to do a merging journey to an aspect of an element. In this way we learn about the elements by becoming an element. Here are just some examples that will inspire you to find an aspect of an element with which you would like to merge.

For earth, you can merge with the desert or a forest floor. For water, you can merge with the ocean, a river, a teardrop, the morning dew, or a cleansing rain. For air, you can merge with a strong wind or a gentle breeze. And for fire, you can merge with the flame of a candle, a raging forest fire, or the sun.

Another interesting journey is to merge with your internal fire. I find that people who suffer from anxiety need to learn how to manage their inner fire, while people who are depressed need to learn how to stoke their inner fire.

I have been doing merging journeys for years. Each time I merge with an element I keep learning more about myself and the world around me. As I learn about my own nature, I reawaken to the fact that I am also earth, air, water, and fire, and I learn about the connection of the elements to each other. We really cannot separate them out—they live together and support the life of one another as part of one organism. As you merge with the elements, notice how they are always in movement. This gives us information on how we can restore our own health and well-being by keeping our energy moving.

You can also do what I call a "gratitude walk" in Nature. As you walk outside—whether it is in a city, or a forest, a beach— you give thanks to the elements for all that they give you. What we bless blesses us in return. As you learn to honor and respect the elements, they will reflect that same respect back to you. This is the principle of reciprocity.

As you walk in beauty and honor the elements, you may also find Nature responding back to you through signs or omens. As you feel gratitude for your life and all you are given from Nature, you might find a butterfly landing on your hand. As you walk in an honoring way, a gentle breeze might caress you. As you pass a beautiful tree and acknowledge it, you might see the branches move in a way that lets you know your heartfelt thoughts were heard. Or as you are giving gratitude to Nature, the sun might come out when before the sky was filled with clouds.

As you find ways to reconnect with Nature and its elements you will find that the life of Nature responds in a way that reminds you of the magic of life, a truly wonderful gift.

We all embody one of the elements in one way or another, notes Hank, so merging with the elements can be particularly revealing:

Within the indigenous cultures of West Africa where I lived for many years in the 1960s as a U.S. Peace Corps volunteer, it is widely understood that we as individuals are born embodying one of the elements as part of our life essence. This is most important because your essence also contains your genius. Since no one can be just one element without the presence of the others, we also carry the others as support elements.

The tribal peoples believe that the element we embody is predestined, perhaps even reincarnational. All elements exist to some degree in each person, but one tends to be predominant. This brings up the issue of what it is to be a gatekeeper, a shamanic healer who is able to use his or her body and mind to form a bridge between this world and the sacred realms, which allows the healing gifts from the spirit world to flow into ours. In his book *The Healing Wisdom of Africa*, Malidoma Somé reveals that gatekeepers have a primary affinity with one element; their genius, their essential character, embodies the gift conveyed by that element. By virtue of the fact that every person carries a certain gift, we are all then given a special relationship with the element from which that gift originates. In this sense, everyone can become a gatekeeper.[1]

Among the peoples of West Africa, the carriers of these gifts, or gatekeepers, are known to be servants to the particular gate from which the gifts originate. This allows them to convey the resources and qualities of that element to their community. Although every person embodies one element in primary focus, all elements must be present in each person in order for him or her to blossom fully.

In this regard, you might make a journey to connect with an elemental spirit. How will you invite fire, for example, to appear to you in your journey? Once it does, you may either merge with it, as Sandra suggests, or you may just allow a respectful relationship with it to come into being.

Ask this elemental spirit what qualities and abilities it conveys. What does it mean to be a gatekeeper of fire, for example, and what gifts are conveyed by this gateway? If you feel uneasy about fire, you may perceive or imagine it as "light."

Do the same for all the other elements as well—water, earth, stone, air, even the spiritual mosaic of Nature herself. In this way we discover what our primary element may be, as well as the qualities and gifts conveyed by that element.

USING THE ELEMENTS TO RECEIVE GUIDANCE

Sandra teaches that working with the elements in Nature is a great way to help us listen to the deep calling of our soul. Nature can move us into a trance state where our rational mind quiets down and we can listen to the deep guidance rising from within.

Sitting by running water such as a river, stream, or waterfall can help you be transported away from the ordinary, allowing your inner wisdom to rise up. Watching the waves in the ocean creates a state of opening so you can listen to the messages of your soul.

Finding a place on the Earth where you can look out into the distance can take you away from daily thoughts and allow inner guidance to be heard.

Sitting in the breezes or winds of summer—just listening—allowing your ordinary thoughts to fly away and be replaced by your inner voice can provide guidance for you right now.

Building a campfire in a campground and gazing into the fire is an old way of moving into a deep trance where your own spirit can fill you with the guidance needed to create your next steps in life. Watching the flame of a candle can do the same.

DEEP LISTENING

Among some of the Australian Aboriginal peoples, there is a state of being known as *dadirri,* which translates into English as "deep listening."[2]

Hank notes that through deep listening, we are able to connect to the spiritual mosaic of Nature from which we are inseparable, an essence that is within us all:

> Miriam Rose Ungunmerr-Baumann, an Australian Aboriginal elder, defines dadirri as a special quality that allows each of us to make contact with a deep spring that lies within us. Connecting with that spring requires that we achieve a state of quiet, still awareness, or dadirri. It is similar to what we Westerners call "contemplation." Shamanic practitioners know it well.
>
> Miriam Rose proclaims that this contemplative focus permeates the Aboriginals' entire way of life, their whole being—that dadirri continually renews them on a day-to-day basis, bringing them peace, creating harmony where there is disharmony, producing balance where there is imbalance, and restoring health where there is illness.

There are no great hidden truths here, no "secret knowledge" hidden away for centuries, waiting for a bunch of New Age charismatics with PowerPoint presentations to rediscover them, excavate them, and write a book about them, proclaiming them as the solution to all our problems, personal and collective. Instead, this Aboriginal woman's message conveys a simple and unmistakable truth—that the practice of dadirri can make us feel whole again. She shares that the Aboriginals cannot live good and useful lives unless they practice dadirri and that they learned how to do this from their ancestors.

As a Westerner who has spent considerable time living and working in the indigenous world, I can appreciate this traditional woman's words. During my years spent among the tribal peoples of Africa, for example, I learned that those still living in their traditional lifeways are not threatened by silence. Rather, they are completely at home in it. Their ways have taught them how to be still and how to listen to the silence. Accordingly, they do not try to hurry things. They allow themselves to follow their natural courses—like the seasons—and they wait. Following the natural courses of existence removes worry from their life. They never worry. They know that in the practice of dadirri—the deep listening and quiet stillness of the soul—that all ways will be made clear to them in time.

The Aboriginals are not goal-oriented in the same way that we Westerners are programmed to be from childhood, nor do they attempt "to push the river," which they know with absolute certainty is an exercise in futility. In Miriam Rose's words: "We are like the tree standing in the middle of a bushfire sweeping through the timber. The leaves are scorched and the tough bark is scarred and burnt, but inside the tree the sap is still flowing, and under the ground the roots are still strong. Like the tree, we have endured the flames and yet we still have the power to be reborn."

Miriam continues: "We know that our white brothers and sisters carry their own particular burdens. We carry burdens as well. Yet I believe that if they let us come to them, if they would open their minds and hearts to us and hear what we have to say, we might lighten their burdens. There is a struggle for all of us, but we, unlike them, have not lost our spirit of dadirri. I believe that the spirit of dadirri will help you Westerners blossom and grow, not just within yourselves, but within your nation as well. There are deep springs within each of us and within these springs there is a sound—the sound of the deep calling to the deep. The time for rebirth is now. If our culture (and your culture) is alive and well, as well as strong and respected, it will grow. In such a case, our culture will not die (nor will yours) and our spirits will not be lost. We will continue, together, as this was always meant to be."[3]

Chapter 4

Visionary Work with Weather and Environmental Changes

In addition to being the originators, and thus the source, of the world's first mystical traditions, shamans have always been accomplished in their understanding of Nature and Nature's cycles, and so it would be correct to describe them as the world's first ecologists.

It is through our ancestral shamans that we've learned of the overarching interconnectedness of all life and the transpersonal energetic matrix that connects everything, everywhere, to everything else. It is through their wise teachings that we've come to understand that we are, and have always been, part of these cycles.

Throughout their lives, shamans continually observe the changes of the seasons and the moon, the alignment of the stars, and the movements of the planets. Through practice, they become masters in reading and interpreting what these changes mean, and through the path of direct revelation they communicate with the forces that govern and influence the environment in order to maintain balance and harmony, thus furthering the well-being of themselves and their communities.

THE DRUIDS

According to Hank Wesselman, the Druids were a spiritual fellowship of male and female shaman-priests that spread widely across the ancient world during the classical period. It is well known that the Druids placed the reincarnational cycle and the certainty of our immortality as souls right at the center of their spiritual teachings. This was in direct contrast to the beliefs of the classical Greeks and Romans, among whom knowledge of reincarnation was singularly absent:

> The Druids were the wisdom-keepers of their people, and they were known to be keen observers of Nature. For them, as for shamans everywhere, the gateway into the transpersonal realms lay in their practice of Nature Mysticism, with the many aspects of Nature itself, including our own bodies, serving as doorways into the Other Worlds.
>
> As priests and visionary shamans, the Druids knew that our consciousness could be transformed, allowing us to access the true transpersonal realms and experience them directly through Nature Mysticism. This ability allowed them to influence Nature and especially the weather as will be explored in this chapter.
>
> The Druids also knew from their direct experience of Nature that "God" is not a being, but rather a force or process that can be found within everything, everywhere—one that is both immanent as well as transcendent, one that is densely concentrated in living beings and thus found within all of Nature.
>
> From the Druids' perspective, when we abuse Nature in any way, shape, or form, we abuse Goddess.[1]

NATURE MYSTICISM

As mentioned, we are genetically hardwired with a program that allows us to expand our conscious awareness. We have also discussed how this program on our inner hard drive (our DNA) may be activated by double-clicking it with the right mouse—the drum or the rattle, the song or the prayer, the ritual or ceremony, or even the hallucinogen.

The Druids, like shamans everywhere, were masters of working with Nature, and they knew that through the practice of Nature Mysticism the deep psychic abilities inherent within all of us could become active, enabling us to experience true transpersonal connection with the worlds of things hidden.

Nature Mysticism is an authentic spiritual path with heart that many of us experienced spontaneously as children through our contact with Nature. As adults, we can learn to reconnect with this path, a path that brings us into direct connection with the World Soul—the same multi-leveled archetypal matrix and intelligence of our planet that the classical Greeks called Gaia. In our own time, this concept has been widely embraced through the visionary writings of the scientist James Lovelock and John Lamb Lash.[2]

In Nature Mysticism, we achieve a direct, transpersonal contact with the life-giving force that we summarily refer to as Nature, and this is often sensed by the visionary (and those with psychic awareness) as an immanent and user-friendly presence. Some of us experience it on the golf course, some on a fishing trip or a weekend camping expedition. Sometimes it's a walk in the park, a hike through the woods, a visit to the zoo, a trip to the beach.

However this contact is made, when we sense it, we know with certainty that the soul of Nature is alive. It's aware of us, and it always has been. When we walk the path of direct revelation, we discover that Nature expresses itself through those archetypal forces that traditional peoples call the spirits.

We are not talking about belief systems here. We have now gone beyond them and beyond faith as well. We're talking about direct connection with the real thing. We're talking about communion with the Infinite, and the doorway into that Infinite usually becomes available to us first through a one-on-one connection with Nature at large.

This is considerably easier to feel than it is to describe, and yet once you have had it, the rest follows. We're talking here about the gateway into true Deity Mysticism, in which we may connect with the real transpersonal archetypes.

The great message of the authentic mystics across time is that "Spirit is." And they expect us to take nothing on faith. Rather they have set out the steps of a grand experiment spread out across the time-space continuum that allows each of us to achieve the direct experience of what they experienced. That's what *Awakening to the Spirit World* is about.

REVERENCE AND DEFERENCE

Celtic shamanic practitioner and teacher Tom Cowan teaches that we should show not only reverence and respect toward Nature, but also deference:

> I think "deference" is the key word here because it means
> that we put someone or something else ahead of ourselves.
> We usually defer to an elder or superior, which means we
> concede to their wishes rather than to our own. While it's
> important for practitioners to respect and realize our one
> ness with Nature, I think underlying this attitude should
> be deference. In other words, we can acknowledge that
> Nature is superior to and far older than us. We can then
> understand that Nature is fundamental to our own activi
> ties, needs, and well-being.
>
> We live in an age in which we assume that human
> ingenuity and technology can control Nature to a great
> extent, at least tempering or eliminating its unpleasant
> and uncomfortable aspects. We don't like inconvenience,

and we have become addicted to being comfortable. But if we really stop to think about this, we understand that we are not in control. As the world becomes ever more unstable due to global warming and human activities that disrupt natural rhythms and patterns, Nature is responding by becoming extreme. Weather and seasonal patterns are disturbed, defying our so-called weather predictions even more than usual.

Rather than gripe or sulk over this, I think all people could consider actually reconnecting with Nature's cycles by choosing "acts of inconvenience and discomfort." For example, we could walk rather than drive, dry clothes on a line rather than in a dryer, set the thermostat lower in winter and wear heavier clothes, learn to live with summer's heat as much as possible, find recreation outdoors rather than in malls or indoor recreation centers. Through such conscious acts, we could each become more fully aware of our current lifestyle, and we could come up with several practical, concrete changes in how we live that would make us come face to face with respecting Nature. Such deliberate acts will put us more in touch with the indigenous mind and heart that we still carry within us.

We often forget or ignore the fact that Nature is immensely more powerful than we are. As shamanic practitioners, we like to work with Nature in its more gentle aspects: the gorgeous sunset, the flowering garden, the starry sky, or the gentle brook. But Nature is also the hurricane, tornado, forest fire, earthquake, and flooded river. Faced with these inevitabilities, we then stand in awe of these forces, recognizing their power and even their terrible beauty as we pray they do not damage our homes or kill us. The power that we witness in these and other natural events is far older and stronger than we are. These primordial activities happened before we humans arrived in this world, and they will most likely continue after we are long gone, revealing how small we really are in this great drama of the natural world.

And knowing this, we can defer to these natural events. We can feel confident in conceding that they are going to happen, that they in some way are necessary in some grander scheme than we can readily imagine. We can then accept with grace the discomfort and inconvenience they inevitably produce. And if we have already been disciplining ourselves by choosing to experience the less than comfortable, the less convenient ways that humans have traditionally related to natural conditions, then we may have greater understanding, appreciation, and acceptance of those more serious disasters when they occur.

We will then be living more in alignment with our indigenous mind and heart rather than the foundation of our modern Western mind that seeks dominion and control over Nature.

THE WEATHER

We have all become aware over the past decade of the global changes that are occurring within our planetary "weather machine." We now know, as well, how these climatic shifts are being exacerbated, even caused, by the activities of industrialized humanity. These changes are now well documented and have been validated by countless scientific studies and manifestos from the National Academy of Sciences in the United States as well as from other industrialized nations.

It is vitally important for us to understand and accept that every change, great and small, entails a death of that which was before. These deaths are necessary and inevitable steps before the birth of what is coming into being becomes possible. Seen from this perspective, there is no question that we live in a transitional time in which everything around us is changing—including the weather.

The Druids of ancient Europe would have considered this to be an issue of more than just passing interest. In light of Hurricane Katrina and her descendant Ike, they might have advised that working in partnership with the weather is the preeminent issue that we face in our time. In this vein, Sandra Ingerman teaches, from a shamanic perspective, that the weather may be a reflection as well as a projection of our collective inner state of consciousness:

> There is an aspect of weather that is simply part of Nature and its cycles. At the same time, the environment, including the weather, may be an outer projection of the inner state of consciousness of humanity. In looking at our existing weather patterns, we can work with the spiritual principle of "as above, so below; as within, so without." The condition of the weather, especially in the extreme, calls us to go within and reflect on our own internal state.
>
> When we do this as a shamanic meditation, we realize with great certainty that the weather is reflecting our toxic thoughts. The weather at large may also reflect our societal state of imbalance: the disharmony and violence we see between one another as well as between us and Nature.
>
> When we intentionally shift into a positive attitude and show reverence toward others and to the world around us, however, we tap into our own divine nature and spiritual light. The environment, in response, will reflect this light back to us, thus creating a growing and pervasive state of harmony within us all. This reveals that who we become can change the world.

THE ROLE OF THE MODERN VISIONARY IN NATURE

The Salish people of the Pacific Northwest have a wonderful word that describes the state of consciousness that we, as modern visionaries, are learning to (re)achieve. "Skalatitude" means "when the people and Nature are in harmony, there is magic and beauty everywhere."

It has always been the role of the shaman to mediate between the community and the spirits of weather. There are many stories of shamans bringing rain when it was needed or sending sun to areas dealing with flooding. When we consider the role of the modern visionary in this process, this does not mean trying to manipulate the weather for trivial or personal reasons such as not wanting an outdoor wedding reception to be rained off.

The weather works on a regional, even planetary, scale and the key to working with these truly awesome primordial forces lies in asking for the highest good for all of life in the particular region where you live. In other words, it's not just about you.

This is most important to understand, for we do not want to use our spiritual practice to work with power *over* Nature. Rather, we want to use our spiritual awareness and abilities to bring us into alignment with these natural forces.

According to Hank, the Hawaiian kahuna elder Hale Kealohalani Makua was fond of observing that "the foundation stone for Western Mind, which is the same as Colonial Mind, is dominion. By contrast, the foundation stone for indigenous mind is respect." Thus, the first step for the modern visionary in working with Nature is to show our deep and abiding respect.

As modern visionaries working with the weather, teaches Sandra, we must remember to stay humble:

> When and if you choose to utilize shamanic methods to connect with the spirits of weather, and if you do have success in working in partnership with the spirits, it is important not to take credit for it. When we brag about our power, we lose it. To avoid letting your ego blow out of proportion, consider working with a group when doing a ceremony to connect with and affect the weather. In this way, no one person can take credit for any successes,

and the power of a group is much stronger than the power of an individual working alone.

Another way to keep the egoic mind at bay is to do the weather work at times when it will be difficult to determine your influence on the outcome. You might try calling down the rain when the sky is already thick with rainclouds. This brings in the principle of ambiguity, where you are in the dark as to what forces are really at work. Although this doesn't create scientific proof, it does keep us open to the mysteries of the universe. And as Hank the scientist is fond of observing, all of us discover sooner or later that transpersonal experiences rarely lend themselves to scientific validation. Yet when they happen, we take note, and in response, we are drawn into a deeper connection with the Great Mystery.

ANECDOTAL ACCOUNTS

Here are some examples of how working in partnership with the helping spirits and with Nature can and does impact the weather.

In the year 2000, a fire at Los Alamos was destroying much of the wilderness in northern New Mexico. There were Native American ruins in the area, and some very sacred places were in the path of the fire.

People from all cultures of the region prayed for rain and performed ceremonies to protect the area from more destruction. Yet the wind was the force that ended up saving the endangered sacred sites. It suddenly changed to a direction from which the wind doesn't usually blow. This unusual wind caused the fire to burn back over the same land that was already charred, and so those sacred sites were spared.

This was quite a teaching—a direct revelation of how ceremonies can be performed and how spiritual help can be called in, yet we cannot always predict how that help will manifest.

In this vein, Hank shares a story that has impacted his work. In the late 1990s, prolonged drought and widespread forest fires of great intensity were devastating entire regions of northeastern Brazil. The Associated Press reported that the Brazilian government, willing to explore all options in the face of this overwhelming catastrophe, finally agreed to fly in several indigenous shamans from the Xingu River area in the Amazon region. These power-filled shamans then did a ceremony, using plants (and by association the plants' spirits) from the region they had come from, and within two hours torrential rains fell over the entire region and doused the fires completely. This made international news.

José Stevens shares a story about people working in harmony with the earth and sky and how the weather responded:

> In the fall of 2007, my wife, Lena, and I were leading a group of about twenty Americans and Canadians to the island of Amantani in Lake Titicaca, Peru. This remarkable island lies at an elevation of 12,000 feet and is populated by Andean farmers and shamans. With no electricity or motor vehicles, it hosts two temples, one on each of two peaks. One temple is devoted to Pachatata, the male principle of Father Sky, and the other is devoted to Pachamama, the female principle of Mother Earth.
>
> Early one morning we set out with our group, accompanied by an equal number of village people, to visit the temples about a thousand-foot climb up the mountain. The procession was ceremonial, and with the help of the local shamans we made traditional offerings on the way to the top. First we visited the Pachatata temple and performed a short ceremony to honor Father Sky. The Pachatata temple is a square depression in the ground surrounded by a high stone wall that protects it from intrusion. The gate was closed; we did not have permission to enter, so we remained just outside the gate. We stayed for about an hour to pray and contemplate in this extraordinary setting overlooking the lake and the snowcapped Andes all around.

We then proceeded to walk to the other peak, to the Pachamama temple. Upon arrival we were amazed to find the gate wide open. This temple is a round depression in the ground surrounded by a round stone wall. After serious consultation with the villagers and the shamans we determined that the gate was open for a reason and we had permission to enter. About fifty of us filed in and sat in a circle to perform a spontaneous ceremony to honor Pachamama.

We set up a portable altar, on which we placed coca leaves, condor and eagle feathers, various other fruits, and offerings. Lena stood up, and in her beautiful voice she began to sing a sacred *icaro* (a healing song) to honor Pachamama. Although the sky had been clear and still on our walk up, a sudden wind from nowhere became a minitornado inside the circular temple. Dust swirled violently, and hats, scarves, and the offerings were all taken up high into the sky. Throughout this almost shocking display, Lena simply continued to sing to Pachamama.

Suddenly the wind died and everything became still again just as she finished the song. Not knowing the local understanding of such things, we were a little uncertain about the meaning of this intense windstorm. However, the locals were overjoyed and said this was a rare and special sign that our ceremony was most successful and had been received readily by both Pachamama and Pachatata. They eagerly embraced each member of our party, and a joyous celebration followed with many tears of happiness and much dancing.

Food came flooding out of the women's shawls and soon we had a surprise feast of potatoes, fish, and local beer. After we were done, we did a celebratory dance all the way down the mountain. I cannot remember a more joyous day than this one.

We had no intention of conjuring this weather phenomenon, yet when a group of people are in harmony with the earth and sky, and when they honor the environment properly, the weather responds with its own display of approval and acceptance. While there are shamanic ceremonies and prayers to deliberately influence the weather, more often than not the weather cooperates with activities of people who are in balance with Nature. Sometimes this is all that is needed for connection and cooperation.

USING SPIRITUAL PRACTICES TO HEAL THE ENVIRONMENT

Today, it is quite obvious to both indigenous and modern visionaries of all persuasions that we simply have to change our way of living to create positive environmental changes. In addition, there is much to explore in terms of renewable energy resources and our political leaders who are devoted to working with environmental issues.

It is also time for modern visionaries to bridge our applied spiritual work into the environment. As we have revealed, the spiritual traditions teach us that everything manifested here on Earth has its source in the Dreamtime—in other words in the spiritual worlds. It is there that shamans and visionaries do their best work. We humans are world-class dreamers, and our task in this time of change and societal transition is to dream well. If we do, our world will change for the better. We must therefore begin by doing our own inner work, notes Sandra, because everything in the outer world is now being born from what happens within us:

> When we look at life on earth, everything is being born from within. A baby forms in the womb of his or her mother and then is birthed into this world. In the same way, a tree begins as a seed, filled with purpose and triumph before being born into this world as a manifestation of that potential.
>
> To do our inner work, we must begin to explore what is actually being birthed from within us as well as what is

84

being manifested into our outer world through our dreaming. In this respect, we need to learn how to transform our problematic thoughts and attitudes. We must also work with our thoughts and our emotions so that manifesting those thought forms and emotional fields truly reflects the world in which we want to live. In essence, we all need to dream the world that we want into being.

An important step in this work is performing ceremonies within a group of committed souls with a similar orientation and practice in order to work on behalf of and in partnership with the environment.

We simply have to find and connect with our own spiritual light so that we may shine that light into the world. We are body, mind, and spirit/soul, and when we intentionally peel away the body and the mind, including all our past experiences and wounds of this life, this may allow us to experience ourselves as our original face—as pure divine spiritual light. Meditation is useful for this practice.

As we learn how to express this divine spiritual light into the world, the outer environment will reflect this back to us. This process, called transfiguration, is a process that Sandra advocates incorporating into a shamanic practice:

In the year 2000, I started to experiment with the results of transfiguring into one's divine light in my trainings. We put toxic ammonium hydroxide into pure deionized water, which has no minerals in it. Ammonium hydroxide is a strong base, and with its assistance, we took the water to a pH of 12. This would literally kill anyone who drank the water, but no living being would do so because the smell is so strong.

In the groups that I work with, we do not pray for the water or ask any helping spirits to heal the water. We

simply change ourselves by experiencing our divine perfection and our light. We use the teaching that the outer
world is a reflection of our inner state of consciousness.
If we exist on a moment-to-moment basis as a light, the
world will reflect that divine light back to us.

Since 2000, I have worked with ammonium hydroxide in samples of water with various groups in the United
States, England, Austria, and Switzerland. Together
we have performed ceremonies where I led participants
to experience themselves as more than their body and
mind—as pure divine light. In all our experiments, the pH
of the water changed one to three points toward neutral.
From a scientific view, this would be seen as impossible.

By working in tandem with archetypal forces through
the path of direct revelation, we learn that we all have power
to create change within the matrix of Nature because we
are, and have always been, part of it. At the spiritual level
of awareness and experience, we can and will grow into the
highly evolved beings about which shamans, mystics, saints,
and sages have been teaching for thousands of years.

Remember that we are always dreaming the world
into being with our thoughts and words. As we learn to
uncover, rediscover, and express our divine light, the world
is enhanced and can express its divine light in response.

EXERCISE: A JOURNEY TO YOUR WORLD

It has become apparent over the last twenty years or so that
the world's indigenous shamans have tapped into the dreaming-
at-large of the planet and humanity as a whole. In response,
cultures such as the Q'ero peoples of the Altiplano region of
the Andes have sent representatives to the lowlands to inform us
Westerners that we are dreaming the wrong dream.

To change our distorted dreams—and by association the
world that we live in—the shamans say we must learn to use the

power of our thoughts and our creative imagination. It would be good to journey on those qualities of the world that we want to see—qualities that create balance and harmony. Once we have these, we can then start to engage our senses and begin to dream this world into being.

Consider these questions: What would this world look like? What would people's faces look like? Would they be smiling? What would Nature look like? How would it feel to live in a world that embraced and expressed all these qualities? What would you feel like on an emotional level in this world?

In your journey, walk around and touch all the various healthy life forms with your awareness and even with your "dream fingers." Feel how good it is to be alive in this world. What do the sounds in Nature sound like? Can you hear children laughing? What are the fragrances filling the air? Can you smell them? How does the food taste? Imagine yourself tasting and eating the most delicious and nutritious foods. Taste the clean, pure water. Smell the fragrant, clear air. Listen to the sounds of Nature that surround you. Feel the warmth of the sun on your skin.

By engaging all your senses, you may work with an inner process that engages your body-soul—a process that can be expressed into the physical world. It is important to see, hear, feel, smell, and taste this world as it already is and as it is coming into existence. Otherwise you are always creating it in the future.

It is also important to actually be part of this creation by fully engaging in the world you are dreaming into being rather than watching your creation as if it were a movie or flat-screen TV. The other key ingredient is a passion for what you want to create. Loving your creation fuels its manifestation, and from the mystical perspective we are in training in this world to become creators.

Imagine how society would change if we all held the awareness that consciousness, not matter, is the primary ground of all being. Tom Hurley, the former educational director of the

Institute of Noetic Sciences, once asked Hank, "What if the purpose of business was to nurture and sustain life?" This question deserves our careful consideration—for through our collective dreaming on it, all will thrive.

Chapter 5

The Power of Ceremony and Ritual

THE ROLE OF THE VISIONARY

Ceremonies and rituals are performed to honor the spirits, to celebrate life and changes in Nature, to acknowledge rites of passage, to give thanks, and to create change. Performing a ceremony or ritual creates transformation.

Shamans are inspired visionaries who are able to access information through their invisible allies for the benefit of themselves, their families, and their communities. This process is known as divination, and it is usually accomplished through ceremony and ritual. The ability of shamans to communicate with the spirit realms enables them to act as healers and doctors, priests or priestesses, harmonizers and psychotherapists, mystics and storytellers. Throughout the group process of ceremony or ritual, visionaries are advised by inner sources of power and wisdom—their helping spirits.

Through their relationship with these transpersonal forces, shamans are also able to retrieve lost power and restore it to its original owners and remove spiritual blockages in those who are crippled by them. A shaman can also address the spiritual aspects of illness and mend the fabric of damaged souls through the performance of soul-retrieval rituals.

Ceremony is a vital part of this healing process, and it doesn't matter if the healer is wearing a white lab coat and stethoscope or body paint and feathers. This is because the subconscious body-soul is very impressed by anything physical. In this sense, it doesn't really matter what you do; what matters is that you do it, whatever it is, and that your intentions (and your ritual) come from the heart. By acting from this heart space, teaches Alberto Villoldo, you can more easily access a transcendent state of mind:

> Shamanic rituals are different from ordinary rote practices in that they often create a collective group experience of the transcendent realms and their inhabitants that may utterly transform the experiencer. Rituals are at the core of all religions, but unlike religious ceremonies that must be repeated the same way every time until higher authorities mandate differently (as happened with the transition of the Catholic Mass from Latin to English), shamanic ritual is always different in that its outer form is suggested, not prescribed, by tradition.
>
> Sacred ritual, properly guided by an experienced shaman, can create a "whole brain" experience that awakens the curiosity of the neocortex, satisfies the need for safety of our more primitive limbic brain, and makes ecstatic states accessed by the frontal lobes of the higher brain possible. Ritual performed wholeheartedly allows us to transcend our limiting roles and beliefs and experience more elevated states of being.

A shaman, then, is a facilitator who, through ceremony, can help others achieve a new mind state. According to José Stevens, this is one of a shaman's main tasks:

> The ceremonialist is one of the seven main functions of a shaman's work. The others include artist, storyteller, healer, warrior, leader, and keeper of knowledge. Each function contributes to the others, which makes for a rich and comprehensive array of skills. While all shamans know something about ceremony and ritual, some shamans make this their specialty and are called in for special occasions to preside over larger, more complex ceremonies that may last several days and nights. These may include songs that go on for many hours, complex dances, prayers, and the blessing of hundreds of people. But anyone can incorporate the shamanic approach to more simple ceremonies in their daily practice.
>
> The primary definition of a spiritually oriented ceremony offered by Webster is "a formal religious or sacred observance." Shamans do observe sacred occasions such as solstices, equinoxes, new and full moons, fertility days, initiations, dedications, annual pilgrimages, births, marriages, and so on. But in addition they create formalities around healing practices such as plant-medicine ceremonies and the like. Often shamanic ceremonies are created for the purpose of blessing children, families, animals, sacred power places, and homes.

Ceremonies (in the generic sense) honor the different transitions we make in life. In shamanic cultures, ceremonies are also used to mark transitions; they are performed when children are born into the world, to mark different stages of life including marriage, and to honor our final transition back into the spirit world at the death of the physical body. There may be ceremonies to mourn

91

the death of loved ones and to mark important rites of passage involving transitions in a person's life, especially those initiations that sanctify moving from childhood to adulthood. Ceremonies are also performed to revere our ancestors who gave us life.

Shamanic ceremonies also honor the cycles of Nature. For an agricultural community, for example, ceremony is done at the time of planting to honor the ancient spirits of Nature and invite them to support the people with a good crop. Then, at the harvest, ceremony expresses the collective gratitude for the abundance with which these natural forces graced the community—abundance that allowed them to live and thrive for another year.

Ceremonies open the lines of communication between a person and the powers of the universe and solidify our relationships with our helping spirits. Ceremonies also create change, so they are a potent tool to use when one is ready for a shift in life.

In the indigenous world, war dances, rain dances, or healing rites do not necessarily cause victory, bring rain, or cure a sick person. But the ceremony can and does bring about a remarkable (and measurable) physiological change in members of the group as tension and excitement rise, peak, and then subside. And it still may also bring victory, rain, or healing.

RITUALS AND CEREMONIES

Strictly defined, ceremonies have a predetermined structure and goal. In this sense, everyone participating in the ceremony has a predetermined role, and the ability of highly structured ceremony to create change cannot be underestimated, especially in helping maintain the physical and metaphysical equilibrium of any given community.

Ritual, on the other hand, is much more open-ended. When we are engaged in ritual, we always have intentions for doing so, yet the end result may be quite different from those expectations. This is because there comes a point in every authentic ritual in which the spirits arrive, and then any predetermined structure or form may go right out the window.

In ceremony, the practitioners are in control from beginning to end. In ritual, the spirits run the show and the results can be truly startling as well as life-changing.

José Stevens, who spent years training with the Huichol Indians, was able to see this spontaneous aspect of ritual first-hand:

> The primary purpose of ceremony in my understanding is to create a container for a specific shamanic event. The container focuses the group on the task at hand, helps define the purpose, and offers protection so there will be no outside interference. Ritual, on the other hand, begins with a prescribed or established procedure for a religious experience such as an annual pilgrimage to a place of power, yet most shamanic rituals have a high degree of spontaneity. In shamanic practice, you find both ceremony and ritual. The Huichols of Mexico create a yearly ceremony of light in November, but the ritual of it ensures that the ceremony is never exactly the same.

According to Hank Wesselman, another way to describe the difference between ceremony and ritual is that ceremony is the prescribed procedure, but ritual is the magic:

> Religious rituals perform several important functions. In a supernatural sense, religious ritual usually involves the manipulation of symbols in order to control, influence, or persuade supernatural powers or archetypal forces to assist us in achieving some given end. (And of course, religious ritual can used to express all or part of the complex drama of human life from birth to death.)
>
> In a political-ideological sense, religious ritual reinforces group solidarity. Group prayer, choir singing, dancing, feasting, or having a pep rally all involve acting as a group that integrates individual behaviors into a community structure. This communal experience helps reduce

tension and allows individuals to feel a sense of belonging. And it is here that we can bring up the subject of magic.

True magic involves specific ritual procedures that if followed precisely are designed to bring about specific desired results, usually by enlisting the aid of supernatural forces. The recitation of the Lord's Prayer is a good example of using magic in ritual, so allow me to (respectfully) offer two versions here, one from the religious perspective (on the left) and one from the mystical/visionary frame of reference (on the right).

Our Father	*My immortal oversoul-self*
Who art in Heaven	*Who exists in the Upper*
Hallowed be Thy name.	*World*
Thy kingdom come,	*Sacred is your symbol.*
Thy will be done,	*Grant us access,*
On earth as it is in heaven.	*Let your wisdom and inten-*
Give us this day our daily	*tions be manifested,*
bread	*On earth as they are in the*
And forgive us our	*spirit world.*
trespasses	*Nourish us*
As we forgive those who	*Be forgiving of our depar-*
trespass against us.	*tures from the path,*
Lead us not into	*And help us to be forgiving*
temptation	*of others.*
And deliver us from evil	*Protect us from craving,*
For thine is the kingdom	*Protect us from the dark*
and the power and the	*forces,*
glory forever.	*For you are the source of*
	my power and my
	being forever.

This is magic in every sense. We invoke the archetypal forces, in this case our own higher self, to be of service to us; state what it is that we need/want; and then honor the source. And as is true with any authentic ritual involving magic, we have no idea of what the outcome may be, but we hope for the best. And when this takes place in culturally meaningful ceremony in the company of other like-minded folk, it enhances both the process as well as the power of the process.

In summary, true magic involves a ritual in which an accomplished practitioner accesses or even steps into the transpersonal realms, connects with the power that is available there, and then bridges this power back into our everyday world to manifest something—healing for example.

Another way to distinguish between ritual and ceremony, teaches Sandra Ingerman, is that ritual can be as simple as a healing process that is incorporated into your life on a daily basis:

> In my own practice, I use the word "ritual" to imply healing work that will be repeated every day, once a week, or once a month. For example, I might have a ritual that I perform daily to honor the helping spirits who reside where I live. A ceremony is something I might perform once by myself or with a group, usually for a desired result.
>
> You can perform a ceremony or ritual for just about anything. In my workshops we perform ceremonies in order to curtail beliefs and attitudes that prevent us from using our creative energy to create a good life for the planet and ourselves. We use ritual to create agreement between ourselves and the power of the universe for what we wish to create in our lives. When we use ceremony for manifesting something we want, we can add to the power of our creative potential by working in partnership with the creative forces of the universe.

KEY INGREDIENTS OF CEREMONY AND RITUAL

There is no correct way to perform a ceremony or ritual. What is important is that you use your own creativity to come up with a ceremony to perform. Here are some key ingredients:

1. Set a strong and clear intention about what you want to accomplish.

2. Concentrate and stay focused on what you are doing. If you become distracted, your energy becomes disconnected from the spiritual forces within.

3. Create a feeling of harmony with yourself, your helping spirits, and, through them, the power of the universe. When we are in a state of harmony, our hearts open and we become one with the universe, and it is this union that mystics use for creation and healing.

In addition to these guidelines, take the length of your ceremony or ritual into account. Hank, for example, stresses the importance of keeping it relatively short:

Shamans, unlike medicine people and ceremonialists, tend to keep their rituals simple and keep them short. From the visionary perspective, the most powerful ceremonies and rituals get right to the point. They open the door, connect with the powers that be, state the intention, then honor those allies that will help with the manifestation of what is needed, including the process.

In order to create your ceremony or ritual, it might be helpful to write out a plan beforehand. José Stevens, through his participation in a variety of shamanic ceremonies, has noted that they almost always have some key elements:

Design your own ceremony with all the elements (listed below) or as many as are appropriate. Be sure to allow plenty of opportunity for spontaneity. When you carry out the ceremony, perhaps give participants different duties or parts to lead the rest of the group in. Later you can repeat the ceremony—on a different day with different people. Include the elements you used before and see how different the ceremony can turn out.

1. An opening song or statement that greets all the participants and makes the purpose of the ceremony or ritual clear.

2. An offering of gratitude to Spirit for the good fortune to have come together.

3. A calling to the land, the elements, and the directions that contribute and support the ceremony.

4. A calling in or petitioning of other allies or helping spirits to support the ceremony and its purpose.

5. A cleansing of all the participants, which can be a way of initiating participants into the ceremony or ritual. Burning incense and using the smoke of the incense to clear the energy of a person is a common way of cleansing. Different cultures use different incense from plants where they live. In the Native American traditions, sage or sweetgrass is often used for cleansing purposes.

6. A blessing element designed to increase the health or good fortune of all attending.

7. Prayers asking that the goodness of the ceremony may radiate to others not in attendance, perhaps the whole planet.

8. Songs and dances with instrumentation such as drumming, rattling, flute playing, clapping, foot stomping, bell ringing, and so on. This may occur throughout the ceremony or at certain transition points.

9. A closing announcing that the ceremony is terminated.

10. A thank you to all the helping spirits and a message that releases them from the sacred space.

11. A releasing of the directions (described in Chapter 3) and an unwinding designed to return the participants to an ordinary or normal state of awareness.

Singing and Dancing

The spirits tend to read our hearts and not our minds, so we want to make sure we begin our ceremonies and rituals with an open heart. Furthermore, an open heart will help us imagine that our work will be successful; if you can't imagine a successful result then it may not happen.

Singing and dancing are wonderful ways to enhance harmony during a ritual or ceremony. You can sing songs you love or do some drumming and rattling and let your own soul sing a new song that comes through you. When you sing with passion, the energy moves from a mental state into your heart, and your heart opens.

Participants

You can perform ceremonies or rituals alone or with a group. When you work with the support of a group, you add your intention and power to the work you are doing. We have found over the years that when a powerful group focuses on healing or on helping someone manifest a dream, there is more power than when one works on his or her own. A collective focus creates a more successful outcome.

Intention

Though the number of participants plays a strong role in the outcome of a ceremony, according to Sandra it is not the most important ingredient. She emphasizes the need to be clear on your intention and wording when performing a ritual or ceremony:

In my practice, sometimes I work alone and sometimes I work with a group. I perform ceremonies when needed and when the time is right, but sometimes I can't always wait until I am with a group of people to do my work. What is most important, then, is my intention.

Ceremonies are so potent that it is important to get very clear on my intention. Working with your helping spirits to find the right words to use is pivotal.

I have a funny story to share about this, one that happened when I was presenting at a conference years ago. As I have written in my book *Medicine for the Earth,* I often find myself meeting people who know how passionate I feel about using ceremonies to create change and to help manifest what it is that we desire in life.

On this occasion, a woman came up to me and introduced herself. She then informed me that she had performed a ceremony to find a rich man, and then she turned and introduced me to her husband, Rich, who she announced was poor. They both laughed as she told me this story.

When I first began to practice shamanism, I thought I had to learn how to perform ceremonies because they hold so much power. And then I met a teacher who regularly led ceremonies in Northern California. The most important piece of information she gave me was that there is no right way to perform a ceremony. You just have to set a clear intention.

With that statement, she gave me freedom, and I then started to perform ceremonies for all sorts of different reasons.

In response, I experienced how powerful they were in creating change in my life. It was then that I learned that I had to be careful about my wording. For example, my own ego did not always know what was for my highest good, and sometimes I did not understand how my wording was affecting my results. There are many stories from different traditions about people asking for an open heart. And the next thing they know they are in the hospital having open-heart surgery. So be careful what you ask for.

Your power animals and teachers in nonordinary reality can give you guidance on right intention and the correct wording to use. I highly recommend that you consult with your helping spirits as you create an intention for a ceremony. Make sure what you are asking for is for your highest potential.

Myth and Legend in Ceremonies

One way of getting creative with your ceremony, shares Carol Proudfoot-Edgar, is by incorporating the mythic into it:

Bring more of the mythic and legendary into your ceremonies. Myths and legends take place in a world half-formed, where humans and animals interact or share identities, and the entire cosmos is dominated by legendary figures such as White Buffalo Woman, Kokopelli, Spider Woman, Raven, Heyokas, and Bear Mothers—just to mention a few found in North America. I have spent a great deal of time in various methods of research exploring these myths and legends, and they have become a central part of my ceremonies.

I do this because I believe a new myth is seeking to be born through us. This new story or way of being has more chance of being born if we carry the seeds from previous myths into today and if we are taught by the figures of legend.

Every ceremony I do includes some ancient story because the realm of story can reinforce our collective experience of these wonderful archaic realities.

Here is an activity you can try. The next time you, or your Circle, does a ceremony, journey to see what mythic figure wishes to be present in your ceremony—or search to see what ancient story illustrates the purpose of your ceremony. Then include that mythic figure or that story in your ceremony.

TYPES OF CEREMONIES

Ceremonies can be performed to honor a life transition or the cycles of Nature. They can also mark a time of letting go of something that no longer serves you or to bring in something you want in life.

Here are examples that might inspire you to find your own purposes for a ceremony or ritual:

- You can perform a ceremony at an important birthday when you feel you have reached a new stage of life.

- You can perform a ceremony at each solstice or equinox to honor the change in seasons.

- You can perform a ceremony when getting engaged or to break the connection between you and another if you are getting divorced.

- You can perform a ceremony if you want to manifest a new job or a relationship.

- You can perform a ceremony when a death of a friend or loved one has occurred to wish them well in their journey back to their spiritual home.

At the end of the chapter, we will give you an exercise to create a ceremony that will speak to something you personally need right now in your life.

One especially helpful subject for ceremony, teaches Sandra, is to release blocking beliefs from your life:

> One of the central questions my clients and students need to address is, "What core belief or attitude do you hold that blocks you from using your energy to create a joyful life?" I have discovered that the beliefs that have the most power over us are beliefs about ourselves that we picked up from our family at a pre-verbal age—the belief that we are not good enough or the belief that we are not lovable, for example.
>
> Before performing a ceremony to release those blocking beliefs, it is good to identify what negative belief or attitude you took on at a very young age. Every time you attempt to make positive changes in your life, there is often something held in your unconscious that sabotages you again and again.
>
> In response, we can journey to a helping spirit with whom we have developed a good relationship and whom we trust. We might ask them the following question: "What is the core belief or attitude that I am holding that blocks me from using my creativity to the fullest?"
>
> The reason I insert the word "core" into this question is that this is the key word in uncovering what you picked up at a non-verbal age. Once you have diagnosed the nature of your block, it is your choice to let it go. For this purpose I like to work with fire ceremonies.

Another possible theme for your ceremony is fire. From a visionary perspective, fire is a living being whose nature is to transform and transmute. In this sense, we can ask the fire elemental spirit to work in partnership with us to transform the energy of our blocking belief into pure light.

A Fire Ceremony

You can perform a fire ceremony alone or in a group. Ceremony done in a group magnifies its power. You can work with just a few other people; the group need not be large to experience an exponential effect.

The first step is to create a power object that will embody or symbolize your blocking belief or attitude. Have fun with making your power object, suggests Sandra:

Let your intuition guide you when developing your power object. For example, you can find a stick in Nature and wrap some yarn around it. When you wind the yarn, it symbolizes the unwinding from your held belief. Some people draw a picture; some write a letter. I have found that people are infinitely creative in coming up with a power object. Just make sure that you always treat whatever you take from Nature with honor and respect.

Once you have made your power object, you can journey on how to fully infuse the power of the belief into your object. One way I work is to rattle and sing and really shake out of me what I want to get into my object.

Again, it is important to understand that the shamanic art you create does not represent power. Shamanic art is power.

Next, bring the fire into your ceremony, which, Sandra notes, can be done in a myriad of ways:

You can use a fireplace for your ceremony, or, if conditions are safe outside, you can build a fire on the ground or use a barbecue. In one group I worked with years ago, we could only use a sewer grate on a street on which to build a fire. While working in the darkness, we felt that we were in the middle of the wilderness. The power that the group generated was so strong that the location of the fire no longer mattered.

Be responsible and avoid building an outdoor fire where there would be any danger of sparks creating a major problem. Always put out the fire after you are done, and do it with gratitude.

While building the fire, tell the fire what you are doing; remember that you are working in partnership and collaboration with the element of fire in your ceremony. You also might want to burn some incense or sing or meditate to create a sacred space. In North America sage is often burned, in South America copal or special tobacco is used, and in Australia eucalyptus is an effective incense.

Some people are sensitive to incense smoke, so there are sage sprays that you can buy or make. You can also use organic rosewater sprays where the fragrance dissipates quickly.

For many, including Hank, burning incense is an integral part of any ritual or ceremony:

> Incense cues the subconscious body-soul that you are doing sacred work, separating what was a few moments ago from what is now. Remember, the body-soul is very impressed by anything physical. Ritual, ceremony, and incense will alert your body's soul, and in response to your focused intention, it will obligingly open that inner doorway in your heart so that the rest can happen.

Remember once again that intention in a ceremony or ritual is the most important key. So if you can find an incense that you like, burn it with intention to honor the spirits of the earth, air, water, fire, your helping spirits, the helping ancestors, the moon, the stars, and the spirit that lives in all things. By doing so, you extend the invitation to all your spiritual allies and helping spirits to join you in your spiritual endeavor.

If you are working in a group during your ceremony with fire, sing and dance together to create a beautiful heart-filled space. You can keep up the drumming and rattling as each person comes forth when they are ready to place their power object, infused with their limiting belief, into the fire. With community support, we feel the power needed to let go of beliefs that have been running our lives. They are old attachments that need to be released.

As each person leaves their object on the fire, each should show gratitude toward the flame that everyone is working in partnership with. "You might wish to give the fire an offering in thanks after placing your object in the fire," says Sandra. "In my fire ceremonies I give cedar to the fire in gratitude. Others offer tobacco."

If you are working alone, create your fire/belief-blocking ceremony in the same way as you would with a group. Instead of having a large fire, you can use the flame of a candle to burn a note in the sink or bathtub. When finished, invite the spirit of water to clear the space.

Once your ceremony is complete, thank the spirit of fire and the helping spirits that you invited in to witness your work, and then acknowledge that your work is done. You don't want to walk away from a ceremony without acknowledging the spirits whom you invited to provide you with power, protection, and support. This is common courtesy—and correct protocol.

Once a ceremony has been performed, an intention has been set into motion, creating movement and enabling you to let go of the past. You may then move forward onto new roads that are not looping back to your childhood and your past wounds. You can now live out ways of being that support you in being able to fully express your soul's purpose. Creating a positive present and optimistic future for yourself is not only healing for yourself but also for humanity and the planet at large. Fully remembering who you really are and living your soul's purpose is your destiny.

EXERCISE: CEREMONY FOR STEPPING INTO YOUR TRUE IDENTITY

Sandra shared with us a ceremony to let go of blocking beliefs. Alberto Villoldo shares with us the need to look at the labels we cling to and how to let go of ones that no longer serve us. This next ceremony will help you to redefine who you are.

For most of us, our self-definition is so important that we cling to our labels and roles and never explore how we can redefine ourselves. Our roles are our ego; without them, we feel that we'll be losing the essence of who we are and, in a sense, "dying."

Through ceremony you can incinerate your roles in order to let go of your limitations. Afterward, you'll discover the possibilities of those very same roles—without getting stuck in the story you created around them. Your roles then become what you do instead of who you are.

To perform this ceremony by Alberto Villoldo, you will need some twigs, several strips of paper, a pen, a fire, and your courage. Gaze into the flames (a fireplace, barbecue, or firepit) and let your thoughts slow down and fade in intensity. Cease to give them weight, and watch as they begin to dissipate. Fire has a mysterious ability to help you enter a state of lucid reverie in which you can access the Dreamtime.

On each strip of paper, write a role, label, or self-definition that you identify with. Be sure to include them all: husband, wife, father, mother, doctor, breadwinner, shaman, nurse, recovering alcoholic, student, lover, or whatever your roles may be. All of these roles, no matter how exalted, have bound you and kept you stuck. Wrap each strip around a twig, and thank each role for the lessons it has taught you and the powers it bestowed upon you. Bless each role and then place the twig in the fire and watch it burn. Continue this process with all your roles, and know that you are creating a sacred ritual for yourself.

Feel the heat as each twig burns, making sure that you witness this from a still place. Imagine the demands of your roles disappearing into smoke and ash as you're freed from playing the part of mother, spouse, son, or employee, and open your heart to receive the gifts that each of these roles present to you. Know that you cannot be defined by your roles, but you can perform them with beauty and grace.

Cairn Ritual

As we have said, ceremonies can also be performed to honor ourselves and Nature. Historian Tom Cowan—who teaches workshops and writes about Celtic shamanism—shares a ceremony that you can perform to honor yourself and a symbolic force in your life.

In some of the Celtic shamanic work that I do with groups, we honor and journey to the Dark Mothers, such as the Cailleach or the Old Bone Mother, by building a cairn to her and using that as the entry into her world.

Each person in the group brings a stone about the size of a computer mouse and places it on the pile in a ritualistic way, usually accompanied by soft drumming. Then we bless the cairn by crumbling sage or dried leaves over it, and sprinkling it with water. We might also smudge it with the smoke of burning sage. We build this cairn in memory of our most ancient ancestors who built cairns over passage tombs and dolmens in Western Europe, many of which still stand today.

The pile of stones contains numerous cracks and entries, so when we journey we allow our spirits to enter at one of these openings. Each person then wanders through the crevices and spaces inside the cairn until a "room" is found. On the wall of the room we sketch a representation or symbol of our power animal or some other pertinent symbol, thus making the space a sanctuary. Then we return and dance around the cairn.

Next, we make plans to reenter the cairn to meet the Dark Mother with our intention, whether it be to gain knowledge, wisdom, insight, or spiritual help in our lives.

If we are in a workshop of several days, we leave the cairn in the center until we are finished. Taking the cairn apart must be done in reverse order from how it was built in order to get back the stone you put on, although each person does not need to get their exact stone back unless for some reason the group decides to do so.

An optional follow-up is to scry the stone you take back for a symbol or message of peace. Each person then speaks the message of peace either in a circle or outside, where the cairn can be rebuilt as a "peace cairn" that will remain as a beacon or permanent prayer for peace and as a memento of the shamanic work you did there.

Working with ceremony will bring a richness into your life and will lead you back into a place of appreciation, awe, wonder, and connection with the invisible worlds. The ceremonies described in this chapter are meant to be an inspiration so that you can use these principles as guidelines in creating a powerful experience. They will allow you to apply your own creative brilliance to come up with a ritual for the healing and transformation of yourself and your community.

EXERCISE: DESIGNING YOUR OWN CEREMONY

Now that you have learned some key elements that go into performing a ceremony and have seen examples of ceremonies, it is time for you to design a ceremony you can use for yourself.

We suggest that you perform a journey to a power animal, guardian spirit, or teacher and ask them if there is a particular ceremony that would be helpful to honor yourself or Nature, to bring something to you, or to let go of something that no longer serves you.

Ask your helping spirit to assist you in coming up with the right wording for the intention for your ceremony. Then ask your helping spirit to help you design a ceremony that you can perform.

You might find that it is important to invite friends to your ceremony or you might wish to perform it alone.

As you become comfortable with performing ceremonies, you might find yourself journeying on ceremonies for another person or for your community.

Chapter 6

Dreams

THE MASTER DREAMER
IN THE IMAGINAL REALMS

We have revealed the shaman to be a man or woman who may intentionally dissociate his or her conscious awareness away from the physical body (and this physical world) and enter into an alternate reality—the shaman's world of "things hidden." Once there, he or she discovers through direct revelation that this subjective, dimensional level of reality, awareness, and experience is inhabited.

The dream world is also a level of consciousness—the level of spiritual consciousness, and the indigenous peoples universally refer to this timeless archetypal field as the spirit world—revealing that the spirit world and the dream world are experientially one and the same.

In Western psychology, the dream world is interpreted and understood in various ways according to various schools of thought, but most agree that it is a mysterious place we go into when we are asleep—a place where we have strange, numinous experiences and encounter people and localities that we may know, yet are always different in some way. Often elusive, the images from our dreams can evaporate from our conscious awareness shortly after we awake, revealing them to be idiosyncratic or self-determined.

But there are ordinary dreams and then there are shamanic dreams or "big dreams" that we may remember throughout our life—sometimes called lucid dreams in which we become aware that we are dreaming, and yet we remain in the dream, acting and directing the context of the dream. These are literally visionary experiences of the transpersonal realms that may be accompanied by connection with spirits or with soaring feelings of power that may be transformative.

The shaman and the modern visionary alike learn to enter this level of experience while very much awake. In fact, notes Hank Wesselman, from a shamanic perspective we are dreaming throughout our entire lives:

> We might begin by emphasizing a point mentioned in the Introduction—a deep insight that I gleaned from my years of living with the tribal peoples in Africa.
>
> Right at the core of their indigenous worldview is the perception that the multileveled field of the dream is the real world, that we are actually dreaming twenty-four hours a day, throughout our entire lives, and that the everyday physical world came into being in response to the dream, not vice versa.
>
> These assertions were always accompanied by a conviction, strongly held, that the dream world is "minded"—that it is consciousness itself—alive, intelligent, and power-filled, and that it infuses everything that emanates from it with awareness, vitality, and life force.
>
> This means that we are always dreaming, even as you

read these words, wherever you are. It also means that the experience of dreaming when we are asleep and the experience of the shaman who journeys into the dream worlds while very much awake, are experientially and phenomenologically the same. Both paths give us access to the same levels of reality, awareness, and experience revealing that the dream world serves as both the source of this physical reality in which we live, and yet it can be affected by what we dream as well. This reveals that our relationship with the dream world/spirit world is a co-creative one.

The process involves shifting the focus of our awareness from "here" to "there." This is a learned skill, and a shaman's ability to do this through their focused intentionality reveals why the shaman is called "the master of dreaming."

Because we are always dreaming, Sandra Ingerman notes, we have great power over our lives:

It is with our creative imaginations that we dream the world in which we are living into being. This gift of imagination is a gift of power. We create our lives with our thoughts and words. In our culture, few are encouraged to use their imaginations in a way that helps develop creative abilities. Most of us are taught early on that there are only a few creative geniuses in the world and that we are not among them. Throughout our lives, we were taught to give our power away to authority figures who then determined the shape of our world according to their wishes.

Well, that was what was. We live in a time of great change and now is the time for us as modern visionaries to own our power, to make our lives better, and to use our creativity to find solutions for what is happening in our world. All of this becomes possible through our focused dreaming.

Both shamanic journeying and dreaming are very creative endeavors, and they are experientially similar, yet there are differences between them. According to Sandra, many students of shamanism don't always see this difference—but it is important to make the distinction:

> In a journey, for example, you might choose to go to the Lower World or to the Upper World where you may engage your helping spirits for healing and problem-solving, ask questions, and receive answers. In our ordinary dreams at night, we do not typically have that kind of conscious control. Such dreams are idiosyncratic—unique to the dreamer—and usually quickly evaporate upon awakening. In ordinary dreams, things happen without much conscious choice on the part of the dreamer.
>
> Lucid dreaming, on the other hand, is a kind of in-between state in which the dreamer's body is asleep, but their mind is awake and aware that they are dreaming, allowing them to direct the dream to some degree. Such dreams, like shamanic journeywork, can be life-changing, with the dreamer remembering all that occurred in great detail, often for the rest of their lives.

So, from a Western perspective, dreams and journeying are different activities. From a shamanic point of view, nighttime dreaming while asleep is not viewed differently from the shamanic journeys we take while very much awake. Shamanic journeywork is, in short, a form of dreaming—but dreaming while awake. A shaman thus places great value on the world of dreams. According to Hank, there are many names for the dream place, and the world of dreams is honored throughout all shamanic cultures:

> As we have mentioned, the dream world is the level of reality called the Dreamtime by the Australian Aboriginals, the

Other Worlds by the Celts, the Po by the Polynesians, and the Spirit Worlds by the shaman. It is often simply referred to as The Sacred, and, as such, it is the astral level in which our personal oversoul, our higher self, lives as an immortal being of pure energy rather than as form.

This is the plane of realization in which there is nothing to gain and nothing to experience. Yet it is also a level of consciousness in which the knower, the knowing, and the known are one. It is in this manner that perception, knowledge, and action can occur simultaneously, and in these dream worlds, all space is here and all time is now. This is why it is often referred to by the indigenous peoples as The Timeless and why we here are often referred to as "the people of Time."

THE DREAM ASPECT OF
SHAMANIC JOURNEYING

The great three-leveled world system of nonordinary reality is the shamanic dream world. As discussed in Chapter 2, these beautiful, awesome regions in which the shaman connects with the spirits are perceived in every shamanic tradition, and all shamanic cultures agree that these worlds exist in layers. The various levels are distinguished by their density, as well as by who and what may be found within them. And as we have already mentioned, they are commonly known as the Upper Worlds, the Middle Worlds, and the Lower Worlds.

Right in the center of the stack is the Middle World, the locale of human dreaming. This is also where we find ourselves right after the death experience—the postmortem *bardo* states of the Tibetans and the Purgatory of Judeo-Christianity—regions populated largely by the souls of recently deceased humans. *The Tibetan Book of the Dead*[1] reveals that when we die, it's like going into a dream and not waking up. And the dream that we go into is our own unique dream—the one that we create for ourselves during our soul's transition from the physical world into the dreaming of the spiritual worlds. This reveals that the Middle World has two aspects, an ordinary physical aspect and a nonordinary dream aspect. And everything that has a physical aspect here seems to have a corresponding dream aspect there. Nobody really knows why this is so. It just is, and as such, it is part of the great mystery of existence.

Our Sacred Garden, discussed previously, is usually found on this dream level of the Middle World. As we remember places in Nature where we have felt connected, at home, or at ease in a spiritual sense, we are actually connecting with the dreaming of that place—and this dreaming is a fluid and ongoing process associated with that place that emanates power.

Below the Middle Worlds, we find the Lower Worlds, which are formed by the collective dreaming of the spirits of Nature. This is where the shaman journeys to connect with the spirit of wolf or bear, raven or tiger, eagle or deer, oak or corn, healing herb, or even with the elementals—the spirit of fire, water, earth, or stone. As we have discussed, shamans and visionaries of all traditions across time have discovered that many of these spirits are willing to come into relationship with humans as spirit helpers, providing us with protection and support, and by association, with the power that they possess.

The shaman as the master dreamer may work with everything in creation dreams or even manipulate "the dreaming" to create effects in this world here, revealing the accomplished shaman to be the master of dreaming as well as the magician who can manifest a wide variety of effects—healing for example.

Above the Middle Worlds are the Upper Worlds, which are formed by the collective dreaming of the gods, goddesses, angelic forces, and the spiritual heroes and heroines of the past. These dimensional levels were brought into existence by these highly evolved beings or organizing intelligences. Within these luminous, light-filled regions, we may find connection with our spirit guides, ascended masters, and the members of our council of elder spirits.[2]

Many of the beings who exist in the Upper Worlds may serve us as spirit teachers, and it is among them that we have a very special connection indeed—our personal oversoul.

Interestingly, these imaginal realms are perceived in much the same way by visionaries of all cultural traditions, everywhere, implying that all human beings may be linked by a basic psychic unity, as some anthropologists and psychologists have claimed. It also suggests that these dream worlds are separate from the one who perceives them and that they have their own autonomous existence, a claim that shamans and visionaries everywhere affirm with confidence.

In our time, it is remarkable how the spirits who reside in the dream worlds—Upper, Middle and Lower—may often appear spontaneously to Westerners in psychotherapeutic sessions. Using guided visualization and various hypnotherapies, increasing numbers of therapists are encouraging their clients to interact with and learn from these imaginal beings.[3]

KAHUNA INSIGHTS INTO DREAMING

According to the Kahuna of Hawai'i, the spiritual worlds of the Dreamtime operate under three distinct assumptions: 1) everything we experience within the dream worlds is symbolic; 2) everything we encounter there is part of a pattern and exists in relationship to everything else; and 3) everything at this level means what we think it means.

According to the first assumption, the symbols we perceive reveal dreams to be the archetypes that are well-known to mythologists, psychologists, and shamans alike. According to the second assumption, the pattern is the great tapestry into which these archetypal forces are woven. The fabric of this tapestry, spread out across the continuum of the dreaming, *is* the spirit world. Part of the great mystery of living involves the realization that the dream world and the spirit world are actually one and the same.

Last, the third assumption presumes that everything in your dream means what you think it means. Thus, each of us must interpret our symbols, as well as our dreams, for ourselves. No one can do this for you with accuracy, because your dreams, visions, and symbols have come to you for a reason and often from many sources. Your job is to figure them out, a task that will deepen your awareness of your self, as well as just about everything else.

Hank, who studied shamanism in Hawai'i among other places, stresses the fact that we are the weavers of this fabric:

> We accomplish this extraordinary task of weaving our lives though our actions in the physical level of the Middle World—which the Hawaiians might call the First Level of Reality—through our thoughts, intentions, emotions, and dreams. Everything that we have become and accomplished on our long voyage across time is woven into the tapestry.
>
> Considered from this perspective, the spirit world can be thought of as a level of relativity, in which space and time, galaxies and stars, animals and plants and humans achieve meaning only through relationship with each other.

DREAMS FOR HELP AND GUIDANCE

We can also begin to learn how to ask for help in our nighttime dreams just as we do in setting an intention in a shamanic journey. Sandra, who receives a great deal of guidance from her shamanic journeys, gets the same kind of information from her night dreams as well:

> This began when I was a child, when I regularly received a tremendous amount of information in my dreams to help me find solutions to issues in my life.
>
> In 1998 I started to write my book *Medicine for the Earth: How to Transform Personal and Environmental Toxins* just before taking a travel group to Egypt. When I returned, I had a very powerful dream in which the Egyptian god Anubis introduced himself. He shared

with me that the missing piece of my work in reversing environmental pollution was "transfiguration," and then he disappeared.

I woke in the morning and discovered that transfiguration means "shapeshifting." Transfiguration became the foundation of my work in *Medicine for the Earth,* using light for healing others and the planet. I will share more about this in Chapter 8 on sound and light. This is just one example among many of how my work was guided by information that came in a dream.

Hank adds that with this perspective, consciousness becomes "geographied" when journeying—it becomes the spirit world in which the shaman will travel. And shapeshifting? In this case, consciousness becomes objectified in some other thing or being. Shapeshifting is consciousness as object; journeying is consciousness as landscape.[4]

How to Ask for Guidance and Healing in a Dream

When you begin a new project or need some advice, you can simply ask for a dream to provide you with guidance. Before you go to sleep at night, set an intention that you would like to receive helpful advice in a dream.

Many of Sandra's students have reported that a helping spirit they already work with comes into their nighttime dream or that a new spirit they have never met gives them the help they requested.

As with a shamanic journey, write down a dream you have received that gives you guidance. Sometimes the answer will be very clear to you, and sometimes you have to sit with the message you received in order to understand the meaning. As with a journey, keep working with how the symbols or message answer the intention you set for your dream.

Dreams can help you solve major dilemmas, and they can

bring on healing—even on the physical level. Sometimes you need to be patient with your dreams; they don't always bring healing right away, teaches Sandra:

In the 1980s I had a physical condition that created a great deal of pain. Many medical doctors told me I was going to have to learn to live with the pain. I went to my helping spirits and asked for help. I had others journey on my behalf. I collected quite a lot of spiritual information, but no relief came.

Every night before I went to bed I asked for a healing dream. I was very persistent and did not give up. And after months of asking the dream finally came.

A Native American man wearing blue jeans and a blue denim shirt came out from behind my couch. He said he had always been there. Then he proceeded to show me a beautiful blue rattle—a blue that was very vibrant and I had never seen such a hue before. The man pointed to the place in my body where I was in pain and said, "You have a pain right here." He then shook the rattle over that place on my body, and in the dream the pain disappeared. When I woke, the pain was gone and has never reappeared. You can imagine my gratitude over this healing.

Ever since that dream I have instructed people dealing with an emotional or physical issue to ask for a healing dream. The key is persistence. You must ask every night.

It is quite extraordinary how many of my students share that they had a soul retrieval or some other spontaneous healing like the one I had. You simply need to ask for a healing dream.

When you go to bed at night, hold the intention that you are seeking a dream that can give you guidance and healing. Many of my students report that one of their helping spirits has appeared in a dream to offer healing, but as in my dream, it is also possible that an unknown being may come to offer help.

GROUP DREAMS

When a group gathers to do spiritual work together it is sometimes noted that the different participants begin to have dreams that overlap in meaning and have relevance to the entire circle—not just to the individual who had the dream. Sometimes participants will receive a message or information that is for the entire group.

Carol Proudfoot-Edgar, who encourages group interaction with dreamwork in her workshops, notes the value of sharing dreams in a community:

> In every workshop I teach, no matter how long, I ask participants to journal and then share their dreams in Circle during the next morning's session. In workshops of more than fifteen participants, we form Dream Clan groups. Within these groups we speak and draw our dreams. Each Dream Clan has a Dream Keeper who notes the similarities among the dreams. The last full day of the workshop, a major portion is given to mapping the whole Circle's dreams and working to both understand and enact these dreams (when appropriate).
>
> As images appear in our dreams, it is helpful to draw the images in the same colors as they appeared in the dream. Once the drawings are completed we can see where images overlap.
>
> For example, if a bird shows up in the dreams of five different participants we will discuss or journey on the significance of what the bird has to share with the group. One time I was teaching in Montana in a location where there were caves sacred to the Native people of the area. When a cave appeared in the dreams of three of the group's

participants, we made a decision to actually go visit the caves. Through journeying, we all received very important messages from the ancestral spirits who lived there.

From sharing our dreams in a circle, we are shown the work we are doing as individuals and as a group. Our dreams are a major way that the spirits are speaking to us—informing, guiding, requesting. The dream drawings become part of the published material available to participants after the longer workshops. They record journeys much the way writing in a journal does, and we reflect on them to see how they have impacted our life as time goes on.

I encourage participants to do this dreamwork at home, too.

We also construct "dream gatherers," usually using natural materials in the landscape where we are meeting. Dreams are a doorway into another world, and the dream gatherer is the door. Think of the wreaths that people make at Christmas and hang on their doors. There is a circle within the wreath. The dream gatherer is made from things from Nature and has a circle that represents the doorway into the dream world. These are then placed somewhere close to each dreamer and used to entice the dreamer and the dream spirits to join one another in mutual collaboration.

EXERCISE: MAKING YOUR OWN DREAM GATHERER

Carol Proudfoot-Edgar has been impressed by how the dream gatherers that each person makes seem to promote stronger dreaming. It can be very valuable to make your own. You can gather materials from the landscape or from your home. For example, tie twigs together with feathers between them or tie some thread around a simple piece of wood. The thread represents the fringed pathway that may reach out and draw the dreaming world to you.

Try using your dream gatherer for a period of time, such as a month, and see if your nighttime dreaming world becomes more active, vivid, and informative. It is important to make note of your dreams, and for some of us, it is very helpful to draw our dreams because the image world speaks to us in ways words do not. It is also important to be willing to follow through on teachings you receive from the Dreamtime—otherwise this gateway may close until you are ready to respond accordingly.

INTERPRETING NIGHT DREAMS

Many therapists study for years to learn the symbolic interpretation of dreams. You can write them down, or draw them—and even then the meaning might be unclear. Shamanic practitioners have found journeying to a power animal or teacher to ask for the meaning of dreams to be a great way to work. One such journey, which Sandra suggests, is a journey to the Land of Dreams:

> Years ago I discovered a territory in nonordinary reality called the Land of Dreams. It is a wonderful place where you can enter into a dream that you have had before to learn the interpretation of the symbols.
>
> To begin, think of a dream that you would like to work with and ask a power animal or teacher to take you to the Land of Dreams. There you will find a guide who will help you to understand the important elements and meaning of your dream.

Another way to uncover the meaning of a dream, suggests Tom Cowan, is to utilize the power of a group:

> A dreamwork process developed by psychiatrist Montague Ullman more than thirty years ago has been used by groups of lay people as well as professionals to

study, reflect on, and interpret their dreams. I've created a shamanic adaptation of this process by incorporating it into drumming circles and other shamanic groups since the 1980s.

First, a dreamer tells a dream. Others take notes for two reasons: For one, it helps the others remember the key parts of the dream. Second, it slows down the dreamer in the telling so there is more time for elements of the dream to sink into everyone's unconscious.

Next, people can ask the dreamer clarifying questions. These help the others "see" the dream more accurately. Examples of clarifying questions are: How many people do you think were in that "crowded" room? What kind of street were you walking down in the dream? What did the man/woman/child you saw look like?

Clarifying questions are not *interpretive* questions, such as: What do you think the crowded room means? Did the man remind you of anyone that you know? What is your relationship with your mother? At this point in the process, the people in the group do not want to know how the dreamer would interpret the dream or anything in it. Such interpretations from the dreamer will cloud and confuse the others working with the dream. Furthermore, the point of working with a dream is to find ways to interpret it; the dreamer will probably not be sure at this point what the dream means.

Next each person journeys into the dream *as if it were his or her own dream.* So if the dreamer sees his mother in the dream, each person journeying would see his or her own mother in the dream, not the original dreamer's mother. This way the dream becomes personal for each individual. On the journey, each person can talk to anyone or anything in the dream because everything is conscious and can communicate.

For example, we can ask the elements of the dream why they are in the dream. We can extend the dream beyond where it ended for the original dreamer to see what happens next. Similarly, we can journey to the events leading up to the dream to see what happened before it began. And if the dreamscape shifts into something very different from the original dream, that is okay also. Dreams are alive and become even more alive inside a shamanic journey.

After the journeying, each person relates his or her journey and speaks of it as if it were based on his or her personal dream, not the original dreamer's. This is important to make the dreamer feel safe. In other words, *no one tells the original dreamer what his or her dream means.* No one plays psychiatrist here to psychologize the dreamer or the dream. Everyone speaks about the dream in terms of what the dream and journey mean for themselves. But as the original dreamer listens to all the various ways that the dream unfolded for others, the dreamer begins to see possible interpretations. From this smorgasbord of interpretations, the dreamer will find those meanings that make sense. Ultimately only the dreamer knows what the dream means. This process respects that.

After all the dream journeys are related, then the original dreamer (who also journeyed into the dream) shares with the group what he or she thinks the dream is about, based on what happened in the dreamer's journey as well as from the possibilities that emerged in the dream journeys of others in the group.

WORKING WITH NIGHTMARES

People in indigenous traditions take nightmares and dreams of tragedy and great difficulty very seriously. One way to work with a dream of this nature is to gather a group of friends or peers and then tell them the dream in great detail, leaving nothing out.

Then you may ask your friends to create a drama in which various people take an active role in the dream and then act it out like a play. According to the shamanic path, once the dream is acted out, it is done, the prophesy fulfilled, the objective accomplished.

For example, if you have a dream that your house is burning down, you might engage your circle of friends to build a miniature representation of your house using cardboard. Once it is done, have someone light a match to it. Have some people act out being the fire crew coming to put it out. Dowse the fire with water. Feel your emotions and say out loud all the words that go along with seeing your house on fire. Breathe a sigh of relief when the fire is out. The act is now done and you no longer have to worry that the prophetic dream will come to be, that your actual house will be destroyed. The dream has been manifested and it is done.

A Healing Nightmare

If you are struggling with a serious illness, addiction, or chronic affliction, you might encounter it in your dreaming in the form of a nightmare. This experience can be disturbing to say the least, or terrifying at its most extreme. However, the shamanic perspective allows us to take a more informed look at what the message of the dream may actually be. It also allows us to take an active role in our own healing. You can turn the tables, so to speak, by meeting with the spirit of your illness or affliction in your journeywork—in your Sacred Garden, for example—and there, you can confront it directly. This could also happen spontaneously as a healing dream.

Hank is one of many who has been able to resolve an issue through a vivid and potent dream:

> I remember a nightmare I had almost forty years ago—an extremely vivid dream in which I was in Africa, wading along the edge of a shallow, jungly river looking for fossils in the eroded silty clays of the riverbank above me. This is also what I do as a scientist (I search for fossils),

so this experience was not unfamiliar to me. As I slogged along, knee-deep in the muddy water, I suddenly turned a corner and found myself face to face with a crocodile. It was a really big one, a fifteen-footer at least, and it was much too close to me.

After a moment's hesitation, it started to close in. Not surprisingly, I began to panic, and as I desperately tried to escape up the steep riverbank, the sticky brown mud impeded my progress. In no time at all, the croc was almost upon me. Perhaps the shock of knowing that I could not possibly get away triggered what happened next.

While my physical body continued to sleep, I "woke up" in my dream, which means I entered a state of lucid dreaming, and I realized that the whole scenario—the African river, the mud, the crocodile—was a dream. With that understanding, I swiveled around and, raising my arm, I pointed at the giant reptile and shouted "Stop!" The croc slid to a halt an arm's length away.

I stared into its yellow eyes and demanded to know why it was pursuing me. A telepathic response came immediately: "I am your tobacco addiction." Stunned, I stared at the creature and noticed for the first time that the brown mud caked all over it looked like the tar I cleaned out of my pipes. Suddenly, I smelled that familiar, rancid tobacco odor emanating from the croc.

Then something unexpected happened. The reptile shifted somehow, transforming itself from pursuer into pal, appearing more like a pet or a harmless circus animal, but it was too late. I had seen it for what it really was. My resolve formed, and I proclaimed with absolute authority, "You're outta here. I no longer need you in my life," and instantly the croc was gone.

This was the turning point in my battle to give up smoking. From that day forward, I never had another cigarette and I never looked at crocs in quite the same way either. From the perspective of the shaman, I confronted the spirit of my addiction in the dream world, battled it, and won. Even though it tried to shapeshift into an ally, I saw it for what it really was and remained steadfast. I have not smoked tobacco since that dream.[5]

A fantastic dream perhaps? Then again, maybe not. If you are dealing with an addiction or illness and you haven't found solutions through your dreams, here's a suggestion for how to journey to its spirit. While listening to the CD that accompanies this book, go to your inner place or your Sacred Garden and practice relaxation. Feel the tranquility of this wonderful place. Allow it to calm you.

When you feel settled, call for your most powerful spirit helpers to come. If you are not sure about who your spirit helpers are, you should journey to find them first. When your spirit helpers arrive, tell them that you plan to confront the spirit of your illness (or addiction) and that you need their support. We are not meant to go through things like this alone. Ask them to provide you with power, protection, and support.

When you feel yourself become power-filled, find a trail at your garden's edge, one that leads off through the foliage or trees or grasslands down into another lower area that is clearly separate from your personal place of refuge. This will be your battleground. Ask your helpers to accompany you, and then go there. This is where you and your helping spirits will confront the spirit of your illness.

Hank stresses the fact that the more vividly you envision everything in your dream, the more powerful your battle with your addiction or illness will be:

Pick a spot that appeals to you in some way, a place of advantage, perhaps a large stone with a flat summit upon which you can stand high up above the ground. Then, call for the spirit of the illness to come. Remember, everything

128

that has a physical aspect here in this world has a dream aspect there in that other world, and this includes illness.

When the spiritual aspect of your illness or addiction appears, observe it closely. What is it? How does it look? Does it seem threatening? Friendly? Remember, your helping spirits are with you, and so there is nothing to fear. You are safe and just about to reverse the course of your illness or addiction.

Enter into brief conversation with it, just as I did with the crocodile, but don't be fooled if it shifts to appear charming or amiable. This is not a good guy. This is not someone you want connected with you. Think about your spirit helpers and how they have filled you with power. Allow your inner director, your inner chief, to emerge.

Bring up your full power and confront the illness spirit. Order it to leave you. In your mind's eye, see it diminished, beaten down, and defeated, and banish it from your life forever. If there is any resistance, ask your spirit helpers to flex the spiritual muscle for you, and they will. Don't be surprised if someone unexpected shows up to assist. If your illness spirit has chosen to manifest itself to you as a crocodile or a dragon, the new ally could be St. George—or even Archangel Michael with his sword of light.

This doesn't mean that crocodiles or dragons are evil, by the way. It is simply a form that your illness has chosen to take in confronting you. The spirit of your affliction could appear as anything, even as a sacred being, a saint or a prophet or an angel. Your task lies in seeing through its shape-changing trickery—in seeing it for what it really is and remaining firm in your resolve.

When the sickness spirit has vanished, return up the trail to your garden. Does anything appear different? Ask your defenders to join you and have a talk with them.

Express your gratitude and ask them to remain on guard until all vestiges of the illness have left your body.

There is one more aspect of this healing dynamic that needs to be considered. Since your subconscious body-soul is the self-aspect through which you journey into your garden, it has witnessed all that transpired, and it takes everything literally. So while you are still in your garden, address your body-soul directly, in the same way that a kindly, wise chief might speak to one of his or her servants. Ask your body if there is anything it needs or wants. You may get a surprise. It could be an espresso at your favorite cafe, a long hug with your lover, a swim at your favorite beach, or even a hot fudge sundae.

Use your mental egoic soul to create a thoughtform—a visualization of whatever it is your body-soul has asked for and offer it, right there in your garden. Take your time and allow the experience to be savored, like a fantasy. Remember, your body-soul does not distinguish between reality and illusion. So from the body's perspective, the visionary experience that you just had is real, and so is the thoughtform of the gift you have created for it.

This is active dreaming, or what Jung called "active imagination."

Next, when your body-soul is sparkling happily, instruct it to start restoring your energetic matrix to its former undistorted state. One of the primary functions of your body-soul is memory, much like the hard drive of a computer. It can remember the original pattern of your energetic matrix before any distortions occurred, and it can rework your energy field accordingly now that the illness intrusions have been removed. As the blueprint is repaired, your inner healer will go to work once again with a clear pattern to work from, and your health will be restored. In this way, utilizing the shamanic journeywork method, you can infuse your own inner healer with an enhanced sense of purpose as well as with power and support from your helping spirits. Knowing this, you might adopt a healing meditation, repeated at regular intervals, to reinforce your command—to heal the body.

So many of the things that appear in your dreams and journeys can be a source for healing. Hank often shares a story about a particular journey one of his students had, as it reveals how transformative shamanic journeywork may be, as well as how the Sacred Garden in the Middle World of dream may be used as a place of power and healing:

Many years ago during a workshop in Sacramento, California, a woman in her early fifties had a particular place in mind to be her Sacred Garden. When she returned from the journey, she seemed agitated and on the verge of tears, and during the break, she asked if she could share her journey with me privately. This is the essence of what she told me.

She described how since childhood this particular locality was her special inner place where she had daydream-like adventures with her imaginal friends. She spoke of how it resembled an English garden or park with rows of flower beds and trees, including a small thatched cottage where she had teddy bear tea parties with all her stuffed animals (who came to life, of course, in this magical place), and so forth.

On this day, she had journeyed back to this locality, but it was not as she remembered it. For starters, it had thorny, unfriendly looking vines growing all over everything, choking the trees and blanketing the elements that made the place so charming. They were actively growing even as she saw them, and as I listened to her account, a message arrived in my mind, a download from my over-soul/spirit teacher. On impulse, I took courage and asked her if she had cancer.

Her eyes widened as she confirmed my intuition. She told me that she had recently been diagnosed with this dreaded disease and that it was metastatic in nature and dangerous. She was still in the denial phase and only she and her husband (and of course her doctor) knew.

Now, from the shamanic perspective, the unrestrained growth in her garden was symbolic of the out-of-control cell division in her body (remember—everything in the garden is symbolic of some aspect of yourself or your life experiences). I asked her another question, and again her answer confirmed my suspicion. A series of traumatic life losses had recently created a profound sense of dishar-mony within her. "What shall I do?" she asked me with fear growing in her eyes.

"Well," I responded lightly with a reassuring smile, "you've come to the right person. You could begin by sharp-ening up your metaphysical machete and then go back into your garden and start chopping the vines out. Or you could do what I do. I was born in New York and lived in an apartment during my early years. I'm great with plants in pots, but I'm not skilled at full-fledged landscaping. So when something really big in my own garden needs my attention, I invite master gardeners to help me."

She laughed as I suggested that she do the same—invite a team of spirit gardeners into her garden to help her chop all the vines out. And at that moment—her laughter—is when her healing began. She followed my advice in the journeys that followed, yet when the week-end workshop came to a close, she and her gardeners were still chopping. The vines were still growing, and they had barely made a dent.

I then suggested that she go to her garden at least twice each day, as time allowed, and that she continue to work on chopping out the vines with help of her spirit gardeners. She followed my advice, journeying to her garden twice a day, and three times on Sundays, calling in her spirit helpers to help her chop vines (in addition to her chemotherapy).

A letter arrived from her several months later, and it contained good news. She and her spirit helpers had finally succeeded in removing all the vines from her garden. Not a sprout or shoot or sprig remained. Not surprisingly, when she next visited her oncologist, it was discovered that she was cancer-free, and as far as I know, in the twelve years since her healing, she still is.

YOUR LIFE AS A DREAM

So far we have talked about the dream aspect of shamanic journeying, working with nighttime dreams, and how a group can use their nighttime dreams as a way to work on a collective level. As we mentioned earlier in this chapter, our ordinary everyday life can also be seen as a dream.

José Stevens, who says that shamans worldwide believe dreaming is central to their reality, describes how to use the principles that go into working with dreams to navigate our lives:

> Shamans see the world as a dream and view the art of dreaming as a tool to be mastered to navigate infinite states of reality. Although the details of dreaming may vary from culture to culture or from shaman to shaman, the overall understanding of dreaming is basically consistent. Shamans hold that all worlds are dreams and that these dreams can be shaped, altered, re-dreamed, and navigated by the dreamer who is also dreaming him- or herself and being dreamed by the dream. Rather than the

world being a fixed reality as it is seen by today's mainstream approach, the shaman's understanding of the world is much more optimistic and flexible because it holds that since everyone is collectively dreaming, each person can, with awareness and an act of will, change the dream. This understanding allows the shaman the liberty to act with abandon, experience massive freedom, and apply strong intent to whatever he or she wants to accomplish with the certainty that results will follow.

Perhaps the greatest enemy or obstacle to a man or woman of knowledge is the belief that one can be victimized by outside circumstances or trapped by fate. By definition, this is an admission of intolerable weakness where all power is projected externally onto outside forces. A shaman can never afford to take this stance because the results of doing so are disastrous. Shamans therefore study the art of dreaming, the art of influencing the collective dream in order to accomplish what to others seems impossible.

Clearly you do not have to be a shaman to adopt this powerful approach to your life. However, you would do well to study the shamans' understanding of the dreamscape because this will grant you a measure of freedom not provided by mainstream thought. Here are some shamanic notions about dreaming that you may find useful:

- In the deepest of terms, all of life consists of a range of dreams, some with more solidity than others. Your house and your car are dreams of great solidity, whereas your daydream about winning the lottery is more fluid and may or may not take physical form. Your house or car is more of a collective dream because your neighbors and friends dream that you have a house too, but they may not dream that you have won the lottery so that is more a personal dream. Sometimes, with enough intent and focus, a personal dream will become a collective dream; this in fact happens all the time.

- Shamanically speaking, dreams have so many functions that they cannot be lumped into one or two categories. Dreams are communication highways through which much information is exchanged and processed at all levels of reality. This information from all parts of the universe moves about through "wormholes," or pathways, that make travel over great distances in the universe possible and that connect everything to everything else. When you dream, you make use of these wormholes, and this is often accompanied by a rushing feeling.

- Dreams connect your everyday personality with your soul. And soul is defined as your essence. Dreaming carries the experiences of the body to your soul and conveys your soul's guidance to the body personality. These very same dreams can be influenced by your allies and spirit helpers to assist with plans or visions. Dreams also connect individuals separated by space and time. They allow you to maintain friendships with beings who are not currently physical or may never be, to communicate with friends who are a long distance away on this planet, to exchange information with your own other personalities in other time frames and probabilities. Through a dream you can receive help from a future "you" in this lifetime or a future "you" in another lifetime.[6]

- You can also send help to a "you" in trouble in a past lifetime. Through a dream, you can retrieve lost parts of yourself or restore that which has been temporarily misplaced by another. In fact, conscious dreaming is what makes soul retrieval possible.

• Dreams are a projection of consciousness via the language of symbols. As with shamanic journeying, it is important to learn how to work with and interpret the symbols you receive in your dreams. The better you understand the symbols, the better your exchange of information via dreams. However, even under the best of circumstances, some dreams fail to communicate information because the symbols used are obscure or not understood. That is why you often have recurring dreams or dreams with similar themes but different circumstances. They are being re-sent by your spirit self, your oversoul, in hopes that the communication will be gotten right this time.

• The symbols of your dreams are the alphabet of consciousness, the art of thinking in images, vessels of energy, the language of emotions, multileveled carriers of information, transforming agents, magnetic in their ability to draw attention to themselves. Dream symbols draw things together of like rhythm and frequency, unite paradoxes, shape and determine perception, and are used throughout the universe. Symbols unite the spiritual with the physical, as in the age-old statements "As above, so below" and "As without, so within."

• Symbols can become worn out or go out of date with changing times. On the other hand, new symbols may appear with the advent of new technology, fashions, or customs. For example, the symbol of an old man or woman with a scroll may be replaced by a computer or cell phone revealing a text message for you from Spirit.

• Symbols are the language that your spirit self uses, and for the average person, they are largely confined to the subconscious mind. Shamans make it a point to take charge of the subconscious and make it conscious, so they learn to direct symbols and utilize them to advantage. For example, a shaman may communicate with the spirit of eagle and arrange for a physical eagle to fly over a ceremony at a specific moment. Everyone there may look up in amazement to see the eagle, but the shaman knows the eagle is part of the dream and both Spirit and the shaman have dreamed the event.

EXERCISE: SEEING YOUR LIFE AS A DREAM

During your waking hours, practice looking around you and seeing everything as a dream symbol, suggests José Stevens. Remind yourself often that what you seem to be taking for reality is actually an amazingly detailed and solid-appearing dream. Practice realizing that you are dreaming yourself and that all sensations coming from your five senses are actually hallucinations of the highly symbolic dream state you find yourself in. This will not only keep you busy in a highly entertaining way, but it will begin to unravel your concrete and reactive way of being in the world. It will put you more in the driver's seat of your life because, shamanically speaking, you are in fact the dreamer at all times.

The more you practice this exercise, the more powerful you will become. You will gain tremendous insight into your everyday activities, your worries and concerns, and the bigger themes of your life. More importantly, you will begin to see solutions to many of the things that stumped you before. Simply changing your perspective is enough to transform many of your patterns in a beneficial way.

Chapter 7

Creative Art As a Bridge

Another doorway into the hidden realms is through shamanic artwork or participation in a creative activity such as spinning fiber into yarn.

Our uniquely human capacity to create helps dissolve the veil between ordinary reality and the spirit worlds, but acquiring a visionary state of consciousness through art requires both practice and discipline. It also requires balance between the mental egoic soul that is the source of our creative imagination and the subconscious body-soul—the self-aspect that manifests the painting or drawing, sculpture, or poem or song.

When that balance is achieved, the doorway through the heart opens and the created object can take on truly amazing levels of expression, for that open channel allows inspiration and intuitive guidance to flow into us from our oversoul that resides always in the dream worlds.

These activities reaffirm the shaman as a person who can move out of the mental state and become a "hollow bone" or "hollow reed" through which the Navajos say the many colored winds may blow. Inherent in the practice of shamanism is the understanding that the shaman opens himself or herself to allow the power of the universe to flow through them and bring healing to those in need. By serving as the bridge between the worlds, the visionary can literally merge with and act as a conduit for the power of the universe. One way to do this is through making art.

SHAMANIC ART'S ANCESTRAL VISIONS

Many archeologists consider the painted caves of the Late Stone Age to be examples of shamanic art. The earliest of these sites dates back to 32,000 – 36,000 years ago in Europe, and perhaps to even earlier in Africa and Australia, yet there is controversy among the primary researchers of prehistoric art over the art's interpretation and purpose.

On one hand, many claim that we simply cannot know the minds of our prehistoric ancestors, and these investigators affirm that the rock art itself becomes more and more cryptic the more they study it. On the other hand, others proclaim with equal fervor that as far back as 36,000 years ago, the artwork, such as that painted on Europe's cave walls, depicted the visions of entranced shamans, suggesting that the art makers were the shamans themselves.

From this standpoint, French archeologist Dr. Jean Clottes and South African researcher Dr. David Lewis-Williams have suggested that the purpose of making the art was magical—that it gave the shamans access to the spirits of the animals, who provided them with food (meat), clothing (leather), and shelter (tents) across tens of thousands of years.[1]

Animals completely dominate these earliest compositions; the human figure is almost absent. An exception can be found at Grotte Chauvet in southern France where a sketch in charcoal, deep underground, depicts a human-animal figure with the head and shoulders of a bison and the lower body of a human. Perhaps this too is shamanic art, and it is a depiction of a shaman merged with a power animal 32,000 years ago or perhaps a mythic figure such as the minotaur from Greek mythology.

Peoples of the Gravettian culture, which dominated Ice Age Europe 30,000 to 20,000 years ago, carved into rock, ivory, and antler what appear to be fetish objects of animals as well as images of pregnant women like the famous "Venus" of Willendorf found in Austria. They also made the first sculptures combining animal and human form such as the bipedal lion-man from Hohlenstein-Stadel, Germany, fashioned from a mammoth tusk—a power animal or perhaps a shaman merged with an animal spirit ally.

Hank Wesselman, a paleoanthropologist, has studied shamanic artwork and emphasizes how it played a role for an entire tribe or community:

Shamans created art in order to maintain equilibrium, both physical and metaphysical, between the community and the archetypal forces that affected the well-being of the community. They knew that one of the ways in which we may honor these wise beings is through our art, for we humans are the only ones on this planet who make art. The shaman has always been the mediator between the forces of Nature and the people, and the continued survival of their bands most likely hinged upon their ability to do this.

Today's modern visionaries must play a role similar to that of the visionaries and shamans of ancient cultures. In a world that is increasingly out of balance, most of us live in a state of ongoing and pervasive disharmony for much of the time, and so the role of the visionary in restoring equilibrium and harmony and thus contributing to the greater good of their communities cannot and should not be underestimated.

ART IN SHAMANIC HEALING

The shaman is the master healer in the imaginal realms and is able to perform a variety of healing rituals and ceremonies on behalf of individuals in his or her community who are emotionally or physically ill.

From Hank once again:

For the shaman, the emotional or physical manifestation of the illness is not the primary issue. The spiritual healer is concerned first and foremost with the cause of the illness—with the loss of personal power or the damage to the fabric of the soul that allowed the illness to enter and manifest itself within the body in the first place.

Drawing on her study of the Ulcchi shamans of Siberia, Sandra Ingerman notes that shamans often bring about healing by journeying and using artwork in the same session:

There are many different ceremonies that can be done to restore power and, by association, harmony within the client. The Ulcchi shamans in Siberia, for example, might work for a person who is ill or suffering from a loss of power in a way that incorporates shamanic art.

The Ulcchi shaman will journey into the spirit worlds on behalf of the client to find a power animal or helping spirit who is willing to come into relationship with the client to help restore the client's personal power and provide him or her with support and protection. Then the shaman will commission a carver in the village to make an image of the power animal—a bear, for example. From the traditional perspective, shamanic art does not represent power. Rather, it *is* power. The carving of the bear becomes the vehicle, the embodiment, of the spiritual power of bear, so the next step is for the shaman to imbue the carving with that power. Then the carving will be placed by the shaman in the client's home in order to serve as a literal and symbolic bridge between the person and the bear spirit.

Most shamanic cultures have traditions of using art for healing. The Navajo peoples of the American Southwest say that sometimes it is necessary to create a doorway between the two halves of the world—the inner and the outer—and between the people of time (ourselves) and the timeless people (the spirits). This is a poetic and symbolic way of referring to the relationship between ourselves and the helping spirits. The Navajo accomplish this with sand painting.

At a healing session to cure an emotional or physical illness, for example, a group might gather in a hogan, the traditional Navajo one-room, circular, dwelling. On the sandy floor, the shaman will create elaborate iconic and symbolic designs of the spirits using colored sands. When the healing ceremony commences, the shaman sings a very long prayer such as the Blessing Way while the patient sits right on the painting in the center of the room. This healing ceremony traditionally continues from dusk to dawn for two consecutive nights, and the painting serves as the doorway through which the spirits come into the hogan and into the patient. Through their grace, the sufferer is cured. Its work accomplished, the painting is then obliterated.

Among the Shipibo Indians in Peru, illness is understood as a breakdown in the body's energy system. To restore harmony, Shipibo shamans make visionary journeys into the Dreamtime to receive healing symbols from the spirits. When they return from their journey, they use a strong dye to actually paint these energetic symbols on the body of the patient, or they will embroider energetic patterns accessed through a healing song into the clothes the patient wears. These designs are colorful and filled with power, thus creating a strong impression in the subconscious body-soul of the sufferer and enhancing his or her own inner-healing abilities.

José Stevens, who has worked for a number of years as an apprentice to Herlinda Arevalo, a Shipibo woman in the Peruvian Amazon, notes that some visual shamanic art works hand-in-hand with musical art:

> Most of the Shipibo women—as well as many of the men—are highly skilled artists and craftspeople who embroider their textiles with brightly colored and distinctive designs of many varied shapes. According to Herlinda, these designs are in actuality icaros (healing songs) embroidered right onto the cloth. She and other shamans are able to sing these songs in a beautiful, melodious voice as they trace their fingers along the designs like a musician reading notes from a sheet of music.

Sandra adds to this:

> Through José's work I have heard many beautiful icaros and have seen many examples of how the songs of the Shipibo have been embroidered onto their textiles. It is quite a wonderful process, and the designs are passed down through their families.

> For example, a song that would bring protection would actually have a design that is embroidered onto a cloth. The design is akin to how we use musical notation to record music. As José has stated, when the Shipibo sing their icaros they might use their fingers to read the song. It would be like reading the words as they sing.

So far we have talked about the Navajo use of sand paintings, carvings made by the Ulcchi, and icaros, or healing songs, embroidered into cloth to give you some examples of how shamans use art for healing. We continue on with a method for healing used by the Kuna Indians of Panama.

The Kuna create wooden medicine dolls called *uchos* in order to perform soul retrievals for patients. Uchos are figures carved from sacred trees by a medicine man or blessed by a medicine man. The spirit of the tree, as embodied by the ucho, travels through the spirit world to find and retrieve the lost soul part needed to heal the patient. The uchos may also travel into the world to help heal the Earth and to retrieve messages for the Kuna people about how to cope with the changes affecting their lives. The Kuna honor and respect their uchos because, to them, they are alive. In gratitude for their protection and healing help, they sing to their uchos and ceremonially bathe and feed them with the smoke of cacao beans. They are seen as extended family members.

The Kunas are only one culture of many who consider some of their art pieces to be alive. The Zuni people of the American Southwest, who are known for their carvings of animal fetishes, utilize different forms of stone, bone, and shells to create power-filled objects that not only represent a spirit but actually hold a spirit. They treat these fetishes as living beings and believe that they will bring protection to those who own them, as long as the fetishes are fed and nurtured. The Zuni often feed their spirit creations with blue cornmeal or tie turquoise or coral onto them as an offering. A hunter, for example, might use a fetish to invoke the presence and power of Mountain Lion, the guardian of the north in their mythology, the elder brother of all the animal spirits, and the master hunter as well.

We have given you a variety of examples of how different shamanic cultures use art for healing. As we look at the petroglyphs and pictographs on the walls of rock shelters and caves, and as we observe the paintings of Ayahuasca visions from the Amazon,[2] and the visionary yarn paintings of the Huichol shamans in Mexico, we see imagery of the well-traveled territories of the hidden worlds, as well as the powerful helping spirits who are so familiar to the shaman. Through shamanic art, we are touched by the mystery and are given the opportunity to heal and discover more about ourselves.

WORKING WITH CRAFT IN YOUR PRACTICE

You too can make shamanic art. This might take the form of a painting, drawing, or a carving out of wood or bone, or a creation from ceramic or stone. You might journey to invite a power being to embody your creative work, thus bringing your helping spirits into ongoing and dynamic proximity for healing and protection. Your power objects can be placed on an altar that you have created in a room where you meditate or do sacred work, or you might position them on the land where you live or in a garden.

Sandra, who uses spinning as a form of shamanic practice, notes how the act of creating can be a kind of meditation:

> I like to spin fiber into yarn. As I spin, I meditate and focus on the power with which I want my yarn to be filled. For example, I might repeat the words "love," "light," "joy," "beauty," and "peace" as I spin. Then I take what I have spun and crochet a blanket or scarf for someone. With each crochet stitch, I focus on the words of power I am placing into what I am making. In this way what I create is truly filled with power and healing. Many people use knitting in the same way.
>
> Wearing an item of clothing made with this kind of mindfulness brings power, life, and immortal Spirit back into the material world. It is time to once again be surrounded by objects made with love and intention.

You can do this with anything you make, including food. Through daily activities such as cooking, making a bed, or ironing a shirt, we can focus our thoughts on a healing intention, and love will fill our lives with power, harmony, and beauty.

Drawing on his own experience with making shamanic art, Hank emphasizes that with patience, the spirit of what you are creating will come through:

> More than twenty years ago, when my shamanic practice was taking form, I was inspired to make a large oil painting of one of my primary spirit helpers, the one I call the Leopard Man.
>
> In creating this image, I accessed a light trance state and waited. Slowly the image began to take form in my mind. I sketched it onto the canvas, then began to work in color and value. The painting was completed quickly over a series of sessions, and it graces the cover of *Visionseeker*, the third book in a trilogy in which I wrote an account of how I use this image as a doorway to access the power of my spirit helper.[3] Today this painting remains in my care and hangs on the wall of my office where I write. It is a watchful presence, providing protection for my home and family, as well as quick access to this powerful ally in the Lower World when the need is there.

Carol Proudfoot-Edgar calls bringing artwork into her shamanic practice "soul-crafting":

> In some guidance I received in the mid-nineties, I was shown how soul-crafting through the hands was vital to shamanic practice. Following this guidance, I began focusing on crafting activities that would deepen our group work in Circle. Some of the crafting we do allows individuals to take their items home, and some crafts are done and left on the land where we are gathering.
>
> The range of crafting activities is varied. You can make masks, prayer sticks, totem poles, medicine wheels, prayer

beads, designs on the body with paint, shamanic garments, medicine bundles, dream gatherers, healing quilts or blankets, stone pictographs, animal clay footprints, and much more. Something happens in crafting such items that joins all the senses with the heart, mind, hands, and the landscape wherein the Circle is gathering. Throughout history, crafting has been a fundamental part of human activity, and I am not surprised that participants engage in these activities with joy and intense engagement.

After the objects are crafted, they are empowered, blessed by the whole Circle, and used according to the intention with which they were formed. But the main intention of this work is to craft our souls through our hands—to create art and objects infused with spirit power.

EXERCISE: **FOR CRAFTING**

Meditate on what area of your life you would like to infuse with more spiritual vitality: this could be your garden, home, or a relationship with one of your helping spirits, says Carol Proudfoot-Edgar. Ask your heart and hands to join together in creating something that will remind or assist you in accomplishing this infusion.

With soft eyes, take a walk through the landscape of your home and see what materials you are drawn to for creating a "reminder" for you. Do this walk without preconceptions—sometimes unusual materials wish to be joined. Gather the materials and set aside some time to work with them. Crafting is the art of shaping forms. We cannot fail in such explorations; the very activity of crafting imprints body and soul with ancient memories as we shape modern materials. As you craft, you might look into where the finished item wishes to be placed—and be sure to place it where it can serve the function for which it is crafted.

HEALING WORDS

We have mentioned that when the modern visionary steps onto the path of discovery, it becomes a way of life in which he or she gradually incorporates the spiritual teachings learned from many sources and traditions into his or her practice, which enables the visionary to live more consciously. One of those spiritual teachings includes the importance of being conscious of the words we use with ourselves and with others, and even the words we use about our wider community and the planet.

Words are power. Words are seeds. Every time you say a word, a seed is planted into yourself, others, and the world. This seed will grow as you continue to use those words. This reveals that it is important to reflect on whether you wish to plant seeds that create sabotaging thoughts, fear, or hate or whether you wish to plant seeds that create hope, love, and inspiration.

All indigenous cultures have creation myths upon which their way of life and their perceptions of themselves are built. In most of the creation stories, the world was created by a sound or a word. In this same manner, words can be used to create the world we live in.

In her teachings, Sandra stressing the need for us to remain mindful of the words we choose:

> The Navajo people have a saying, "May you walk in beauty." Whenever there is someone from the Navajo nation at one of my lectures, he or she comes up to me and tells me about this term. It means that one can choose to speak words that are loving and that will be healing to others—words that create beauty.
>
> One of my favorite teachings is about the true meaning of *abracadabra*, which many of us used as children. This word comes from the Aramaic *abraq ad habra*, which literally translates to "I will create as I speak."
>
> Indigenous people take words very seriously because they can be used to heal or to curse, yet the modern

person tends to speak very quickly without really considering his or her words. When we say things like "there is
no hope," we are creating no hope. When we say things
like "I am grateful for all I receive in my life," those
words of gratitude become affirmations that reverberate
back to us and ripple through the web of life.

The first time I did a journey about this, one of my
teachers had me sit in a beautiful place in Nature. He
asked me to say the word "brilliance" out loud and watch
as the vibration went up into the universe and then
"rained back down on me." Then he had me repeat words
to create a vibration that I would rather not see the manifestation of. I have guided many on such a journey and
it has always been an eye-opening experience.

EXERCISE: JOURNEYING ON THE POWER OF WORDS

Journey to a beautiful place in the Middle World, perhaps to your
personal place of power and healing: your Sacred Garden, suggests Sandra. Ask your power animals and teachers to meet you
there, and request a teaching about the power of words. Next,
begin saying words you commonly use out loud. Observe the
vibration of the words and see how they manifest a particular
energy in your life. Notice if the intention behind the word creates a different manifestation.

In your daily life you might start to make lists of words that you
would like to incorporate into your daily vocabulary. Be conscious
also of those words that you would like to avoid using. Incorporate
healing, loving, and inspiring words into your life as you speak
about yourself, others, and the planet. When you engage in conversation, always be conscious of the seeds you are planting.

Another powerful journey to make is to actually merge with a
seed. Seeds are very potent; they contain the code for the manifestation of a living being and are an expression of the collective
wisdom of the universe. They are small packets of the universal life

force itself. When you can experience the true power of a seed, you will receive a real appreciation for the power of the words you are planting into yourself and others.

Word Blessings

Shamans are masters of the power of words, as they know what words need to be spoken aloud to create change and healing. The words that shamans use for healing are known as blessings. A blessing is created by words and actions—such as making art to create beauty, love, light, inspiration, hope—that affirm healing and success for yourself, others, and the planet. What we bless with our creative acts, thoughts, and words blesses us in return.

Many people feel they are not poets or songwriters or believe they cannot use words in a magical way, but, as Tom Cowan teaches, each of us has the poet/songwriter in us:

> We just need to learn how to encourage that part of us to express itself. One way to do this is to find short prayers or blessings that can be used as formulas for your own words and sentiments. Once you know the formulas, you can slot in your own words or lyrics whenever needed. The more you practice this, the more you will remember phrases and images that are important to you.
>
> For example, take the Scottish blessing, *You are the wife/husband of my love* (a variation is *You are the wife/husband of my joy*). In rural Scotland these phrases are used to bless people, animals, even features of the landscape: *You are the neighbor of my love, You are the cow of my joy, You are the mountain of my joy*. With this little formula, you can bless anything in your life for which you wish to express love or joy.
>
> Another formula you can use for blessings comes from a medieval poem called "The Loves of Taliesin":
> *Beautiful the rising sun, beautiful too the shadows it casts.*

Beautiful the morning dew, beautiful too the grass where it lies.
Beautiful the passing clouds, beautiful too the blue sky behind them.

The formula is simple. "*Beautiful . . . beautiful too . . .*" As you walk through the woods or down a city street, let your attention focus on places of beauty and honor them by inserting your own words into this formula. Don't worry if it takes a few moments to think of what you want to say and how to word it. The moments you spend considering how to express yourself are meditative and create an intimacy with the object. Notice in the original blessing how the second half of each line is connected in some way to the first half. This is not absolutely necessary, but it expresses how things are connected and interdependent.

A third blessing you might use comes from the Scottish Highlands:

As the mist scatters from the crest of the hills,
May each ill haze clear from my soul, O God.

The formula is to notice something happening in Nature and then find an analogy to something that is happening in your soul or life. The following are some samples:

As the sun rises and warms the earth,
May my soul warm with gratitude for the good
*   things in my life.*

As the rain falls gently on the grass,
May any hardness in my heart soften and grow moist.

As the stars shine brightly overhead,
May my heart sparkle with gratitude for all that blesses my life.
As the road stretches to the horizon,

May my life go forward with joy and hope.

As the bird sings in the tree,
May my heart sing with joy for my life.

The idea is not to memorize these examples (although you can to get started), but to create your own blessings from them. When you use the same blessings over and over, they become second nature to you. And you can always create a new one based on what you are doing or the place you find yourself at the moment. Again, if it takes a few minutes to come up with words and phrases that please you, don't get discouraged. These are meditative moments when your attention is deeply focused on something. Such deep attention can be prayer in itself.

The above are just three examples of formulas, but as you find poetry, prayers, chants, or sacred song, look for the formula in them and learn it. Then find ways to put your own words into that formula to create magic.

In this vein, we might say something else about prayer, for these are words of power that we speak aloud or in our hearts when we wish to talk to the gods or our own immortal self-aspect.

Interestingly, the word for "prayer" in Old English is *bede* or *bed,* the origin of our word "bead." When you string your beads, you string your prayers or blessings, and the beads then become objects of power imbued with your words and intentions. This, of course, is no news to anyone who uses a rosary or prayer beads.

The Practice of Truth

There are many ways that we can use words to create blessings. It is also important to remember that the words we use in our daily life make a difference in what we create for ourselves and for the planet.

In his book *Courageous Dreaming*, Alberto Villoldo teaches us how we can change our self-talk so that we can live from our highest potential:

> The discipline of self-talk is one of the most difficult to practice. It states that when we practice truth, everything we speak becomes true: whatever we say comes to pass because our word is golden. When we don't practice it, everything we say becomes a lie.
>
> The practice of truth requires vigilance, honesty, and acceptance of ourselves and others. It begins with mindfulness and with not pretending that little acts of cowardice are unimportant. When we are not mindful, we are sleepwalking; when we are, we notice when something isn't sitting right with us, which opens us up to ask the question, "Why am I so uncomfortable?" "What thought is making me unhappy?" and "What unsettling feeling am I experiencing?" There are a few core practices within the discipline of truth, including those of nonjudgment and transparency, that help us understand how little control of our lives we actually have and how Spirit is always in charge.
>
> Whenever you are hiding from an uncomfortable truth, life will draw your attention to it by providing you with situations that will challenge you to stop the charade. If you choose to ignore these signals, your body may very well give you a wake-up call. A story created when you avoided a painful realization will become buried in your subconscious. Eventually, it will manifest as a physical ailment.
>
> Practicing truth means being willing to consider that everything we say and do might be a mirage designed to perpetuate the nest we've built for ourselves in the material world: our reputation, our marriage, our career, our house, our credit rating, and so on. So often we tell ourselves lies about who we are so that we'll feel secure in our

identity, thus not having to do the hard work of facing our failings. When we believe our own press releases, we're like the fellow driving the car with the bumper sticker "Practice Random Acts of Kindness" who cuts off someone else to get into the parking space first.

Accept who you are, laugh about your foibles, and allow others to see the real you rather than presenting them with a smoke-and-mirrors act designed to trick them into believing that you are someone you are not. To let others know who you are, you must be willing to *see* who you are, with all your beauty and ugliness. This is the practice of transparency, where you allow yourself to be seen by others for who you are, having nothing to hide. This does not mean that you go around sharing your dirty laundry with everyone, but rather that there is congruence between who you say you are (to yourself and others) and who you really are.

In Judaism and early Christianity there is a sin known as *loshon hora*, which refers to engaging in gossip. According to loshon hora, speaking negatively about someone is equivalent to cursing them, and listening in on gossip is as bad as spreading it yourself, because you are actively participating in it. It's best to remain silent and not speak poorly about anyone, regardless of how great the temptation is.

Every great spiritual tradition speaks of a universal truth that can be experienced by all, whether it is known as the "perennial philosophy" or by the Greek word *logos*. A personal truth, on the other hand, is always a lie designed to justify the terror felt in the face of the mystery of creation. If my truth is different from yours, it's because we are both latching on to a limited idea, mistaking our own perspective for universal truth. The minute we become attached to our personal dogma, we start justifying it, and that's when we slip into the nightmare of judgment, bigotry, and discrimination. The way to peace is through the practice of universal truth—it takes you out of the story of who's the good guy and who's the bad guy, and it helps you create your life journey with creativity and courage. But universal truth can only be experienced through your spiritual practice.

Making art and working consciously with imagery and words have been used by shamans worldwide to provide a focus for bringing the energies required for healing an individual, community, or the planet from and through the transpersonal worlds of things hidden.

We suggest that you use craft to bring spirit and power into your house, your community, and into society at large. Work consciously with weaving blessings into the words you use throughout the day. Start to observe your self-talk. By doing all of this you will feel a shift in your consciousness which will bring healing into your own life and into your everyday world.

Chapter 8

Working with Sound and Light

The fact that sound can heal has been known since the beginning of time. Shamans all over the world have used songs and chants to heal illness. Vedic chants, icaros in the Amazon, and the mantras of yogis all are used in healing. The great Egyptian physician and architect Imhotep, the "man who became a god," created a temple designed for sound divination and healing near his step pyramid at Sakkara almost 4,000 years ago. And today Navajo healers sing long healing prayers over their patients—whose conditions then improve.

We can even see in the creation myths that many different cultures teach that matter and life were formed through the sounds and words of some creative force. You may be familiar with the biblical teaching in Genesis that says, *In the beginning was the word* (sound) and *God created the world with the words "Let there be light."*

For the past forty years, Westerners have been rediscovering the power of sound to heal. For example, vocal "toning" and using Tibetan singing bowls, crystal bowls, and tuning forks are all being explored as ways to heal emotional and physical illness. The same holds true for monotonous drumming and rattling. Working with the vibrations of sound—whether from a musical instrument or from the toning or chanting of one or more voices—has been revealed to be a way to restore harmony to the body.

The musician Robert Gass, who has written on sound and healing and has made extensive cross-cultural sound recordings, observes that the healing power of the harmonics of sound can be seen as the "light" in music. He also states with conviction that one of the definitions of healing is to make sound.

In support of this, Hank Wesselman adds that the name of the Polynesian healing god Lono ("Rono" or "Rongo" in the southern ocean) means "to listen" or "to make sound" when it is expressed as a verb: *ho'olono.*

We have observed that the subconscious body-soul is very impressed by anything physical. So when a sufferer sits in the center of a circle and receives ritual sound vibrations that amplify the person's own healing intention, the body-soul (whose job is to restore and repair the physical) goes to work with an enhanced sense of power and purpose.

DRUMMING AND HEALING

Many of us who serve as shamanic practitioners work with drums and rattles in our healing rituals. Over the past decade, numerous scientific studies have been published that demonstrate the enhanced health benefits, such as positive immune system changes, provided by exposure to recreational music-making, especially drumming.

For example, a 2001 paper published in the peer-reviewed journal *Alternative Therapies in Health and Medicine* by a cluster of investigators headed by Barry Bittman, MD, demonstrated that group drumming definitively strengthens the immune system. To be precise, statistically significant increases in the activity and number of cellular immune components called natural killer (NK) cells, which seek out and destroy cancer cells and viruses, were seen in the subjects who drummed.[1]

POWER SONGS

We have observed that a shaman is a person who learns to move his or her ego out of the way so that the power of the universe may work through and within them. For this reason, the shaman is often described as a hollow bone or empty reed. To move their egos out of the way, shamans traditionally use singing and dancing to build their connection with this universal life force, and they frequently sing and dance for many hours before they do any journeying or healing work. Singing is an extremely powerful tool, and Sandra Ingerman teaches that when you truly sing with passion, energy moves from your head into your heart:

> The forceful breathing associated with the singing allows oxygen to flow through us, saturating our tissues and brain, affecting our arousal centers, and awakening our entire body. In response, we may feel ourselves being filled with power. I have found that singing is an extraordinarily potent way to relieve depression or feelings of powerlessness.
>
> However, many of us were told as children that we were not good at singing or our voices hurt the ears of others. In accepting this belief, we lost our power—for we are powerful when we sing. Everyone can sing, and it is a great way to activate and experience our own healing process.

Finding Your Songs

Shamans have power songs that they use for different healing ceremonies. To find your own power songs, you might first do some drumming and rattling. Listen to the sound and allow your awareness to shift until you begin to achieve inner focus—and then allow your consciousness to travel inside of yourself. Notice if you are feeling any vibration in your body and let that vibration surface. Find your voice and allow this vibration to express itself as a sound, chant, tone, poem, or song.

It is easier for some people to find their song while they are alone in Nature. You might sit by a tree and hold the intention of having a song sung through you. Or you might find that by taking a walk and incorporating some movement, a song will flow out of you. Often a song begins as a repetitive humming that grows and increases as we continue to hum. Sometimes words begin to take form as phrases.

Notice the energy you start to feel in your body. As you continue to sing, you may find feelings of joy returning to your life.

You might find your song(s) by journeying to your place in Nature—your Sacred Garden. Before journeying, try doing some drumming, rattling, and singing to move the chatter of your mind out of the way and to open your heart. Your journeys will be deeper and clearer when you take some time to prepare yourself before visiting your garden or connecting with your helping spirits.

As your conscious awareness "geographies" itself into this place—literally re-forming itself as though you are actually there— allow yourself to settle, then create your intention to "capture" a song and move into a state of deep listening. Just wait and let the song come to you. Once it does, allow yourself to hum along as it takes form. Repeat it over and over so that you won't forget it.

As Hank has discovered, sometimes your song can come to you at an unlikely time or place, such as in a car:

> I received my first song in the 1980s when I happened to be driving around the Big Island of Hawai'i. I was alone in the car visiting my favorite places of power that are scattered around the immense slopes of the volcano Mauna Loa. A song appeared in my mind as I drove—a repetitive rhythmic melody without words. I sang it over and over all day.

I held my focus as I drove on this largest mountain in the world (if you measure its height from the ocean bottom). I also focused my attention on the spirit who lives in this mountain, the one the Hawaiians call Pele. In the Andes, she would be considered an Apu, a tutelary spirit who resides within a particular mountain of great power. She has been one of my "friends" for more than thirty years.

On that day, I came to believe in and accept Pele as one of my protectors who also serves me as a teacher on occasion. The song she gave me is about power. I sing it when I need to power up. Because it was my first song, it could well be the last one that I sing to release my breath before I make my final transition into death.

I have also received other songs since that time—healing songs, for example, and songs for bringing myself "into alignment with." I sing one of them when I arrive in a city, town, or place I have never been before. Singing is a way of making contact with the spirits of that place and of announcing my presence. It's also a way of saying something about myself and my reasons for being there—but ultimately, it's about "finding connection with." It's about correct protocol.

Gods of the Harp

Songs can be used to raise power, and they are also used as a way to perform a healing.

Tom Cowan points out that in the Celtic tradition, the idea of God or the Creator is referred to as the Òran Mór, or Great Song:

> This is in keeping with other cultures that see the universe as something vibrational or something created by a voice, song, or sacred word.

In an old Irish myth, the goddess Boann (later her name becomes Boyne, one of Ireland's sacred rivers) gives birth to three sons who become harpers. As each son is born, Boann's husband, Uainthe, plays music on his harp to accompany her experience. The first birth is difficult, so he plays a lament or song of sorrow; the second birth is joyful because she realizes she is having another child, so he plays a happy tune; and she falls asleep during the third delivery because she is tired, so he plays a lullaby. When the boys become harpers, each specializes in the type of music he heard when he came into the world. I think of them as the gods of the harp.

In many myths and folk tales we hear about a harper who knows how to play these three strains of music as a healing technique. The harper plays laments and listeners weep, then songs of joy and listeners laugh, then the lullaby and listeners fall asleep. Later they wake healed of their sufferings. My take on this is that these three categories of music reflect the matrix in which we live, which is composed of sorrow, joy, and peace. I interpret the sleep/lullaby music as a means for creating peace, not necessarily sleep. This is in keeping with the non dualistic (we are one with the web of life) teachings of the Druids. In other words, our lives are not just a tug of war between sorrow and joy, but also a yearning to move beyond these two states into something that transcends the dualism—and perhaps this state is peace.

I think of sorrow and joy as categories into which we can place all our dualistic feelings, thoughts, emotions, and situations that occur in life. While we might think that the healing solution is to move from the negative into the positive, we know that everything contains its opposite and will revert to it at some point. So moving the distressed person into joy is only temporary. The real healing solution is to move beyond the dualities to a place of peace—a more abiding state that can be present whether one is in sorrow or joy.

A simple way to use this matrix for healing is to hum these three strains of music for someone as a kind of prayer. Visualize the person in distress or pain and hum a low tone, then watch the person's face begin to smile as you move up a couple notes on the scale, then see the person in total peace as you move the hum up a couple more notes (C, E, and G work well). This can be done in one slow breath as you exhale. Then keep repeating this as a kind of breathing-humming meditation for several minutes in which you send out healing with your breaths and intentions. Not surprisingly, you'll find that this brings you too into a wonderful state of peace.

Singing and Healing Patterns

In Chapter 7 we shared how the Shipibo use icaros, or songs, for healing. José Stevens, who has studied with the Shipibo, has experienced shamanic healing though their songs first-hand:

> During an all-night Shipibo healing ceremony in Peru's upper Amazon, the presiding shaman healer whispered to me that I had a growth in a specific location of my body. Although I had mentioned this to no one, I had noticed a hard lump under my skin in just that location, and it worried me some, so I was startled when he mentioned it. He said, "Let's take it out," to which I readily agreed. He proceeded to sing several icaros, or sacred healing songs, and he passed his hands over the spot and then blew smoke over me. The next morning I checked the spot and noticed to my great relief that the hard little lump was totally gone. To this day it hasn't returned.
>
> In contrast to removing what should not be in the body, the Shipibo also utilize icaros that can have a positive healing effect or create a cocoon of protection. Indigenous people know that inside the body there are

vast open spaces, plenty of room for things to go in or come out. One of the things that can travel in and out of these open spaces they like to call *mal aire,* or bad air, or cold. They believe that the icaros can be inserted into these spaces as well. This is not in contradiction to the understanding of quantum physicists and neurobiologists who are beginning to uncover how empty the human body actually is at the subatomic levels. Inside the human body are vast reaches of space—just as in outer space. Shamans say that these spaces are not empty but are filled with patterns like radio waves. These waves can have a positive or negative impact on the person. In these terms, mal aire inserts itself in the body just as song patterns that penetrate the subatomic structure of the body and impact it at the subtlest of levels. As the shaman removes the mal aire, he or she burps long and loudly to help release it. The burps are a great metaphor for getting rid of whatever is not good. Burping, which, like song, is another sound vibration, makes the release real for the body.

According to the Shipibo, each icaro has a subatomic pattern with a specific purpose. When this pattern is sung into the body with intent, it begins to create a set of outcomes that would not have occurred had it not been inserted. The icaro is intended to stay within the body for a long time—sometimes even permanently. A shaman or healer can actually see the icaros in the body. They say, "Oh, I can see the icaro placed in you by Shaman X or by me six months ago. It is still there working away." In order to reinforce the inserted icaro, they might sing into a bottle of water and tell the patient to carry this water with them and drink a little out of it every day or two. They also might provide the patient with a bottle of icaro infused with perfumed water to sprinkle on the patient's head. Or they might give the patient some *mapacho* (tobacco) with icaros sung into it to be smoked a little each day and blown around the body. Anyone who knows about the latest research into water understands that water responds to chants and prayers by changing its molecular structure. Although this has not been scientifically proven, the same is true for tobacco.

Healers and shamans actually create changes in reality by singing their intent into the "now point," or what quantum physicists call the quantum field. Shipibo healers use their heartfelt intent and subatomic vibratory patterns carried by icaros to extract negative or disease-oriented patterns from the body, and they replace them with positive harmonious ones. They are effective only to the degree that the patient goes along with the program. If the patient does not believe in the process or does not accept the healing, they can easily counteract the effects of the icaro and remain sick. This is the bane of some people who say, "How could that work?"

For the Shipibo, the universe is made up of songs that the healing plant, animals, and elements teach them. One can make a point of learning these songs and then become a co-creator with Dios, or God, in shaping reality. Thus, the Shipibo culture is filled with singing just as is true for most of the indigenous peoples of the world. Many shamans say that because we have lost touch with our songs we are experiencing grave troubles. For those in the know, it is anathema to go songless, for then one has no capacity to shape his or her world and one is at the mercy of delusion and less than beneficial forces.

I asked the Shipibo to help me learn to sing, which has always been difficult for me since I am so intellectually centered. They provided me with a cloth embroidered with specific icaros, which I was to wear over my shoulders in ceremony to help me learn the songs. Then they sang some icaros into me that would help me learn more rapidly. At first I had doubts, but I was amazed at how quickly I began to learn. Songs started flowing through my head morning and night, and I found myself singing them over and over even when I tried to stop.

According to the Shipibo, everyone has a song, everyone can sing, and Spirit gives everyone songs upon request. All that matters is that you are willing to sing. These songs may or may not have words. Often they begin with just a simple repeated melody that can be whistled or hummed and over time becomes more complex with words and content. Many icaros are dedicated to gratitude or honor a spirit helper. Others are used for establishing protection, requesting assistance, or giving direction to an ally to carry out a desired task. The Shipibo, like most shamanically oriented peoples of the world, believe that if one does not sing, even poorly, then one is prone to depression and fearfulness. They say we must sing every day without fail, and this will keep us healthy, happy, and protected from harm. If you wish to follow the shamanic path, then you will not be able to avoid songs, just as you will not be able to avoid Nature.

Carol Proudfoot-Edgar speaks more on how important it is for all of us to find a way to use song:

The use of sound in shamanic practice is as necessary as breathing is to human life. We can't live without breathing, and we can't follow the shamanic path without working with sound healing in some capacity. Sounding ourselves and sounding with others is part of all shamanic practice.

She shares the following way of working to start to incorporate this teaching into your work.

EXERCISE: FINDING THE SONG OF A PLANT

Find a plant in your landscape: it can be any plant, including a tree, suggests Carol Proudfoot-Edgar. In altered consciousness, sit beside the plant. Close your eyes, quiet your mind, open your ears, and listen to the sound or song of this being. Let that sound begin vibrating with you—rising up from the base of your spine through the top of your head. This is similar to sound rising through the stem or trunk of a plant. You will know when you have found and become the sound this being makes because you will sense a deep oneness. When you are done singing the song of this plant, tell it how beautiful its song is and thank the plant for sharing with you.

WORKING WITH STONES OF LIGHT

Crystals have been used in all cultures where they exist in the land. The Manang shamans of Southeast Asia call quartz crystals "stones of light." Carol Proudfoot-Edgar, who has found crystals to be effective tools for healing, sometimes combines them with sound healing in her practice:

Crystals are great holders and conductors of sound-light. The main way I use them is to sing songs into the crystals, soak them in appropriate light (sun, moon, complete dark), then sing again. Once this is done, I place them in various ways on or around the body to bring healing. A special method is to use the crystal for spreading sound-light around the auric body (the energy field) of a person. Such activity seems to energize the individual and to bring forth their own light, their own sound.

WORKING WITH LIGHT

In today's world we say that we are a composition of body, mind, and spirit. But often people don't understand what we mean by spirit. If you take away the body and the mind, you are left with the spiritual aspect of yourself. And that aspect is spiritual light.

For shamans and mystics, the visionary experience inevitably brings them into relationship with their spiritual aspect—"the light beyond the form." Not only are we in relationship with this light, teaches Sandra, but we *are* spiritual light:

The light we are talking about here is a transcendent experience. In one of my past dreams, I met the Egyptian god Anubis, and he shared with me that the missing piece of my environmental work was transfiguration. This dream led me to stories about the miraculous healings that were performed when Jesus transfigured into light. Stories of mystics such as Ramana Maharshi, Krishnamurti, and Krishna transfiguring into light and affecting people by their luminosity are quite common. Iconic images of Christian saints are often portrayed with a nimbus—a halo—a symbolic expression of their ability to transfigure into luminous beings, into solar beings.

The most highly gifted shamans are masters in healing others and creating harmony between the environment and the people. These shamans have had a deep and powerful initiatory experience that comes through a vision, from recovering from a life-threatening experience, or through a near-death experience.

In this type of initiation, everything that keeps the shaman separate from the power of the universe is stripped away—the body and ego—so the shaman becomes formless and pure spirit. The shaman transcends his or her ego and allows the body, mind, and emotions to be bypassed by spiritual forces so she or he can be reunited with the source of life. This is called a shamanic dismemberment, and we talk more about this in Chapter 11. The dismemberment experience is a level of initiation followed by a feeling and vision of the body being renewed and by the acquisition of magical or healing powers.

After a shamanic dismemberment, Inuit shamans are filled with light, which gives them their psychic and healing abilities. During initiatory experiences among the Aboriginal Australians, a creator being in the Dreamtime gives these shamans their psychic sight by placing a crystal in their body. Experiences of being transformed by light are spoken of among shamans in Siberia, Malaysia, and North and South America. Rock art all over the world repeatedly shows depictions of shamans as human forms with solarized heads—with the head literally replaced by a symbol of the sun.

This transformation of the physical being into light is seen everywhere as a spiritual rebirth in which the visionary becomes a luminous being who has access to the spirits and spiritual realms. Knud Rasmussen, a well-known Arctic explorer, shares that the Eskimo shamans believe that the light within the Shaman's body enables them to see in the dark, into things that are hidden, and into the future.[2]

In case after case of miraculous healings, the message is quite clear: true healing is not about encountering luminosity but rather embodying it. By transfiguring into divine light, we convey the luminosity needed to heal others and ourselves, our societies and our planet.

The light that is in us, Hank points out, is the light and love of the universe:

To make the direct, transformative connection with our immortal spiritual aspect through the path of direct revelation is to experience a sense of extraordinary perfection accompanied by an overwhelming feeling of love. When Jesus of Nazareth proclaimed, "I am the light," the message was actually, "You and I and all of us are the light." Our immortal soul aspect is the light and the love beyond the form.

EXERCISE: TRANSFIGURATION

To experience this divine state of your own immortal light, it is good to do some preparation. It can be experienced in a myriad of ways. According to Hank, many discover that it is like a tightly woven basket or cloud composed of lines of light that create an elongated, orb-like luminous field. For some it is the bright darkness of the void. Some will see this field visually; others simply sense utter peace and tranquility in which they often feel the light expand within themselves or perceive it behind their closed eyelids. But each person will have a unique way of experiencing it.[3]

First, find some music that you can listen to that will relax you but also give you a sensation of expansion. You can use the CD enclosed in this book.

It is important not to feel burdened by ordinary reality. This means you want to let go of all that you have to do, where you need to be after the experience is over, what is going on with loved ones in your life, etc. You can release constraining thoughts by doing some singing, dancing, or walking—always with the intention of letting go of anything that is burdening you.

Sandra uses her imagination to find relaxation:

> I often use the metaphor of a ship going to sea. Unless you take up the anchor, you as the ship will not move. It is good to use singing, dancing, or walking as a way to let go of thoughts that might anchor you into ordinary realms through your concerns.

Hank also uses the metaphor of the ship because it can help us in envisioning ourselves moving outward and upward:

> This is a good metaphor because the anchor leads downward, connecting us to our memories, habits, and our everyday habitual behavior patterns held in the body-soul. In this journey, you are not going

170

down into "your stuff." You're going within yourself to connect with the seed of light that was planted within your heart by your transpersonal god-self when you drew your first breath. By turning your focus within and toward it, you are activating that probe and letting your own inner light shine through you. Then you are going to focus your intentions on going up.

We can think of the connection as being similar to the string of a kite. The string is a line of light that leads upward, a connection from the light within your heart to the spirit (the kite) that hovers over you—the self-aspect the Hawaiians call 'Aumakua, or your immortal oversoul.

After you have done some preparation and let go of burdening thoughts and everyday concerns, find a comfortable place to sit or lie down. Make sure you are in a space where no one will come into the room to disturb you. Make sure your phone is off, then put on the music you have chosen or use the last track of drumming on the enclosed CD.

It is important to note that in this experience you are not journeying outside of yourself into another world. You are actually traveling within to experience your inner light so that it can shine through you. Many people actually perceive it as a luminous visual phenomenon against the darkened field of their closed eyes.

You might begin the journey by repeating the following intention: "Thank you for taking from me that which keeps me separate from my spiritual light, my divine perfection, the source, and the state of oneness."

This intention at the journey's onset tells your helping spirits and the universe that you want to transform the form of your body and the thoughts that fill your mind. This, in turn, will bring you into a state of oneness with your source, your personal creator, your god-self, and beyond that with the god or

171

the goddess, the power of the universe, or whatever you wish to call the source of all things.

As you repeat your intention you will find that your helping spirits may help you create a way for your body and mind to dissolve so that you may begin to experience yourself as pure spiritual light. Keep breathing and experience this wonderful state. Soon you might feel a change in the vibration of your body. You can stay in this state for the length of the drumming, or for anywhere from fifteen to thirty minutes while you are listening to the music. This is enough time to truly give you the experience of transfiguration.

When we keep up our transfiguration work and have an experience of our inner light, we also start to find our eyes shining—reflecting that we have touched into the place of inner joy and inner wealth as the indigenous shamans do. In this way we bring more light into our own lives and the world.

The direct experience of your spiritual light can be greatly transformative because you have touched your own divinity, and through it, the greater divinity beyond. Whenever you experience this inner light, it is good to give thanks for the experience and to feel your awareness coming back into your body while you, at the same time, hold onto the light shining through you. With practice, you will find you can hold a bit more of this light throughout the day. And it is in this way that you will be a light in the world.

THE HUMAN SPIRIT

We have emphasized more than once that the goal of the authentic mystic, both tribal and modern, is to access the true transpersonal archetypes—the "lights beyond the form." Within these numinous experiences, mystics say they also perceive a sound. Like the spiritual light, this sound is perceived and interpreted in different ways according to the psychological framework of the perceiver, but all spiritual traditions converge on a singular truth—a deep understanding that this is "the sound that creates all."

The monotheistic religions conceive of it as a primordial word of a fatherly mono-god, the Logos, through which this deity created everything in the universe and all at once in a singular event. Others affirm that the primordial creative vibration was actually a sound, such as the Om of the Eastern traditions. Still others affirm with equal confidence that the first sound was the breathing out of the universe, an extraordinarily long breathy whisper—Huuuuu—a whisper that went on for eons, the echoes of which can still be perceived today by mystics, shamans, and by astronomers using radio telescopes.

In Hawai'i the name of the healing deity is Lono, a word that as a verb—*ho'olono*—means "to make sound" as well as "to listen." Hank provides some information from the mystical Polynesian traditions whose traditional wisdom sheds light on who and what we really are:

The kahuna wisdom-keepers of Hawai'i know that we, as embodied oversouls (Aumakua), are part of a still greater spiritual composite—the collective spiritual essence or field of all humanity. We often refer to it as the Human Spirit. The Hawaiians call it *Ka Po'e 'Aumakua* (the great collective of human oversouls, or the ancestors).

This greater human spiritual field is often perceived by the kahunas as a vast, borderless sea of brilliance that has a drawing power, a luminous expanse compared to which all other lights are pale expressions. It can be thought of as an entity or being, a collective mosaic of billions of oversouls that carries within itself the composite spiritual essence of our entire species, *Homo sapiens.*

The psychologist Carl Jung thought of it as the "collective unconscious"—a hidden field of awareness to which all of us theoretically have access—a field that contains within itself the so-called Akashic Records, an Eastern concept of the collective wisdom and experience of all humanity in our long journey across time. Contact with the greater Human Spirit is achieved through our personal oversoul, a smaller spark of that still greater light.

Interestingly, these insights of the kahuna mystics are very much in alignment with those of the quantum physicists who claim that each human being (our physical embodiment) can be thought of as a "particle" that exists within a greater personal wave-field (our oversoul) that in turn exists within the still-greater collective wave-field of the Human Spirit.

From this view, several conclusions can be drawn—conclusions that can be verified by each of us using the shamanic journeywork method. First, each of us is truly a microcosm within a macrocosm; second, we are all interconnected to one another forever; and third, when we are embodied, each of us exists as a point of focus within which heaven (our spiritual oversoul) and earth (our physical aspect) achieve unity to become one.

From the kahuna perspective, through our personal godself, each of us can thus make contact with an unlimited sea of energy. This is the power that shamans, mystics, and medicine makers have always been able to access through the spirits. This is the energy that Hawaiians often refer to as Ke Akua, Teawe, or what we call the Source.

In monotheistic religions, this power is usually thought of as God, YHWH, Jehovah, or Allah. In the shamanist traditions, it is considered to be the life force itself, highly dispersed throughout the universe, and found within everything everywhere. The life force is not a being or personality to be worshiped, nor is it a thing to be revered. It is not a noun; rather, it is a verb, a process that flows through life everywhere and forever—an energy in action with which we all may come into a more intimate relationship through the shamanic path of direct revelation.

This life force that the Hawaiians call *mauli ola* is available to us at all times, providing us (on request) with access to tremendous energy—enough energy to heal any illness, from aggravating chronic afflictions to serious life-threatening conditions.

In relation to this, it is important to return from a journey that provides us with a transfiguration experience in a way that enables us to function once again in the world. We need to learn how to ground ourselves in ordinary reality—yet without totally disconnecting from this transcendent light. We want to continue to embody this light as we go on with our lives because by embodying and experiencing our light throughout our days, we change. And as we change, this will also change all those who come into contact with us.

This light, flowing within and through us, creates a vibration that ripples throughout the entire web of life, ultimately healing us, those close to us, the rest of society, and even the planet itself.

When we work in this way we are working with divine essence of all of life including the divine light of the planet. Once we tap into the divine, we go beyond physical and emotional pain. For when we transcend our body and its emotions we move into a spiritual state where pain does not exist. The shamans of antiquity knew this and drew upon it. It's just that we have forgotten.

MAINTAINING A SPIRITUAL STATE

It can be difficult to maintain a state of spiritual light if our thoughts break our concentration. You might find yourself being in a true transcendent state—in both states at once, both here and there—and all of a sudden your mind invades your serenity with lists of things you need to do later on the day. The experience of mental chatter is a common problem in all spiritual practices.

According to Sandra, there are tools to enhance your ability to practice transfiguration:

I have found that by toning, you can deepen this experience of transfiguration. Toning is where you sound out a vowel (a, e, i, o, u) and hold it. Allow one vowel to flow into the next and keep the reverberation of sound going. Most of us are familiar with sounding out Om, or Aum. You can use the sound of Aum and hold that too. As we've mentioned, Hindu scriptures teach that Aum is the sacred syllable from which the entire universe is manifested.

When I teach the practice of transfiguration in my workshops, lectures, and conferences, I have the group stand up and tone once they are in a transfigured state. I find this helps maintain a divine state of consciousness while keeping out interfering mental thoughts. Try doing some toning and experience how the vibration affects your consciousness and state of well-being. This is a way to combine the healing power of sound and light together.

A JOURNEY TO A DESCENDANT

The use of sound and light is becoming more and more common in the healing modalities of today. Many healers believe that there will be a time when using sound and light becomes the predominant form of healing.

We can actually journey into the future and learn from descendants how they have evolved with their healing practices and how they incorporate sound and light for healing.

In the shamanic traditions, it is understood that when you journey into and through the Dreamtime you are outside of the time-space continuum of the physical world. This means you can journey back in time to meet with ancestors or even forward into the future to encounter descendants. Sandra, who leads these time-travel journeys in some of her workshops, loves to see what the future has in store for us:

Since the early 1990s, I have been leading journeys in which my workshop participants are encouraged to connect with descendants. This can be quite an experience—because our descendants may have evolved beyond where we are now, and in the process, they may have learned a great deal about how to thrive. In other words, we may find that they are a wealth of information.

Even if you don't have children in this life, you will have spiritual descendants. So when you do this journey you are asking to meet with descendants on a general level.

Hold the intention to journey into a time in the future when life is good and harmonious. You might journey into a time where sound and light are predominantly used for healing. There might also be other advanced healing methods used in the future. Ask to meet with a descendant or a group of descendants who can show you how they use sound and light for healing. Then ask for something simple you can bring back into your practice today.

One time when I was journeying to descendants, they tried to show me a musical note to use. They felt that I would not be able to get to this pitch using my voice. They suggested that I get a tuning fork of the pitch A, which I could use in place of my voice. This is an example of something simple and practical the descendants shared with me.

I have led descendant journeys throughout the United States and Europe. People often report having similar experiences. They say that life has become simpler than the way we live now and that in the future people work together as a community when someone becomes ill.

Working with descendants can provide an abundance of information. It is a journey you may want to practice again and again. Try to build a strong and healing relationship with one descendant or group of descendants. They will keep sharing more information with you over time. They can be very joyous, and this will instill hope for the future of the planet. Remember that our descendants have an investment in our healing and our evolution of consciousness, for we are creating the world they will live in.

Hank, who has written about his experiences with one of his descendants, believes that the person he met in the future is actually an aspect of himself:

> After a continuum of spontaneous visionary connections that I had over a twenty-year period with a man named Nainoa who lives in the future, I realized that he is actually one of my descendant selves.
>
> My ability to make this claim comes from direct revelation, and as my journeys into the future deepened and stabilized over the years, the process became increasingly easy to access, creating the certainty that both Nainoa and I are embodiments sourced by the same oversoul.
>
> Although these visions began spontaneously—much like lucid dreams in which I could act and think and maintain my own integration as a personality separate from him—both he and I were eventually able to bring the process under our conscious control.
>
> I seem to have been given a glimpse of the future—the future that we are walking right into if we continue to do business as usual. And why would I be given this knowledge? This question has kept me awake many nights. My recent connections with the indigenous world have suggested that when "the hand that writes all" reveals the future to a prophet (shaman), it is for one reason only—so that this potential future can be changed.
>
> Needless to say, this assemblage of visionary narratives is quite unique, further revealing what is possible using the shamanic method. On the path of direct revelation, there are no limits.

Chapter 9

Death As a Rite of Passage

In traditional societies, the visionary abilities of the shaman, refined and deepened over a lifetime of practice, enable her or him to explore the spiritual realms into which we pass when we die. The shaman knows that death is not an ending, but rather a natural passage into a transcendent level of reality that occurs at the culmination of life. Their knowledge, gained through direct revelation, allows them to prepare the dying for what they may experience, thus easing their transition into the afterlife.

In today's Western societies, doctors and psychologists have replaced the shaman as our socially sanctioned healers, and our organized priesthoods serve as our official religious practitioners. Yet most members of these professional hierarchies lack the shaman's visionary abilities. And nowhere is this reflected more strongly than in our fear (and ignorance) of the death experience.

This has created a lot of pain and suffering for the people facing death and their families and friends. When someone starts to speak about impending death, the usual social response is, "Don't talk like that, you are going to get well and you will be back on your feet before you know it." Yet we are all going to go through the death experience sooner or later.

Denial that a big change is coming, and that this change is inevitable, blocks understanding. It also blocks true loving and supportive communication on all sides. As a result, many people die in a state of acute fear and anxiety, while their families and doctors try to hold them here for as long as possible. Such a dying process lacks dignity and grace—a grace that we must re-avail ourselves of through the teachings of the visionary.

According to Alberto Villoldo, Western attitudes about death make it difficult for us to find closure when someone we love dies:

> In the West, we no longer remember how to die with grace and dignity. We shuttle the dying off to hospitals where death is considered a disease and extraordinary measures are taken to prolong life at all costs. Families do not know how to come to closure with the passing of a loved one. Many people die in fear, with unresolved issues, not having said the "I love you"s and "I forgive you"s that would be so healing for them and their families. We have tried to make death invisible; we think that if we ignore it long enough, it will go away.
>
> The body knows how to die the same way it knows how to be born. We return to Spirit naturally. Nine times out of ten, we journey to the world of Spirit with ease. Similarly, nine out of ten births happen these days without complications. It is rare for someone who is dying to not make the journey to Spirit naturally, but when there is resistance, we can become earthbound. If this occurs, assistance is needed to help with the journey. Yet as a culture we have forgotten how to offer this spiritual aid.

In the Western world there are not many maps for the afterlife. Most of these maps have been drawn after brief visits during near-death experiences. The shamans of Tibet and the Americas have mapped the landscape beyond death in great detail.

So let us draw from many shamanic sources and examine the visionary perspective about death as a rite of passage. At the outset, allow us to affirm that we understand very well that different spiritual traditions have different cosmologies about where the soul travels after death, but throughout all shamanic societies there is agreement that some part of us continues to exist after we leave our earthly life.

THE LIFE AND DEATH CYCLE

Hank Wesselman draws on his inner scholar to offer these thoughts:

In his seminal book *The Pagan Christ,* Tom Harpur, an Anglican priest and theologian, reveals that the singular mystical teaching of all religions in all cultures, both ancient and modern, concerns the descent of spirit (divine light) into form—the human embodiment (incarnation).[2]

Harpur adds that while the sun is the source of all that is in our solar system, it is also by its light alone that we are able to see and know everything that exists. For this reason, the sun was the natural symbol in antiquity for the ultimate being, for God. Thus the radiant figure of the sun god, who is at the same time divine as well as human, was at the core of the Christ mythos found in virtually all cultures in ancient times.

In the various mythic sun gods, from Helios of Greece to Horus or Iusa (Jesus) of Egypt or Mithras of Persia, humans could perceive their own history, their destiny, and their eventual conversion at death into angels of light. All the myths, allegories, parables, rites, and fables were formulated to support this central play—that we are light embodied and destined for eternity . . . and eternity is a long time.

Harpur emphasizes this with a wonderful allegory. Like the sun setting in the west, our divine light (our immortal oversoul) divides itself, and part of it descends into the darkness of our mortal bodies at the beginning of life. There it remains within us, ensouling us as we live and learn, increase, and become more than we were. Then at life's end, just as the sun rises daily in the east with renewed power and vigor, so our soul-light will rise again to become one with our immortal source in the afterlife.

This is the true meaning of the resurrection of Jesus, of Osiris and Horus in Egypt, and of Mithras. It is a spirituality filled with hope and power.

The visionaries of all times and all religious traditions have always understood that each of us is an embodied seed of light. The same holds true for the Polynesians. The divine breath that the Hawaiians call the "Ha" is the vehicle of transfer through which this light is gifted into us. When we take our first breath, our divinity is seeded within us. It is in this way that spirit (oversoul) breathes life into form, allowing heaven and earth to become one.

And when that life cycle comes to its conclusion, we release our last breath, and with it our light (soul) is liberated from the dying physical form. This seed of light then returns to its source, our overarching ancestral oversoul, bearing as gifts all that we have done and become during life. And what happens to it along the way is part of the great mystery of what we experience when we die.

STAGES OF THE DEATH EXPERIENCE

There is a general agreement among shamans and mystics that when we die, we move out of the ordinary aspect of the everyday Middle World and into a transcendent reality—this is the dream aspect of this world, the same dream world that we access through dream every night while asleep. This is also an aspect of nonordinary reality to which we can journey—the same level in which our Sacred Garden is usually located.

According to Hank, death is a transition that takes us through several different stages:

> There now exists a large body of literature about near-death experiences recorded by researchers such as Dr. Raymond Moody, Elisabeth Kübler-Ross, and others, and the general outline of the stages that we pass through is now known.[3] The transition back from the physical to the spiritual plane of existence usually begins with a pervading sense of peace and well-being. This is often followed by feelings of surprise at finding oneself out of body and able to see and hear everything going on in the immediate vicinity of the (deceased) physical body.
>
> There then follows a sequence in which the newly liberated soul often moves through a dark tunnel toward a blindingly bright light at the passage's end. Often the presence of others is sensed in the passageway, and many perceive being welcomed across and into the light by some sort of greater intelligence. Sometimes these presences are perceived as relatives or friends who have already crossed over—beings who loved us in life. Sometimes they are seen as spiritual figures derived from the dying person's belief systems such as Mary or Jesus, Moses or Mohammed, the Amitaba Buddha or the communion of saints, or the company of angels or one's own ancestors.
>
> With help from these transpersonal beings encountered in the passing from this world to the next, the discarnate soul journeys through the light and into the dream world of spirit. In many cultures, such as that of the Tibetans, collective wisdom about the death experience is recorded in

extraordinary esoteric documents such as *The Tibetan Book of the Dead*, a literary work more than a thousand years old that reveals the Tibetans' culturally determined perspectives on the transition from life through death.

Tibetan visionaries know that when we die, it's like going into a dream from which we don't wake up. And the dream that we go into is our own unique dream that we dream for ourselves. The Tibetans call these postmortem dreams the bardos, or "in-between states."

THE BARDOS: THE AFTER-DEATH REALMS IN THE MIDDLE WORLDS OF SPIRIT

It is understood by shamans and visionaries alike that the bardo dream states exist in the nonordinary aspect of the Middle Worlds, the same mysterious regions that we go into when we dream at night. In the Eastern mystical traditions these states are sometimes called the Kamalokas; in Judeo-Christianity they are known as Purgatory. The modern mystic and visionary explorer Robert A. Monroe calls this place The Park, a locality that serves as a waiting stage where we may get used to our new out-of-body state and where we may do our life review.[4]

The Tibetans say that these in-between states last for only about forty days and so *The Tibetan Book of the Dead* is accordingly a long prayer that may be recited over the deceased for the full forty days in order to remind the discarnate soul (who may maintain connection with his or her physical body and be able to hear all that is said) that all that he or she is experiencing in the bardos are illusions and dreams. The main job of the discarnate soul in the bardo is to remain calm and unmoved by what it may be experiencing, much like the Buddha in deep meditation.

It is during this period that the discarnate soul may be approached by many spirits, including his or her spirit guide, a godlike being of grace and profound wisdom, the keeper and teacher of their oversoul, who therefore is in partnership with the deceased. Then, with the life review accomplished, the deceased being—now a soul-spirit—ascends in the company of this higher spirit into the transcendent realities of the Upper Worlds (Heaven in Judeo-Christianity, Paradise in Islam) where it re-merges with its source and becomes one once again with its immortal soul aspect—its evolving god-self, higher self, or oversoul.

MAPS TO THE LANDSCAPE BEYOND DEATH

As we mentioned earlier, the cosmology of where we go after our own death varies in different shamanic/mystical traditions. Yet we offer just a couple of examples of the landscape that awaits us beyond the death of our physical bodies.

Many shamanic traditions, teaches Alberto Villoldo, believe that this landscape beyond death is like the dawning of a new world:

In the Amazon there are shamans who claim to have journeyed beyond death. Their stories are very similar to the ones told by Tibetans who have mapped the journey across thousands of years.

The first stage of merging into this landscape is the experience of the sun rising as if it were the very first day of creation. This is the dawn breaking on a cloudless morning, a state of primordial purity—immense and vast. The blackness of death, caused by the collapse of the senses, is dispelled by the light of Spirit.

At that moment, you perceive the dawn as if from the top of the world itself. Not only is the breaking dawn occurring outside you, but you simultaneously feel the sun rising in your belly, and all of creation is stirring within you. You recognize that you are one with the dawning of the light; you surrender to the luminosity around you; you are enfolded by it and become one with it. Inca legends say that we are star travelers. At this point in the dying process, we can embark on our great journey through the Milky Way.

In the second stage, the shaman recognizes his own luminous nature and is no longer identified with his or her body, but with the light. If the person fails to recognize the dawn as the awakening of consciousness, the sun continues to rise in a million dazzling colors. All of nature comes alive in a stunning display of sound and light. On this stage, the forces of nature manifest in their pure essence. Water appears as both fluid and light; the Earth itself appears as light; and all of the elements are represented in their luminosity and coalesce into balls of energy. In this stage we have a second opportunity to recognize that we are not separate from the dazzling light and the energies around us.

These two stages are where the person attains freedom and has the opportunity for their Great Awakening. If these two opportunities are missed, then everything shifts back into form, and this usually happens for most of us in a flash of light. Total and complete awakening, if not acknowledged and recognized in that eternal moment, becomes a lost opportunity, and then the next stage begins.

The next stage is the dawning of the light of awareness where the sun rises and the day breaks within you. The windstorm of death is so mighty that many people become awakened only at this stage of their journey through existence. So, death allows us to sense the totality of our being, and in this state we realize that everything around us is alive.

After this we are met by celestial beings (our spirit guides) for our life review and our return back home to the original source. Our goal is to die consciously. My mentor, don Antonio, joked to me that the purpose of all of the shaman's training is "to learn how to get out of this life alive."

Again, all shamanic cultures have their own way of speaking about where we go after the point of death. In truth, none of us will really know until we get there, but it helps to have guidelines. It may be, teaches Tom Cowan, that we each have our own unique experience of the death process:

"Death is the center of a long life" is an old Druid saying that continues to intrigue, and even haunt, our consciousness today.

From the earliest Upper Paleolithic graves with their elaborate grave goods and ritual lay-outs of corpses, it appears that humans have always had some sense that not everything ends with the death of the body. Over the centuries, various cultures and religious systems have worked out different explanations and descriptions of what happens after death, and I like to think that the rich diversity of opinions reflects the fact that there may well be diverse experiences awaiting us. In other words, whatever fate awaits us on the other side will not be the same for us all. Collectively, human beings have had intimations of immortality that cannot be described as one-size-fits-all. Certainly life on Earth is a unique experience for each of us; we are not all leading the same life shapes except in certain broad strokes.

Maybe life after death will be a unique experience for each of us, even though there may be some general similarities in format or structure just as our earthly life has created for us.

But in spite of the differences, there seems to be remarkable agreement that *something* awaits us, that death is truly the center of some larger life experience. If so, each of us incarnates a life force, which extends back before our most recent births and outward after our present bodies succumb to old age, disease, or a fatal accident.

Another way to think about this is to consider the fact that so many people have recognized a certain incompleteness in human life that results in spiritual longing and questing. Even when we live a full and happy life, we can feel that something is missing, even though we are not sure just what that is. Life *feels* like a quest, and we are searchers in the terrain of earthly existence for something we can't quite name.

Dying then is a kind of un-creating in order to be re-created somewhere or sometime else and perhaps as some*thing* else to continue or complete the quest. Existence may be a kind of shapeshifting experience for us all. Perhaps we are meant to be much more than human beings, just as shamans realize when they shapeshift in nonordinary reality.

When people have near-death experiences, they often look down on their physical bodies that seem to grow diaphanous, foggy, gaseous, or misty. They look like what the living often describe as ghosts. The body seems to fade or disappear. We've heard this idea before in fairy tales and legends in which a person or animal "vanishes in the mist." But it's possible that what is actually happening is that the physical body *turns into mist* because the gaseous state is a type of betwixt-and-between state where the energy or life force of the body is being purified, rarified, and cleansed. When this happens in fairy tales, it often indicates the beginning of a journey into the Otherworld. When it happens in a near-death experience, it may also presage a passing into another world.

The shamanic journey is a method for exploring the realms that lie beyond our physical existence. Shamans relate what they see and hear in those realms and in so doing create patterns or structures for that Otherworld that make it familiar and acceptable to our imaginations.

188

Journeys reassure us that the tendencies of life and death that we see in this world are turnings of the tides in which neither life nor death wins.

When poet William Wordsworth titled one of his odes "Intimations of Immortality," he was right in step with the course of human history. We have always had those intimations, those hints, those intriguing glimpses through the misted veil that another world, or possibly many worlds, await us. And it has been an equally human characteristic to have a yearning to know what those worlds are like.

PSYCHOPOMP WORK

Shamans, in their essential work as healers, are able to heal both the living and the deceased. As we wrote in the beginning of this book, shamans heal the living by performing rituals for power augmentation, for soul retrieval, for illness extraction, and for depossession as well as other transpersonal healing modalities in which they are guided and assisted by their helping spirits. Shamans heal the deceased through what is called psychopomp work.

"Psychopomp" is a Greek word that literally translates as "leader or guide of souls." In this sense, a shaman tracks the soul of a recently deceased individual, locates it, and guides it to where it is supposed to go in the afterlife.

In some circumstances, a soul gets stuck in the Middle World and so will not make the transcendent journey back to its source. This might happen in response to a traumatic or unexpected death from murder or suicide; a plane, auto, or train accident; or even a war death or a drug overdose. These are just some circumstances that can lead to a soul getting stuck in the Middle World, yet not everyone who has died in a sudden, unforeseen, or tragic manner will get stuck in this way.

In some shamanic traditions, such as those of central and northeastern Asia, it is believed that a discarnate soul may choose to maintain its integration for a long time after the death experience. The reasons for doing so vary from individual to individual. For example, the discarnate soul may feel the need to be of service to family members and descendants, or it may have strong connections with places or persons from the life just lived. Some shamanic traditions reveal that it can take four generations or up to a hundred years for an ancestor's energy to completely disengage from this world.

In Hank's words, this means that any of your ancestors who have passed over in the past hundred years may still be available to you—they may still be in the Middle World of dream because they have chosen to maintain their integration as a personal pattern that reflects who and what they were in life for reasons that may have something to do with you as their descendant. Ancestors have a particular concern for the well-being of their descendants, and your Sacred Garden is the perfect place to meet with them, should you choose to do so.

According to Sandra Ingerman, some recently deceased souls need the guidance of a psychopomp in understanding what is happening to them:

> Sometimes the practitioner might need to convince a discarnate soul that it has in fact died, for sometimes the death of the physical body may have been so unexpected and sudden that the person might not know or understand what has happened to them. In the same vein, the shamanic practitioner might also be able to assist whole groups of people who died in a war or a catastrophe that has taken the lives of many.
>
> When a soul is ready, the shaman journeys to locate it in the Middle Bardo Worlds and then escorts this "stuck soul" to a transcendent reality or into the company of a deceased loved one or spirit guide who will help to guide it into the afterlife.

Psychopomp work takes in-depth training that is beyond the scope of this book, yet in the next chapter we will share some practices and rituals around the death process that you may incorporate into your life and work.

From a shamanic point of view, death is not an end but a transition. In this chapter we have given you some examples of how shamans see the cosmology of death.

You can also perform a journey where you visit a helping spirit and ask it to show you where people travel after death. This will help you understand how death is a rite of passage, and it will assist you in developing your own map of life beyond death.

Hank adds that once we have found and established our Sacred Garden, it can become our bardo experience—a familiar territory in the dreaming of Nature (here) in which we can adjust to our new state—a place where our ancestors and even our spirit guide can find us, visit with us, and convey us back to where we are supposed to go in the afterlife when that time comes—back into relationship with our god-self, our oversoul, in the Upper Worlds of heaven.

Chapter 10

Experiential Work with Death and Dying

As we bring more consciousness to the dying process, there are different issues that are important for us to look at and work with. There are ways for us to speak truthfully with others as they are dying to help them transition gracefully. There are ways for us to share our feelings with loved ones who are dying so that we feel complete in our relationships. In this chapter we will share with you ways to communicate with people who are facing death.

After more than one near-death experience, Sandra Ingerman has been able to clarify what we, as modern-day visionaries, can offer others in terms of the death experience:

In my own life I have had three near-death experiences. The experience of losing my ego and sense of self and the peace and beauty of being once again with the source of life, has allowed me to feel very comfortable with death.

There was no fear or suffering once I left my body. During these experiences, I had the direct revelation of being held in complete and unconditional love.

My experience with dying has made it very easy for me to talk to people about death. The best gift we can give someone in this end-stage of life is to listen to what this person's feelings are and offer support and comfort.

I teach an experiential workshop on death and dying in which I offer spiritual practices to help participants understand death for themselves. Part of this involves engaging in shamanic journeywork in order to be shown, through direct revelation, the cosmology of where we go when we die. I also teach simple spiritual practices that can help people facing death establish their own spiritual connections through which they may receive spiritual guidance to help with their process. I have also found that for some, the next step in their healing process is actually their transition into and through the death experience, and usually that person is given assistance and support by the helping spirits in letting go of their body. For others, spiritual help sometimes comes through to actually cure the person of illness, and life is the next step in their healing process.

No one, not even a shaman, knows when it is someone's destiny to die physically.

In 1990, I was teaching a workshop in which one of the participants was dying of leukemia. She was getting ready for a bone marrow transplant, so she had not given up on life, but she was preparing herself for her eventual death.

This woman shared in our group that she had phoned all of her friends and family. To each person she announced that her death was imminent; she told them, "Let's say everything we need to say to each other now so that you are not left with unfinished conversations and feelings. And then we need to say goodbye."

What a gift to give her loved ones. I have found in my own counseling practice that the grieving is often extended because of all the unfinished conversations and feelings that were not shared. There was no closure. To be able to truly share what is in one's heart and to have closure is such a gift for all concerned. It helps everyone move on after someone dies. Without that closure, the soul might have trouble in its transition as it is still tied emotionally to people here.

Those who walk the path of direct revelation know with absolute certainty that even if a person is in a coma or unconscious, the person can still hear you, so you can sit by a dying person's bed and speak the words that are in your heart. These words can bring great peace to a loved one who is making a transition. This is also true once someone has actually died. For a period of several days after their release, this person can still hear words that are said in the presence of his or her physical body.

From a shamanic point of view, there might be a loved one already on the other side who shows up to help with the transition of the one dying. Often people who are very close to death speak about seeing a loved one who has already made the transition by their bedside. This person is there to offer comfort. We can validate such a person's experience by knowing and accepting that this is a possibility, although we may not perceive this ourselves. As Sandra points out, we must remain patient and open-minded with someone who is dying. We might not be able to see or feel what he or she is experiencing, but we can validate it through our witnessing:

I had a student who shared that before his grandmother died, she spoke about seeing her mother by her bed whispering words of comfort. The family became frightened by this and called for the doctor. The doctor ordered medicine for her to stop the hallucinations. What a tragedy! A very beautiful scenario would have been created if the family members understood enough to say, "Yes, your mother has appeared to help you."

Another example of this comes from a brilliant retired hospice worker named John who studied with me. John once shared a touching story of working with a dying priest. On a visit one day, the priest said to John, "Tell me what is going to happen to me when I die." He responded, "Father, you know what is going to happen to you." The priest said, "That's just in the books; tell me what is going to happen to me." John replied, "At the point of your death, someone who you once loved dearly will be there to meet you and help you. Can you think of someone you would like to see again?" The priest found peace in thinking about someone he would want to see again.

John was not with the priest the night he died, but another hospice nurse was. The last words out of the priest's mouth were, "Tell John he was right."

As we age, we might find ourselves called upon to help friends and loved ones who are dying. Offering comfort without pushing any spiritual dogma on someone can be just a few simple words. Creating a space that contains love will transmute fear to even more love.

When speaking to someone who is dying, engage the person with your heart. Death is not an experience that we can intellectualize. Although there is a lot of spiritual information on what happens to us after we die, we really will not know until we die. Yet we can die and help others die knowing that we, and they, are held in love. Love and a sense of calmness are the only things you need to bring to the experience of death, teaches Sandra:

People who are close to death are hypersensitive to the energy around them. If I am in a place of fear or discomfort about being in the room, the person I am with will pick this up. It is important when sitting with someone to get into a centered state. Taking long, deep breaths through the nose into the diaphragm and then breathing out slowly can help you attain this way of being. If you breathe deeply, you will find that your own energy shifts the energy in the room and you will find yourself and the person you are with in a more relaxed state. This will move both of you out of your head and into your heart. Just in this act, a tremendous amount of healing will take place.

When I speak with someone who is dying, I stay away from dogma and theory. If I don't know the person well, I try to create a conversation that will give me an idea of his or her philosophical and religious beliefs. From there I use vocabulary that will fit into my client's own belief systems. For example, I will speak to them of guardian angels if they hold strong Christian beliefs. By listening closely, we can find words that will match anyone's belief system. In this way we can use words that heal instead of creating conflict, confusion, or fear.

I might begin by asking a person how he or she is feeling emotionally and physically. If a person says that he is afraid, I don't want to invalidate his feelings by saying there is nothing to fear. This is not a healing action. Just allowing a person to speak what is in his or her heart will allow the nature of those feelings to change. Sometimes the most healing action to take is to be fully present and witness whatever comes up. This act creates a space where change and healing can take place.

If a person complains of being in pain, again I want to acknowledge and validate what is being expressed. I might not have a solution to the problem, as a solution might not exist. But being a listening ear always creates healing energy.

From the shamanic/visionary perspective, there are spiritual forces around us at all times that hear our call for help and have compassion for our suffering. These forces might take the form of guardian angels or spirits; they may also take on the form of God; individual gods or goddesses; our own personal god-self or oversoul; or even of deceased loved ones and ancestors who may appear to us as angels, light beings, or ordinary people.

Another way to support people who are about to make transition, teaches Sandra, is to teach them how to journey:

Depending on a person's spiritual or religious beliefs, I might encourage a dying person to call on a spiritual force that she or he believes can offer assistance. Through the use of prayer and asking divine forces for help, a variety of effects can be achieved. A person might feel peace of mind, or divine intervention might come through to alleviate the pain and suffering experienced in the body.

One of my students taught his father, who was dying of cancer, how to practice shamanic journeying. He gave his father a cassette player with a drumming tape. He educated his father about the shamanic belief that we all have power animals that love and protect us. His father took to shamanic journeying very easily and found a power animal with which he developed a strong relationship. Over time the power animal removed all the father's pain so that he could stop taking pain medication and live the rest of his life pain-free. This, of course, happened through regular journeying, and his father did keep up the practice until he passed on.

When I have presented the idea of teaching people who are facing death how to journey, the typical response in workshops is, "The people I know who are dying would never agree to learn such a practice." Yet I have found that when people are in fear, it is often surprising what they are open to.

Hank Wesselman, who also believes that it can be very helpful to teach someone who is dying how to journey, sees particular
value in helping the dying access their Sacred Garden:

When a person who is dying revisits the memory of his or
her Sacred Garden—the dreaming of a place in Nature in
the Middle World that they have loved in life—they often
discover spontaneously that the spirits of power animals
or deceased loved ones or even ancestors will come to visit
with them there. Then, one day or one night, they journey
into their garden for the last time and they don't return.

In such cases, their inner garden becomes their bardo,
their personal afterlife transition place, to which they may
withdraw and resettle, a place in which their soul in transition may restore itself energetically and adjust to its new
state. This is a place in which they may accomplish the
past life review and where they may await their Guide to
escort them back to their source.

Connecting to the other side before the actual death of the
physical body can help a dying person move more peacefully
toward death, teaches Sandra:

After I have spent a significant amount of time with a
dying person, I ask if they would like to learn a method
that will help them connect with spiritual or divine forces
to which they can speak their thoughts and feelings.

If a person seems interested, I will introduce him or her
to shamanic journeying using vocabulary that fits with their
philosophical and religious beliefs, leaving out all theory
and background information on shamanism. Most people I
have worked with are not interested in learning about shamanism; they are interested in accessing spiritual help. If a
person is not interested in this way of accessing help, I move

on. I can still provide a tremendous amount of support by saying there are deceased loved ones around who can offer help, or by encouraging a person to pray for help.

Today, many people with cancer are given high dosages of painkillers. If the person is on something like a morphine drip, it is not possible to have them do such spiritual work because she or he will not have significant periods of lucidity. If this is the case, I can play soothing music and talk to them, knowing that some part of them is hearing me and taking in what I am saying.

Some people don't want to talk about or process their feelings—yet they also don't want to lie in bed alone. Sitting and maintaining a state of love, appreciation, and compassion can provide a tremendous amount of help. Sitting in silence and continuing to breathe in a normal but deep way will create a healing energy in the room. Often, the most powerful healing is in the silence.

THERE ARE NO UNFINISHED CONVERSATIONS

It is important to complete unfinished business that we have with people before they die. For example, if you feel you have been betrayed by someone who has transitioned, the energy you carry around this issue keeps you connected to that deceased person. You do not become automatically free from them when they pass, and you may feel continually burdened by this connection or issue throughout the rest of your life. In such cases, you might find that the same issue arises in another relationship. It's as if the issue was never completed for you, and so it keeps coming back, over and over again.

The best way to achieve completion with someone who is dying is to give yourself permission to speak what has been in your heart for years. You might want to communicate the positive feelings as well as what you have appreciated about this person and your relationship. But you might also want to mention the struggles or problems that still need resolution between you—and this can be done in a mindful and gentle way.

If a person is unconscious or in a coma, you can still speak the truth that lives in your heart. Sometimes it feels easier to speak to someone who is unconscious since they can't respond in words. Later you might find completion of the conversation in a dream or meditation.

Although the two of you might have some level of discomfort if the person is conscious when you mention difficulties between you, it is best to speak what is in your heart. A person who is close to death will want to unburden him or herself before leaving just as much as you want to have closure.

Sometimes a person close to transition will bring up deeply personal issues. If this happens, practice healthy communication. The key here is to start with what you have appreciated and loved about each other. When moving on to talk about problematic feelings, do not move into a place of blame and judgment. As long as you stick to your feelings, you are in a good place. No one can invalidate your feelings.

For example, communication expressed as, "You hurt me when . . ." can be changed to "Your behavior or your actions hurt me when . . ." Another way of saying this would be "I felt hurt when . . ." Saying "You hurt me" is an attack and can create a reaction that could set up a situation where you feel invalidated. If you say, "Your actions or behavior hurt me," you are not attacking the person, just the behavior. And if you stick to how the actions or behavior made you feel, no one can react to this with rejection or judgment.

If you can do this in a healthy manner, you both will achieve closure. If the intensity of the conversation is too high and you can only communicate in a way that throws you both into a place of blame and judgment, a call to a helping professional who can mediate a healthy conversation might be useful.

It is vital to acknowledge and honor your feelings without feeling guilty about them. We often feel guilty about the feelings we have—especially when we are around someone who is dying or very sick. We can get into blaming ourselves for not having more compassion. But the truth is that these feelings are real and they live inside of us. Either we express the energy or we repress the energy. Repressed feelings, if held for too long, can cause an energy blockage within us that can make us sick. The key is to express our feelings honestly and with integrity, and then with intention we transmute or transform the energy around the feelings so that the energy may become one of love. When we do this, all involved are liberated.

It is always best to communicate what is in your heart and mind with people before they die. However, you can do this with a person who has already died through the use of a shamanic journey. How to journey to meet someone who has died is described later in this chapter.

SOUL STEALING

From the shamanic perspective, when we can't forgive someone, we are "stealing part of his or her soul." It is as though we hold on to a part of their essence. The tricky part about this is that we cannot force ourselves to forgive someone. Forgiveness is something that happens; it is not something we do. But we can set our intention to finding a way for forgiveness to happen so that both parties are set free from each other. As we put our attention to this task, we create an energy where forgiveness can slowly begin to happen.

One way to invite forgiveness into your heart, teaches Sandra, is to create a ritual:

EXERCISE: CREATING CLOSURE

Performing a ritual to break the connection and ask for forgiveness can be very helpful. This can create closure with a person who is still alive or who is deceased. You can do something as simple as walking out into Nature and finding a stick that can symbolize your relationship. Breaking the stick and asking from a place of love that the ties between you be broken sets an intention that will now have its own momentum. It is best not to perform rituals while you are angry as this energy will prevent closure from happening.

You might also build a small fire or burn some incense with the intention of releasing the connection between the two of you. This helps send the essence of this person on to a good place. In addition, you might write a letter expressing your feelings and then burn it. Allow the fire to transform all the energy of your feelings to love. This can help break the connection with another where closure is needed.

It is best to attain closure while a person is alive, but sometimes this is not always possible. You can always journey to the person with whom you need resolution. Use deep breathing to center and change your awareness. Put on the journeying CD. Ask your power animal or teacher to take you to the friend, relative, or loved one with whom you would like to visit.

When journeying to the person with whom you need resolution, it is helpful to meet them in your Sacred Garden, says Hank. The Sacred Garden is a perfect place to accomplish this meeting with spiritual allies or loved ones who have already passed over because it is in the same level in which the discarnate soul finds itself immediately after the death of the physical body.

If you are not successful in finding the person you are looking for in your journey, you can still find ways of making a connection to them. According to Sandra, you just need to remain firm with your intention:

> If it is not time for them to have human contact, they will not show up. This has nothing to do with you. It might be a time out for spiritual healing or their soul might have transitioned to a place where they don't want any human contact.

If they are capable of contact, your intention, as well as the connection that you had with them in life, will establish a line of communication. Tell your loved one what is in your heart. Share what is unfinished for you. Although you might miss them greatly, when you are done with the ritual, wish them well and release them energetically from you so that you are both free to follow your own destiny. Then, you are no longer holding them here and they can return to source.

SAYING GOODBYE

In many native cultures, a shaman performs ceremonies to help people on their way at the time of their death. Among the Pomo Indians of Northern California, a "pushing-through" ceremony might be performed in which loved ones gather around a dying person and actually push their arms up into the air while visualizing the person making a smooth journey back to their original source.

This ceremony adds power to the shaman's guidance at the time of death, but, as Sandra teaches, having a community of loved ones around someone at the time of death is a wonderful gift:

A friend of mine who practiced and taught shamanism called in her community to help her with her own passing. She was at the end of a long battle with cancer. She was very lucky in that she had a loving and supportive community of friends, clients, and students who had helped her with her physical needs as she became too debilitated to care for herself. My friend taught her community a song that she wanted to hear at the time of her death. The song was about a river flowing back to the source.

It was clear to those people who helped with her care that the time had come to call on the rest of her community. Everyone showed up and drummed, rattled, and sang my friend into her transition. Being able to be present in community, or with family, creates closure for all concerned. What a great way to start on the journey back to our spiritual home. And by bringing consciousness and mindfulness to the dying process, the more consciously the rest of us can live.

RECAPITULATION

Alberto Villoldo points out that when a person struggles in their journey to cross over, even with the help of community, it may be that he or she has worldly issues that need to be resolved:

> An extraordinary phenomenon occurs at the moment of death. Shamans believe that when neural activity ceases and the brain shuts down, a portal opens between dimensions. The veils between the worlds part, enabling the dying person to enter into the world of Spirit. When a person has unfinished business in this world, she is unable to step easily through this portal, for we cannot carry our worldly identity into the beyond.
>
> A person who is weighed down by heavy emotional baggage remains bound to the Earth. This soul has to go through a very intensive life review as soon as he or she arrives on the other side. Some people who have had a near–death experience recall a panoramic life review— a very detailed and comprehensive judgment day—even though the experience occurred in only minutes of Earth time. When the person does not return to the physical body, the life review can seem to take years. The toxic energies and relationships accumulated over the course of a lifetime have to be cleared and released, until there is forgiveness.
>
> The vast majority of reports in the literature on near-death experiences recount positive experiences. Yet when cardiologist Maurice Rollins interviewed patients who had died and been resuscitated on the operating table, he

found many people had ghastly experiences. They reported encounters that were frightening, fearful, and painful. And then, within a short period of time, the patients forgot about the painful parts of the encounter. Many of their descriptions were similar to the bardo plains or "hell realms" written about in *The Tibetan Book of the Dead*. This leads us to believe that these patients still had some unresolved business.

Raymond Moody, one of the foremost investigators of near-death experiences, states: "The judgment in the cases I studied came not from the beings of light, who seemed to love and accept these people anyway, but rather from within the individual being judged." This means that our own self-judgment is what causes us a tremendous amount of suffering. Each and every person is the accused, the defendant, the judge, and the jury all at once. How ready are we to forgive ourselves? Forgiveness and closure while we are still living is the focus of recapitulation, a method to heal emotional issues you have with another person so that you can disconnect from them in a healthy way.

In *The Tibetan Book of the Dead*, the life review occurs in the bardo planes or what Westerners call purgatory. We go through a dark tunnel and are met by beings to face our judgment day. It is in these domains where we cleanse; if we don't have a physical body, this is a very slow process— a time of suffering. It is important for the family to give voice to the forgiveness they wish to extend to the dying person and the words of love that have not been expressed during the course of a lifetime. You would be surprised at the healing power of a simple "I love you." This is not always easy, of course, yet a lifetime of mistakes can be undone through forgiveness even at the end of a life.

Thus, the recapitulation journey at the time of death is about saying "I love you" and "I forgive you." It is a form of life-review process that we can do while the person is crossing over to the spirit world, and it saves everyone involved from great pain and effort. According to a lot of near-death literature, for some people who are going through their review, time seems to stand still, but it actually happens in just a few minutes. In our panoramic life review, every action, word, and deed we have performed appears before us and must be accounted for. We observe it, feel it, and relive it.

The sooner you commence the recapitulation, and the more extensive the life review you accomplish, the easier your transition will be. Sometimes it is difficult to begin this conversation, especially if you have not had an intimate dialogue with your loved one in years. Find an entry point for dialogue. A way to initiate or frame this sharing may be to imagine you are both sitting next to a river and that the memories between you are floating by.

Always assist a person who is telling his or her "story." Be a sacred witness without judgment or comment; just listen to their sharing. When were the times this person felt self-disappointment, when was this person of service, loved, or regretful? What does he or she remember? Look at the ways he or she could have honored others and didn't, or ways he or she hurt others. Help them to forgive themselves. Again, it's not about your forgiveness, but that this person forgives him- or herself. Help your loved one recognize that they are the hardest judges.

Recapitulation offers your loved one the opportunity to tell you his or her story, which has cathartic and healing power. It is the equivalent of doing your life review before you have actually died. Recapitulation is not a time for recriminations about past events; it is a time to listen to your loved one's life. Whom does she need to forgive? Remind her that she can forgive through a prayer or a blessing. Ultimately, the dying person needs to forgive herself and know that she is fully forgiven by life. Lastly, ask her how she would like to be remembered. What are the stories she would like her grandchildren to remember her by? Recapitulation brings closure through forgiveness. Assist your loved one in letting go of any feelings of having been wronged or having wronged anyone else.

Tremendous forgiveness can occur in the recapitulation process. But do not expect to be a miracle worker or think that you can heal a lifetime of pain in just a few minutes. People tend to die in the same way that they have lived, which is why it is important to bring mindfulness and communication to the dying process. Dying is a profoundly emotional experience for everyone involved, and it tends to bring back memories and feelings about the entire life of the person. If he was an angry person throughout life, there may well be unresolved anger when people gather. Family dynamics of the past tend to be magnified in such stressful circumstances. Be careful not to react to it or to take it personally.

Powerful realizations often come uninvited as one approaches death. It is possible that the dying person will wish he or she had lived differently, loved more fully, and forgiven more readily. Make it okay for your loved one to voice his feelings, and respond to his anger with physical comfort and support. Hold your loved one's hand as he cries or expresses his ire. Be an unshakable source of love and unconditional support even in a storm of rage. The more willing your loved one is to forgive himself, the more quickly his rage will turn into compassion.

If your loved one's condition is critical and he has not been informed of this, by all means let him know. Most people know anyway. They can feel the change among the family members present—the new quietness in the room, the hushed voices, the forced smiles. It is best to be direct, yet gentle and compassionate. Your straightforwardness will give your loved one permission to be open and disclosing with you. He will know that he can count on you to speak the truth.

GRANTING PERMISSION TO DIE

Some people have a hard time dying if they feel a responsibility to stay and help loved ones. According to Alberto Villoldo, giving someone the permission to die is necessary, and it can also be a tender, loving gift:

An important step in the dying process is that the dying need to feel that they have permission to die. We need to let the person who is dying know that there is no reason to worry about those who are staying behind. Without your permission to die, your loved one might cling to life for months, enduring unnecessary suffering and causing great anguish for the family. Permission must come from the immediate family, and ideally there should be a consensus. If there is a dissenting family member who won't let go, encourage that person to express love and forgiveness nonetheless. Many times the family members who have the hardest time letting go are the ones who have the most unfinished business with the dying person or who are the most frightened of their own death.

Make sure that all immediate relatives voice their feelings to the dying person. Permission from those closest to the person carries the most weight, even if it is a personal friend or confidant and not an immediate family member.

Countless shamans talk about the importance of this step. I had a student who sat beside her dying mother for weeks. The older woman was unable to let go, despite the fact that she was in a great deal of pain and could no longer eat. The student had cleaned her mother's chakras, her energetic centers, and she and her sister had begun to forgive each other and heal the lesions of the past.

She finally said, "Mother, we are here with you and love you very much. We want you to know that we will be okay. We will look after each other and keep our family together. Even though we will miss you, it is perfectly natural for you to go. We will treasure all of the beautiful moments that we had together, but we don't want you to suffer anymore or to continue clinging to life. You have our full and complete permission to die. You know that we will always love you." A few hours later her mother took her final breath and died peacefully.

ALL GOD'S CREATURES GRIEVE

Death is a rite of passage that involves a new journey beyond this life. For the person who is leaving, it can be a time of celebration, for in a sense they are graduating. For those of us left behind, it is a time for grieving, and feelings of sadness and loss are natural. Humans grieve, animals grieve, and even plants grieve.

At Stanford University in California, in a long-term study that has been extensively published, a female gorilla named Koko learned American Sign Language from her keeper Penny Patterson. Through signing and gesture, she has been able to communicate many things, including her grief about the hunters who killed her mother, as well as the loss of the kitten who became her companion in captivity. The observance of such behavior in other animals—including elephants, wolves, birds, and domestic pets—suggests that all creatures experience a period of grief when a mate or offspring dies.

Grief is a natural process that we all experience with a loss. In our busy lives we don't always give ourselves the time to grieve our losses. We try to get on with our lives as quickly as possible. Gone are the days when loved ones and families were left alone to grieve.

If we don't take time to grieve, however, the energy around the loss builds up inside of us as a pervasive state of disharmony that may affect us later on. We might become ill or find ourselves acting out in a way that we don't understand.

Often, we have to return to our jobs and our daily routines, but it is important to create time for ourselves to grieve. You might enter into one of the many grief groups that exist in your area. You might want to create some time during the day where you can be with yourself. You might tell co-workers and friends of your loss or let yourself cry with others.

A good way to support those in sadness and loss is to let them express their feelings without trying to heal them or make them better. A good way for them to heal is to express the energy of the loss until it doesn't exist anymore. Trying to repress it for public appearances just delays healing. One way to work through the grief process, teaches Sandra, is through journeying and ritual:

Once when I lost a friend who was very dear to me, I journeyed on a ritual that I could use to help me deal with my loss. The information I received was that I needed to channel my loving feelings toward this person. I had all this love that no longer could be expressed. I was guided to plant a tree in my back yard that I could care for as I wanted to still care for this lost friend. Nourishing this new life was a wonderful way for me to use my energy that had no other way to express itself.

Sometimes a dear friend or loved one is taken from us unexpectedly. In such an instance, it can be hard to achieve closure, and the shock and grief can be more painful than when you can prepare for someone's death.

I had a good friend who was suddenly killed in a car crash. She had many friends, but most of us didn't know each other. It took weeks for all of us to find each other but eventually we did.

It was important to us to grieve with others who knew her. We created a memorial for her. We met at her house because she loved the land on which she lived. We gathered in a circle, and I asked everyone to share a story about her and what he or she loved and missed about her. After each person shared, I asked him or her to push up with their arms, sending her on in her journey while releasing any attachments to her.

At the end of the ceremony, we all felt that we had achieved a profound sense of closure.

Hank shares this story from his background as an anthropologist and as a workshop leader of more than eighteen years:

About ten years ago, I was approached by a woman at a workshop at the Omega Institute near New York who informed me that she had recently been diagnosed with breast cancer and was approaching the decidedly mixed experience of chemotherapy plus radiation and possibly a mastectomy. As I sat beside her and listened to her story, I perceived wave after wave of her fear about these upcoming possibilities. I then asked her a few pointed questions and learned that she was in a deep state of mourning for her partner who had died (she was lesbian).

A further question uncovered an issue of grave concern. I asked her when her partner had passed, and she informed me that this had happened five years ago. Despite the passage of those five years, she was still in a deep state of grief. She simply could not let go of her catastrophic sense of loss, and from my shamanic perspective this had created a deep sense of disharmony in her soul complex—a disharmony that had been held for much too long and was now generating disharmony in her body, hence the cancer.

We then had a serious talk in which I shared with her my knowledge of an indigenous way of dealing with grief—an account that is published in *The Sacred Pipe* by Oglala shaman and medicine man Black Elk.[1]

When faced with the loss of a loved one and the grief that inevitably follows, the Lakota and Oglala Sioux peoples of the Plains Indian cultural complex traditionally created a medicine bundle—one that could have incorporated an item of the deceased person's clothing or something special they had valued in life. The soul of the deceased was then invited to reside in that bundle so that the grieving person could ritually care for them, feed them with their love, sleep and dream with them, even ritually bathe them. The bereaved would care for this bundle in this way for one year; then after one year to the day, the bundle would be opened. The soul of the loved one would then be released and the grieving would cease on that day.

The Lakota knew that grief held for too long was detrimental to the bereaved as well as to the community in which the grieving person was a member.

As I shared this with my workshop participant, I could see how this indigenous wisdom helped shift her inner sense of balance. She got the message, and she looked much better in the week that followed, yet I don't know how this story turned out as I never heard from her again.

Chapter 11

All Change Involves a Death

In the last two chapters, we have been talking about physical death—the one that can be referred to as "the big death." There are also the little deaths we experience in life that help us grow and evolve. An example of a little death would be the loss of a relationship, and through the ending of that relationship we see how we would need to work on unfinished emotional issues from our childhood. We might suffer from an illness that requires us to let go of an unhealthy way of life. Or maybe we experience the pain that comes from losing a job only to find that a better job was awaiting us all along. Death and, in turn, rebirth surround us all the time, according to Sandra Ingerman:

> When we change jobs, end a relationship, move into a new house, graduate from school, or launch into a new time of life, we are experiencing "little deaths." It is through such deaths that change happens; it is through the death of the

old that something new can be born. Death and change are not something to fear for they allow the birth of the new. By learning how to gracefully let go of the old and accept change, life can become the adventure it was intended to be.

Death is an initiation in which we move from the known into the unknown and from separation to the possibility of oneness. All deaths require that we surrender to the gifts that life has brought to us. Shamanism is a path filled with initiations, and it is through the process of initiation that shamans grow, allowing them to move into their visionary abilities and healing gifts. Initiations are ways for the powers of the universe to shape the ego of the shaman thus creating a person who remembers the power of the universe and the truth of who he or she truly is. There are always new doorways to open when we enter into a new spiritual path, and typically there are things we need to leave behind as we cross over these thresholds.

Shamanic initiations often occur without our having to ask for them. The spirits will create new life experiences to help you move into a new level of awareness. You can also ask a helping spirit to provide you with an initiation through a journey. Dismemberment, which we mentioned in Chapter 7, is one of them.

DISMEMBERMENT AS AN INITIATORY JOURNEY

The experience of dismemberment is a classic initiatory experience in shamanism. In a dismemberment experience, the initiate is usually attacked in the nonordinary dream reality of the Middle World, an experience in which a helping spirit or some force of Nature literally destroys your dream body. Dismemberment isn't given much credit by academia, yet it is an experience that has been reported by many.

There are many ways in which this dismemberment experience can occur. For example, a bear, dwarf, or giant might appear in your visionary journey and suddenly set upon you and rip you apart, or a large bird might peck out your eyes and proceed to reduce you to bare bones. You might be eaten by an animal or a powerful sandstorm might strip off all your skin, muscles, and organs until you are just a skeleton.

Although the process sounds violent, there is no pain. This is an initiation into the shamanic path, and it provides a formidable form of healing, because at the end of a dismemberment experience, you are reassembled once again by a helping spirit but with all the distortions and illness left out. It's a classic way to achieve a new, luminous energy body that is free of the burdens you have been carrying for much of your life.

In a dismemberment experience, you may also lose your ego and your sense of separateness from the power of the universe. It is literally a death experience, yet it is one where you are reconnected once again with the source of life. Through dismemberment you are able to recall that you are in essence pure spirit—and that you are able to remember your true origins.

As Hank Wesselman points out, a dismemberment experience is often a wonderful gift:

> For many of the workshop participants in the circles that my wife, Jill, and I have been leading for the past eighteen years, a dismemberment journey often marks the end of inflammatory and chronic conditions, even allergies, in which the sufferer emerges healed and free of formerly debilitating conditions. The frequency of this happening has impressed my inner scientist beyond measure.

According to Sandra, dismemberment is a kind of liberation:

> I have been leading dismemberment journeys in my trainings for many years, and I have discovered that dismemberment appears in the mythologies of all major

religions, showing that the egoic, self-possessed individual must die so that a new self may be reborn.

In Tibetan Buddhism, it is the dissolution of the ego that liberates one from the limitations of the mind. In the Hindu tradition, it is only when we can allow our attachment to the material to be destroyed that our resurrection is possible. We sacrifice our identity, ego, and beliefs to the divine, and in response we achieve liberation from formerly limiting beliefs and concepts.

The practice of dismemberment clears away and dissolves all the unhealthy aspects of our earthly selves—the ones that keep us from remembering our connection with the source from which we came. In shamanic cultures, having such an experience is seen as a sign that one is destined to become a shaman. Once we remember that we, like the shaman, are more than our bodies and minds, we can open ourselves to the universal forces that provide healing, insight, and guidance.

In my beginning workshops on shamanic journeying, many participants have a spontaneous dismemberment experience in their very first journey. Although the experience sounds gruesome, people come back with a sense of peace and healing—and a feeling that something very sacred has occurred. Or, some participants remember that they had a dismemberment dream as a child. The psychologist Carl Jung taught that many children have dismemberment dreams as an initiation into a spiritual realm of knowledge.

EXERCISE: A JOURNEY FOR DISMEMBERMENT

During the experience of dismemberment you lose your ego and any sense of separation from the power of the universe, Source, the divine, and all creation. During the "re-memberment" you remember your connection to the source of all life.

To accomplish this extraordinary level of healing—a level of dismemberment followed by "re-memberment" (being reassembled) you might journey into your Sacred Garden and invite a power animal or teacher that you met in previous journeys to join you there. You can also do this journey in the Lower World, Middle World, or Upper World. The place is not important. What is important is that you meet up with a helping spirit and state your intention. You might tell them that you would like to be dismembered. Although this may seem a strange and esoteric experience to you, it is well known to those in the spirit realms.

In response to your request, your helpers might find another spirit or elemental force to do the work of the dissolution of your body and mind. Remember to request that you be put back together after the experience. And, as Sandra points out, try to keep your mind open, as the dismemberment experience can occur in a variety of ways:

> The helping spirits are infinitely creative in how they will orchestrate your dismemberment. Allow yourself to be placed into the loving care of your helping spirits.
>
> You might find that you get put back together at the end of the journey, or you might find that the spirits have some more work to do on your behalf and they don't reconstruct you fully at the return. You *will* come back, and you will live your life as usual. But on a spiritual realm the spirits might keep working on you. You can continue to journey to your helping spirits from time to time and check on your progress. Remember that everyone's experience is different.

According to José Stevens, a dismemberment experience can liberate us from our limiting beliefs and habits, and it can free us from our past:

To the shaman's way of seeing, attachment to personal history is the most restricting obstacle that confronts an individual as he or she aims to become free as a human being. Our personal history is the story we tell ourselves about who we are, where we've been, and where we are going.

Through dismemberment, we are given the opportunity to erase our personal histories. Personal history consists of every memory that you have acquired thus far in your life, both conscious and unconscious. It includes memories of people, events, places, and experiences recorded through your five senses—whether positive or negative—as well as your evaluation of them. These memories are chained together to form your story, your identity, your personal dream that entwines constantly with the mass dream that humanity is collectively dreaming. This narrative is what each of us constantly references when we make decisions. The narrative determines our self worth, our willingness to take risks, our confidence, and our sense of shame and guilt.

From a shaman's perspective, personal history also figures in how we age, our health status, and how long we live. Our stories are so powerful (where we think we came from, who we believe we are, what we believe we are capable of doing) that all of our lives are completely overtaken by them. To a shaman, the story of our lives is a trap because even if it is positive it circumscribes our true limitless potential.

Thus, our personal history holds us hostage to an enormous store of energy that, if liberated, could be used for powerful and productive endeavors such as healing, traveling to other dimensions to gather knowledge, and working with the spirit world for the liberation of people everywhere.

For a shaman to make progress, personal history must be erased, which will set the shaman free to fly, to enter the Great Mystery, and to be extraordinarily powerful. A shaman therefore wants to erase the load of emotion that his or her history carries, to render it neutral. This is what is meant by erasing it. It is helpful to remember that your history is nothing more than a collection of thoughts with emotions attached. When the emotion is gone, the story loses its punch and becomes completely neutral, thus freeing us from feeling compelled to act out (or react) due to these emotions.

Shamans know that we each have an official storyline, one that we believe is the way it is for us, yet upon close examination of our stories we can see many possible perspectives on the same set of experiences that make up our storyline. For one person, flunking out of college is a disaster that ruins his life. For another, flunking out frees her to pursue a much more interesting life. The events themselves mean little; the conclusions and assumptions are what dictate our lives. And shamans even question whether these events have any reality at all.

The stories we tell ourselves about our experiences can shift and change through time. Every storyline comes with a complete set of memories that seamlessly move into place, depending on what we want to believe, so that the story seems correct and right to us as we reflect on it. In one story we were neglected and abandoned, and in another we were loved but given freedom to roam and explore.

EXERCISE: ERASING PERSONAL HISTORY

Shamanically speaking, there are various methods of erasing your personal history. One method is to inventory your life in some kind of organized way, perhaps according to decades, or according to places you have lived, or however it makes sense to you. What method you use does not matter, as long as it works for you. This process may take weeks of remembering and making lists, and it can be quite remarkable because it brings up so many charged memories that had been forgotten.

Next, gradually go through each memory and pull the emotion out of it. The simplest technique for doing this is breathing. As you contemplate each memory, breathe in while mentally saying "Accepting," and as you breathe out mentally say "Releasing." While you do this, you can turn in a complete circle to "unwind the emotion," a Mongolian shamanic method for releasing emotions, or you can simply rotate your head from side to side, a Toltec method from Mexico. Shamans the world over have noticed that whirling, rotating, or moving from side to side tends to erase a mental construct and pull the energy out of it. This is why the psychological technique called Eye Movement Desensitization and Reprocessing (EMDR), which involves sliding the eyes from side to side, tends to help people with post-traumatic stress disorder (PTSD).

Another method for erasing personal history, which is used by the shamans of the Mbuti pygmies in Africa, involves ingesting a hallucinogenic plant that helps a person to recall his or her entire past—including genetic history. The Shipibo of Peru use a plant to accomplish the same thing. As a memory comes to consciousness, a person will look at it and then release it with the help of the plant spirit. Sometimes a session like this can accomplish in one twenty-four-hour period what other methods take months to do.

The Huichols of the Mexican Sierras make use of Grandfather Tatewari, the god of fire, to burn away memories and negative emotions. They build a ceremonial fire and then throw into it strings with "memory knots" tied into them. Sometimes they simply talk to the fire and in this way release past events.

These are only a few of the potential methods for releasing the past. Psychoanalysis tries to do the same thing, but from a shamanic perspective, the psychoanalytic approach tends to reinforce memories because they become such a focus with each session.

You need not be a shaman to benefit from releasing your story. Story only reinforces the ego or the false personality created by the ego—the parasite that we may believe is real and that tries to control us. Although it may seem strange, you do not need a story line to live.

Zen masters live very successfully without any attachment to the past. They rid themselves of attachment to personal history by penetrating to the core of who they are in deep meditation. What is most important in achieving acceptance and detachment is the deep desire to do so, as well as the willingness to let it all go.

Shamanic initiations such as dismemberment help us evolve and grow into a deeper understanding of our connection with the web of life. They help us remember that we are more than our bodies and our minds—that we are spiritual light embodied and are connected to all of life. This understanding helps us to remember who and what we really are and to live a spiritual life. For as we have been saying throughout this book: shamanism is more than a series of methods. When it is practiced with humility, reverence, and self-discipline, it becomes a way of life that is utterly free of any religious overlay or dogma.

Chapter 12

Our Children Are Our Future

A recent poll has revealed that as children, as many as 61 percent of us received great comfort and support by communicating with imaginary friends—loving and caring beings who came through from the worlds of things hidden to be our companions. From the mystical perspective, the teddy bears and stuffed animals given to us by parents and relatives were exoteric symbols for esoteric archetypal forces that our parents, often unknowingly, were inviting into relationship with us. Our parents gave us dolls and animals partly because this is common in the Western world, yet on some level they might have had dim memories of their own imaginary friends who came into relationship with them during their childhoods.

At around the age of eight to ten, socialization by our parents, teachers, and friends encouraged the veil to drop, and our imaginary friends departed, their job done. At this point in our lives, we were encouraged to believe that the real world consisted only of what we could see, hear, feel, taste, and smell, so, in a sense, the world became less than it was. Most of us simply went along with it and accepted this as given.

The socialization process that occurs at this age, the "given" that children have come to accept, marks a level of initiation into an existence in which a child begins to feel a sense of separation from his or her ultimate source and, by association, from their spiritual allies. And why, we might ask, is this necessary? Perhaps it is so that we can fully incarnate into our embodiments so that we can learn the life lessons that are available to us on this physical plane of existence through which we grow, increase, and become more. For some, however, the veil remains thin and spiritual allies stay close, often visiting in dreams. For a few people, the veil does not drop at all.

Thus, in some ways, the way of the shaman is the way of the child. And, as Sandra Ingerman points out, beginners in the study of shamanism often immediately see the connection between shamanic journeying and their own childhoods:

> When I teach workshops on shamanic journeying, a large percentage of my participants tell me that they actually journeyed as children. They simply did not realize that this was what they were doing, yet when their attention refocuses into the imaginal realms where their spiritual allies were waiting to companion and champion them, they discovered that these "spirit-friends" were assisting them through the perils and pains of their childhood.

Through the shamanic path, we discover that what we thought were "imaginary friends" in childhood—friends born of our imagination—were actually real spirits who were looking after us, notes Hank Wesselman:

> We use the word "imaginal" when referring to the shamanic path with deliberation, distinguishing it from the

226

word "imaginary" that refers to something that is created by our imagination, yet is not really real. "Imaginal" implies a being that has its own agenda and thus its own autonomous existence in a hidden reality that is quite separate from the one who is perceiving it. This is a concept well understood by the indigenous peoples of the world.

The shamanic path gives us the opportunity to reconnect with these imaginal friends from childhood. Sandra notes that this reconnection can be a very happy reunion:

> Many of my students share with me that they remember the invisible beings who comforted them during times of abuse or some other type of pain and suffering as children. They also share that until this moment (in the workshop) they had forgotten this magical time in their lives.
>
> In response, I have come to understand that as the veils between the worlds closed down for us, a magical and important component in our lives was lost. And since that time, most of us have learned through direct experience that when we acknowledge only the outer material world, this does not necessarily lead to happiness.

In today's world, increasing numbers of us are feeling a growing sense of emptiness and despair, and we dimly sense within our souls a sense of longing for something, some path, that has been lost. As children, we knew the path of the world of things hidden well; it's just that we have forgotten. When we rewalk this path with reverence and discipline, we rediscover that the mystery still sustains us today, just as it always did in the past.

RITES OF PASSAGE

Shamanic cultures give credence to the imaginal friends of childhood, and perform ceremonies to honor the transitions in a child's life, such as childhood to puberty and adolescence to adulthood. In our modern world these rites of passage are not acknowledged in a way that helps children in their understanding of how to move into a new stage of life—and let the previous stage go.

As Hank points out, the "rites of passage" seen in Western culture do not come close to accomplishing what shamanic ceremony does in terms of preparing an individual for a new stage of life:

> Getting a driver's license, going to the high school prom, and drinking alcohol or smoking pot are pale comparisons to indigenous ceremonies in which each boy and girl is subjected to tests, trials, and tribulations that may include social isolation for many days and nights, fasting with no food or water during that extended time, and even enduring physical mutilation—circumcision, tooth evulsion, whipping, scarification, or tattooing, in which the "child" dies and the "adult" is born. During this time, their helping spirits may approach them once again, which is why many groups call such rites of passage the "vision quest."
>
> Hawaiian elder Hale Makua once said that in ancient Hawai'i, each boy-child lived in the house of his mother until he was about six or seven years old. Then the boy went to live in the Men's House, and the first thing that the men taught the boys was how to treat women with respect. In such a society, marital or spousal abuse was virtually unknown. The role of initiation rituals was (and is) the key.

In our Western societies today, many teenagers join gangs as a way to handle their transition from childhood to adulthood in an empowered manner. They are searching for some form of rite of passage to become fully initiated and actualized beings, so that they can discover who and what they are. If society or the community doesn't offer a healthy way to achieve this, they will find some way to create an entrance into their new stage of life—whether by joining a gang or through engaging in criminal behavior in which the boy or girl feels they gain power over the society, family, or authority holding them down.

Thoughts from Hank:

If we were to consider today's world from the male perspective, our young boys are unrelentingly influenced by films, news and social media, peer groups, and by cultural ideals to become warriors. In response, many embrace the ideal of becoming "powerful men" with beautiful and desirable women, money, status, "bling," and the ability to become a dominating force in the world. A spiritual component to this process is nowhere in sight.

In our current world, those who walk the warrior's path include corporate business persons, politicians, world leaders, economists, the military—people who by nature are strong leaders and who ideally should be working for the benefit of all in the positive polarity. When our politicians and our corporados fail in this task, we tend to move into the negative polarity. This is when we turn to covert and coercive ways of manifesting what we want via military, FBI, and CIA operations. Yet we usually discover that the solutions to our problems are rarely achieved through the negative polarity.

Hale Makua, my Hawaiian kahuna friend, was fond of observing that the positive polarity of the warrior is persuasion; the negative is coercion. It's not that the negative is necessarily bad. The negative side allows us to learn our life lessons. And what do we learn in the school of hard knocks? The lesson, as Makua often observed, is about how to lose gracefully.

Our children are our future and it is important that they learn spiritual values sooner rather than later. It is up to us as their elders to provide a spiritual foundation in their lives so that they do not grow up to lead a life of spiritual and cultural emptiness.

REINTRODUCING THE VISIONARY EXPERIENCE

In many shamanic cultures, children are reintroduced to shamanic journeying at puberty during the time of the vision quest. The ultimate goal of this challenging experience is for children to connect with their guardian spirits. In our modern world, children spend so much time watching television and on the Internet that they lack the ability to vision. So what can we offer them and how do we do that? According to Sandra, there are many ways to keep the imaginal realms alive for the children of today's world:

> Parents can help their children maintain this connection with their inner visionary ability by doing simple things such as keeping the conversations going about their child's imaginary friends. Or they can lead their children into a journey to find an animal friend who protects them in life.
>
> Many years ago a brilliant shamanic practitioner brought her nine-year-old son, Matt, to me. A teacher in school was being emotionally abusive to him. I taught Matt how to find what I called his animal friend, who filled him with power so that he did not take on the teacher's abuse. His animal friend filled him with power in another activity, and he became a great tennis player.
>
> Matt never lost touch with this helping spirit or the nonordinary realms. An extraordinary man who is now in his twenties, he is a well balanced, brilliant student who has gone on to very reputable schools and is making a difference in the world—and he is definitely a strong member of the transformational community.
>
> Matt's story is one of many testaments to the positive effects of journeying for a child facing life challenges.

When I teach children how to journey, I drum for about three minutes. Children tend to journey very quickly and might get bored with a longer journey. I then tell them to close their eyes and look for a hole in the ground that they can enter. I then ask them to find an animal friend who is willing to protect them and to whom they can tell their problems. When I create the return beat on the drum, I ask that they say goodbye to their animal friend and come back.

After a few minutes of journeying, most children return and talk for a half hour about all that happened on that journey.

In the early 1990s I taught a one-day workshop in Salt Lake City for six-year-olds. Some of my students there wanted to teach their children how to journey, but they did not feel comfortable teaching it themselves. So I agreed to teach their children. A group of seven children and their parents came to my workshop, and we made rattles for singing and dancing by putting popcorn kernels in plastic cups and taping the cups together. It was truly a magical day, and what amazed me was how each child asked his or her animal friend what they could do in return for the help received. After each journey I asked the children to draw a picture of their journeys and to describe the picture to the group. This worked well as a way to focus the children on the help they received.

The health and well-being of our children depend on our ability as adults to help them remain in contact with the spiritual worlds. It is important for their emotional health to feel that there is more to life than just what they see and hear in the material world. And it is crucial to our future to help our children maintain a spiritual state of consciousness so they find meaning beyond what exists in the material world.

There are many ways we can encourage children's imaginations, emphasizes Hank; for one, it should be encouraged in schools:

One of my former students who teaches in the public school system created what she called "imagination time" and worked it into her sixth-grade curriculum. She began by telling her students that she had read an article in the newspaper stating that today's kids lacked imagination in large part because of television and video games. She then informed them that they would all be working on their imaginations during the course of the school year to help improve their creative writing skills.

She began very simply by having her students close their eyes and imagine picking an apple and tasting it. She then asked what color apple everyone saw, and pointed out that she had not told them what color apple to see. In addition, some kids envisioned sweet juicy apples, while others imagined sour or even rotten apples. They then discussed whether what they had seen was a message just for them, reflecting something about their lives. This allowed them to discuss how our imaginations, that is our dreaming, often communicate with us best by using symbols.

As the semester progressed, the teacher began using a Sacred Garden exercise with the students. They began by imagining a meadow, and then they found a path in the meadow that led to their own special place where they could meet an animal who was there just for them. The animal could talk, and the place was somewhere they could plant seeds for the future, a wish for themselves, a wish for the planet. The children would water the seeds every time they went there. And after each imagination journey, they would write creatively about what they had experienced.

Some days, the teacher asked them to imagine sliding down a rainbow to see where they would land. While studying ancient Greece, they made an imaginal trip to Mount Olympus. While reading about Egypt, they explored a pyramid or dove into the Nile. Some of the children's journeys were quite amazing. One boy came back from a journey and drew an elaborate symbol that looked like Sanskrit. Another boy connected with an Egyptian man named Imhotep who told him that he was one of the architects of the pyramids (which he was). One girl made contact with a Greek goddess, while others met up with grandparents who had died. One boy who was very military-obsessed had a military bunker in his garden.

These imagination journeys began as guided visualizations—no drum—but with very little guidance on the teacher's part. Needless to say, the students loved these imagination exercises. One year they all kept journals, and so they painted or drew pictures of their gardens or wrote poems to accompany their images. And of course, their descriptive writing skills soared.[1]

A BOY'S SPIRIT AND RITE OF PASSAGE

One of our workshop participants in the Pacific Northwest leads a Peace Warriors spiritual mentorship program for boys aged nine to thirteen. This program is inspired by a similar project that has been developed for girls by the Life Blessing Institute (maidenspirit.com).

In essence, the mentors offer the youths an embodied experience of sacred ritual that connects the spirit/soul aspect within each boy to the sacredness of Nature, offering them the tools with which to deepen their own self-knowing through intuition. These include ceremony, meditation, shamanic journeywork, creative art projects, altar-making, movement, and drumming.

These are year-long classes, with each group consisting of a circle of eight youths who meet with their two mentors once a month from October to June for about three hours. They form a circle and make an altar in the center, learn the protocol for calling in the directions, pass the talking stick, engage in a meditation, do journeywork, share, eat together, and create an art project.

In this initiatory program, the topics for the year for both boys and girls might include: The Real Me (who am I?); Our Grandfathers or Grandmothers (where did I come from?); A Wise Man or Wise Woman Knows His/Her Directions (what does it mean to become a man or woman?); Symbols of the Sacred Masculine or the Sacred Feminine (what does it mean to be a sacred man or woman?); Inspired Role Models (culturally immediate accounts of men and women who have embraced the sacred in their path on Earth); The Rite of Passage (a day-long ritual, sweat lodge, or journey up the mountain focusing on connection with the sacred and the nature of one's purpose); and Family Celebration (a ritual in which each boy or girl is given back to their family as an initiated young man or woman).

THE CHILDREN'S FIRE

Indigenous cultures had their individual ceremonies to work with children and pray about their success and future. Today we need to journey to find our own ceremonies that honor our own children and the children around the world.

With relation to initiatory ceremonies that help children step out of one life stage and into the next, Carol Proudfoot-Edgar adds that it is important for children to engage with contemporary shamanism, and that children might have an easier time connecting to shamanic practices than adults:

> The very young have just entered the world from "the other side" and still carry an active relationship from the lands they have recently left—the spirit world. They tend to be comfortable with their invisible friends, whether they be animals, faeries, humans, or beings for which we don't have categories in our ordinary world. As adults we must listen to our children with respect and support these relationships whenever we are invited to engage with them. If we will do this, then the child's transition from There to Here will unfold at a natural pace.

One important issue for the shamanic community is "How shall we inform the young of the sacred nature of *this* new world into which they have arrived?" The ways to do this are as diverse as the many cultures in our world. Common to all these cultures are traditions that include mythic stories, songs, dances, and crafting—ways that allow the very young to continue to engage with the spirit realms. The memories of these traditional experiences will become embedded in their bodies, minds, and hearts and become a critical resource as the children face future challenges or obstacles, which may then become adventures of positive transformation.

This issue of tending the children has arisen in various circles over the past sixteen years. During this time, we have welcomed the birth of several children.

We developed a ceremony to address this issue. On our altar, we have the Circle's Fire (our candle). Around it we create a Children's Fire of seven novitiate candles (a sacred number) that burns through our time of gathering, and we include a daily prayer or activity involved in tending the Children's Fire. At the end of our gathering, one of the women is appointed to take home this Fire and keep it burning until the fuel has been completely used— that is, until the wax has been completely transformed to Light and Fire. During this time, we asked that any dreams, visions, or experiences that come forth regarding the children and the world they are moving into be shared with all of us so that we might, if so called, take thoughtful action upon them. By having and tending this Children's Fire, we have been led to understandings and activities focused on nurturing children that we might not have done otherwise.

Having a Children's Fire is just one of many ways of reaching out in order to help children stay connected to the imaginal realms. The six-year-old daughter of a close friend invited me, many years ago, to her school to share about "Indians and Thanksgiving." This became the occasion for drumming, singing, and stories about sharing the bounty of Mother Earth. This led to further invitations to tell the children stories with a request to be sure to bring my drums! I now see that part of my role in my community is to take these seasonal celebrations (Thanksgiving, Christmas, Easter) as occasions for sharing the mythic sacred meanings that gave rise to these cultural celebrations with children. Beneath all these holidays exists the call to love one another and treasure our planet home.

Our children need to be invited to experience times of shamanic dancing, drumming, singing, and storytelling. I shall never forget one Bear Medicine gathering in which two sisters, aged four and six, were invited to hold a large sculpted MotherBear. They walked around the entire Circle and quite spontaneously invited each woman in the Circle to kiss the MotherBear. As they moved around the Circle, they walked with incredible dignity and delight; they seemed to know they were initiating the older women there to embrace the Mother in the form of Bear. Now when I think of the children, I ask myself, "What can I do today that recognizes the gift of the children to the world and includes them in the Circle?" They have much to teach us; we have much to share with them.

When children are included as part of a ceremonial circle with adults they trust, in which they feel permission to share their stories—including their imaginal friends and the inner adventures they have with them—these young beings experience a form of validation. This validation is the positive polarity of spiritual experience, and once it is acknowledged by their elders, it will serve them throughout their lives.

In our modern world it is rare to see inner light and joy shining through people's eyes. In Chapter 8 we wrote about the extraordinary light that shines through the eyes of indigenous people. This light and joy are the result of people who have a rich inner life from working in the spiritual realms.

We want our children to have passion for life. We want to teach them how to find inner wealth that goes beyond what they can buy in the material world. We want to teach our children how to experience the beauty of Nature and how to honor the earth, air, water, and sun which give life.

You can journey on ways to bring spiritual practices to your children. And as you introduce children to shamanic journeying, they begin to make spiritual connections that will positively shape their lives in the present and will guide them into a good future.

Chapter 13

Working in Community

In the world's traditional cultures, the role of inspired visionaries has always been pivotal in maintaining the harmony and balance of their communities. It is within the shaman's capable hands that the physical and the metaphysical equilibrium of these societies are held.

In modern societies, our doctors and psychologists, our politicians and economists, and even our organized religious priesthoods no longer seem to be effective in creating that harmony, and so the social fabric of our communities lacks equilibrium at virtually all levels. Within such a dysfunctional dynamic, the role of the modern visionary has never been more important.

We most often think of visionaries as developing new technologies and generating new ideas, yet Bill Moyers's television interviews almost thirty years ago with esteemed mythologist Joseph Campbell revealed that the visionaries among us today still play a pivotal role in nurturing us and our communities at the level of our *souls*.

THE ROLE OF COMMUNITY

In a tribal society, every aspect of the community is tightly interwoven. In such cultures, each person is acknowledged for his or her unique gifts, talents, strengths, and characteristics that they bring into the social dynamic, for in this way each person contributes to the wholeness and health of the community.

This means that when someone is ill physically, mentally, or emotionally, or even spiritually, their affliction affects the entire collective of the community itself. Therefore, when someone requires a healing, each member of the collective is needed to provide his or her unique role, and the entire community may show up for the healing ceremony. The community as a whole, as well as the individual's place within it, is honored in shamanic cultures.

Sandra Ingerman, who has worked with many in her shamanic practice, can always tell when a client is from a traditional culture that honors community:

> When I first started performing healing work with individuals in Santa Fe, I always knew if I was going to be working with an Anglo or a Native American by how many cars I heard turning into my driveway. Whenever Native Americans came to see me they brought their children, spouses, loved ones, and even their dogs. It was always a bit challenging for me to have a dog licking my face or a child jumping on my stomach while I was journeying for my client. But there was something special and sacred about this experience.
>
> In such cases, there was so much care and support shown for the individual. And I knew that those who came to the healing ceremony would continue with that support to really anchor the healing within the client over time.
>
> Accordingly, I began to tell all those who came to me for a shamanic healing session that they could bring

friends or loved ones to be part of a support system during the work. I don't force people to do this, and if a client doesn't have someone to bring along, that's fine too. But I have found over my years of practice that by having a client bring one or more support people to the session, the effect of the healing is long-lasting, for the client then has someone who was present during the healing ritual who they can continue to talk to about the experience.

This is healing in itself, for in Western culture, it can be hard for clients to describe the power of a shamanic healing to family and friends who are not educated in or familiar with transpersonal healing modalities.

In today's world, a powerful and pervasive cause of illness can be found in intense and prolonged feelings of isolation. Many people don't know who they are, where they belong, or what unique gifts and strengths they have to share in their community. These feelings of alienation are unique to Western people. They simply do not exist in tribal societies in which every individual belongs in perpetuity to the tribal whole. Although I do not feel that we will go back to living in tribal societies, I do believe that reweaving the fabric of our communities will become more and more important during these changing times.

We can already see this happening as people within communities turn to each other during environmental catastrophes for support and help in rebuilding. I feel strongly that it is not healthy to isolate ourselves from our neighbors. No one is supposed to live in a vacuum. We need the support of others during this great time of change. And I do believe that the inexorable process of evolution is moving us toward a greater level of social cooperation and collaboration, not only in our smaller communities but also in the larger global community.

HEALING CHALLENGES WITHIN FAMILIES

Family and friends can be a great support and a blessing to someone in need. They can also end up unknowingly cursing a loved
one without meaning them harm. Sandra cautions us about pro-
jecting suffering onto others:

> I have had many students who never told anyone that they
> were dealing with cancer. They were afraid others would judge
> them and project a sense of defeat into their healing process.
>
> There have also been cases in which there is so much
> fear about the impending death of a loved one that family
> members projected their fear onto the sufferer or even
> onto others, creating more illness or exacerbating existing
> conditions. Many times, out of sympathy and empathy, we
> feel pity for people we know or for someone we see on the
> news who is suffering a personal catastrophe.
>
> When we project our pity onto others, this act may
> actually take energy and power away from that person.
> On an intuitive level people know this, and oftentimes
> they will hide their major life challenges for the simple
> reason that they don't want to be pitied. We want to have
> compassion for the suffering of others, but when we pity
> someone, we actually push them deeper into a hole.

EXERCISE: JOURNEY FOR A POSITIVE PROJECTION

If you had a way to let thousands of people know that you are
dealing with a serious or life-threatening challenge, would you
prefer people to send pity your way? Would you want people
to say, "That challenge is so big you will never make it?" What
would you ask for?

In this vein, you might make a journey to your Sacred
Garden or other place of power and invite a spiritual team—a
community of healing spirits—to come to you with their wise
counsel as to how you might proceed. This would be a journey

of self-divination in which the team might provide suggestions as to what obstacles need to be removed so that you can achieve a successful outcome as well as how to approach your greater community of kindred souls on this level of reality.

One way to support someone who is ill or going through a difficult time, teaches Sandra, is to envision him or her in divine light:

> One of my discoveries on the path of direct revelation has been that the true help we can give people—family, friends, or strangers—is to visualize them in their divine light and perfection. Just as you can practice experiencing your own divine light (see Chapter 8), you can also visualize everyone you know, or with whom you feel a connection, in their divine light. In this way you are not denying them the challenges they are facing; rather, you are sending them strength and the power to stand strong in the midst of change and even in their transition back into the spirit world.
>
> In quantum physics, there is a teaching that has meaning for us here: lower frequencies entrain to higher frequencies. In other words, if you choose to live and act, think and speak, emote and express your feelings as a true visionary, you must transfigure yourself so that you exist in your divine light and perfection—and then it will be effortless to project that experience onto all of life.
>
> In this way, you as the inspired visionary will help the radiance of life around you to shine strong.

ENVIRONMENTAL CONCERNS

As we shall see in Chapter 14, members of the Transformational Community, a vast national and international social matrix that has taken form over the last forty years, are deeply concerned about the manner in which the environment, including the planetary

243

weather complex, appears to be responding to the activities of industrialized humanity.

From his perspective as both a biological and social scientist, Hank Wesselman offers these thoughts:

> The environmental issues that we face in our time are well known and need no review here, yet we can also observe that much of our current awareness of these problems is due to the expanded perspective of our visionaries.
>
> Members of the Transformational Community are environmentally savvy, and like indigenous peoples they feel an active, almost ritual, respect for Nature. They express a deep concern for the environment and, by association, the survival of the human species. All are seriously committed to stopping corporate polluters, reversing atmospheric warming, and discovering the limits to short-term growth so that we can achieve the long-term ecological sustainability upon which the future of humanity, as well as our civilization, depends.
>
> Unlike many of the hardcore environmental activists of the last several decades, however, members of this emerging social movement are spiritual seekers interested in achieving the direct, transformative experience of the sacred, and it is really this that defines them as both modern mystics and visionaries.

It is our suggestion that each of us begins to extend ourselves in a healing capacity, individually as well as communally, toward the gentle goddess who gives us abundance. In the visionary perspective, this goddess is our planetary biosphere—the ancient progenitor and sustainer of life that is none other than Mother Nature, Gaia-sophia.

It is imperative that we come together with our communities to heal and support the well-being of the environment that provides so much for us. And, as Sandra points out, the work of a community can be much greater than the work of one:

Over my twenty or so years of teaching shamanism, seeing clients, and leading workshops on reversing environmental pollution, I have witnessed countless miracles when a group gathers its energies on behalf of a focused purpose. There are results that happen when we work alone, yes, yet when a powerful, focused group works together with the compassionate spirits who are willing to help us, healing may occur on an exponential level.

Here is an example that comes from my work with Medicine for the Earth. I have already shared how we started by working with water polluted by ammonium hydroxide. After a few years, I purchased a gas discharge visualization (GDV) camera that is based on the Kirlian effect, which measures the life force of the substance being tested. The camera was developed by Konstantin Korotkov, a professor of physics at St. Petersburg State Technical University in Russia who has published more than seventy papers in leading journals on physics and biology and who holds twelve patents for inventions in the field of biophysics.

The GDV camera allows one to image-capture the physical, emotional, mental, and spiritual energies emanating to and from an individual, whether a human, an animal, a plant, a liquid, a powder, or even an inanimate object. The camera captures these as energetic images that it then translates into a computerized model. This diagnostic tool measures and evaluates the energy of an object's auric field and then integrates the information into a computer-generated report with pictures.

In essence, this camera enabled us to document the change in energy that we created inside our shamanic circles during our transfiguration ceremonies. We have worked with different foods, soil samples, and water. (For results and to see the photos taken, you can visit the website shamanicteachers.com and click on "photos/results.")

Years ago, in a Medicine for the Earth training, our group worked with a peach that came from my drought-stricken garden. Because I could not give the trees at my home the water they needed, I walked through my garden each day visualizing each tree in its divine light and perfection.

When we took the first picture of the peach before the ceremony, the light it emitted looked good. But it looked even better, and significantly brighter, after fifty people performed a ceremony of transfiguration. This was a great teaching for all of us about the power of working in a group versus working alone. It also revealed unequivocally the importance of the role of the visionary.

THE CURRENT SPIRITUAL REAWAKENING
As you embark on your shamanic path, it is important to realize that you are part of the Transformational Community, which has an enormous capacity to heal. And, according to Hank, this community is only growing:

The collective beliefs and values of the Transformational Community constitute an emerging worldview that is being embraced by an ever-growing population of well-informed souls. Paul Ray and Sherry Ruth Anderson's research and book, *The Cultural Creatives*, reveals that these visionaries may number more than 70 million in North America alone with another 90 to 100 million in Europe.[1]

These numbers are considerably more than just statistically significant for we are living in a time in which humanity's problems appear to be reaching critical mass, a time in which our leadership is being challenged at political, corporate, military, and even religious levels. Whether the solutions to our issues can be achieved by our current leadership or reached through the increasingly questionable machinations of our military-industrial complex is unknown.

In response, increasing numbers of concerned citizens are considering the possibility that our problems may not have political, military, or even economic solutions. Rather, the solutions may actually be spiritual in nature, in alignment with the beliefs and values outlined in this book.

In addition, as we will discuss in the next chapter, if our children acquire these altruistic, spiritually based values and beliefs within the fabric of their families, this new way of being will spread throughout the larger society, accelerate this spiritual reawakening.

Although this reawakening is most visible in North America and Western Europe, the invasive influence of Western culture upon the rest of the world suggests that it may, in fact, extend deeply into the international community, offering an unprecedented promise of hope for all human beings everywhere as well as a firm guarantee of sweeping changes to come.

Ray and Anderson state in their book, *The Cultural Creatives*, "We should take heart, for we are traveling in the company of an enormous number of allies."

This insight confirms that the Transformational Community emerging in the West is of enormous import and has the power to alter the direction of history in much the same way that the emergence of Christianity utterly changed the Roman world and the Western mind almost two thousand years ago.

While the time frame for this shift may vary with the ebb and flow of current events, there are no maybes about whether it will happen here. The proverbial handwriting is on the wall. The history of the world's peoples will be profoundly and inescapably changed by the spiritual awakening taking place in the West. The results will be felt at every level of society, in every country, and will, by association, determine much of the politics and individual lifeways of this century and beyond.

Your Role as a Visionary within the Transformational Community

Prayer and meditation are two of the great gateways into transcendent experience. As you pray, meditate, or engage in shamanic journeywork for yourself, for people you know, or for the greater world at large, allow yourself to feel part of the global community that is working right along with you. Shamanic journeywork is an ancient yet highly advanced form of meditation.

You already know what it feels like to try doing a really big task on your own. And you already know how it feels so good when others volunteer their expertise and assistance to help you get your project done. Think of this as you step onto the path of becoming a visionary who can be a positive force in the world, and visualize yourself in connection with others who are working spiritually to heal their communities, the world, the planet—for these are people of all different spiritual traditions and cultures who are in service to the greater good. We can join our hearts and spiritual energies together in every spiritual practice that we do and in all accompanying positive intentions that we create.

As the impetus of our collective focus approaches critical mass, exponential shifts toward healing and re-achieving balance will occur. And our world will change—for the better.

LONG-DISTANCE HEALING IN GROUPS

We have discussed how the power and effectiveness of a healing ritual is enhanced when we are part of a group with a common focus. We should also add that under these circumstances you can still offer healing help to someone who is not physically by your side. According to Sandra, it can be done in much the same way as if the receiver is right there with you:

> First, connect with a power animal or teacher in the non-ordinary realms. You can then ask that power animal or teacher to send help to a person in need. Share with the animal or teacher the person's name and their location. You can share the issue as well, but we usually discover through direct revelation that the spirits already know what type of help is needed.
>
> Keep in mind that there are ethical issues in doing this work as you must have the receiving person's permission and know that he or she wants some healing help. If the receiver is in a coma, unconscious, a young child, or even an animal, you could perform a Middle World journey to their spirit and ask for their permission to send help. You may journey from your location and simply shift your focus quickly to the client's location. Once in the journey, you can ask the client if he or she would like healing help from you.
>
> If the client says no, you must respect his or her decision. Yet if they agree, and they almost always do, you may ask your spirits to offer them healing energies, while expressing your intentions for their greatest good. You can also join together with others who know how to journey to ask all of your individual helping spirits to send help to a person or animal in need. In doing so, the power of the ritual is increased exponentially, which is why many people would rather practice shamanism in a group than alone.

Hank, who leads long-distance healing rituals in his workshops, agrees that working as a group can be extra beneficial when performing a long-distance healing:

At my workshops, when we do group long-distance healings, we first wait until each person in the room is "power-filled." Next we connect the circle by joining hands, and then each person brings up an image in their mind's eye of the one in need. When we can see or feel our heart connection with that person clearly, we simply say his or her name out loud, and at that instant, an arrow of healing energy travels from our heart to theirs, nonlocally and instantaneously. The indigenous peoples know a great secret: every time you send healing energy from your heart to someone else, that arrow has two points on it and the energy flows in both directions. This means that every time you offer healing to another, you receive healing yourself, and this is why the healers among us often live to be very old.

This kind of long-distance healing also works well for those who have already crossed over and are in spirit. You can simply say their name or say "my mother's spirit" or "my father's spirit."

As we have indicated, when we are "in community," the power of this method expands tenfold, revealing that for us as modern visionaries there are no limits to what is possible.

FORMING A SHAMANIC CIRCLE

You can gather together with some people where you live to experience the possibilities of the journey together. With practice, each member of the circle can learn how to journey for one another to receive guidance from the helping spirits. Then, when someone is in need, you can work together collectively to perform healing work. This is a powerful way to work.

Carol Proudfoot-Edgar, who founded a nonprofit organization called Shamanic Circles, is dedicated to assisting shamanic communities take form around the world. She has observed that there are many ways in which a new circle can form:

My primary focus in shamanism is to assist in the development of shamanic Circles. These can be local, regional, national, or international. Such Circles may be formed from those simply working with me over the years or from people sharing some common basis who wish to learn how to apply shamanism in their lives. The latter Circles might include groups of physicians, community organizers, women, couples, church groups, or individuals providing ceremonies for the larger community. One of the more intriguing aspects of current shamanism is online networking. The Internet allows for people on this path to focus quickly and strongly on some common concern and to share the results of any shamanic interventions made as well as new shamanic methods that might come through from the Other World.

Each Circle is a constellation connecting with other Circles, with people often spiraling in from different lands, with different experiences. Some of us may have been together at different times, different places. Some of us will be new to each other and by the end of our time together will be One Circle. To have both new and known together is a treasure. This is the very essence of community, of village. For all of us are beginners and all of us have our own life experiences that will make for a bountiful Circle.

From my perspective, Circles within Circles, and Circles joining other Circles, are happening all over the world. Individuals, who might have been strangers to one another a moment ago, are finding that there are strengths and resources that become available when common ground and common yearnings are shared.

In some places, this is happening rapidly; in some places slowly. It is a continuing affirmation to me that the time of loneliness, of only self-enlightenment, of being a lone wolf or a lone bear is over and we are "gathering ourselves" for the changes and transformations needed to be made both in our own lives and in our world, one step at a time, one Circle at a time. Steps upon steps are creating a path; Circles and more Circles are creating the container within which much can be born and held.

If you are not a member of a Circle, go to the Internet and search using the keyword "shamanic circles." Some Circle website have information about the nature of shamanic Circles and articles on the practice of shamanism. If these website interest you, write to the contact for a Circle in your geographical area and see about participating in one of their gatherings or ceremonial activities.

If you belong to a Circle, suggest to your group that it focus on the issue: "What is being asked of us now, in this present age, this current time?" Sometimes Circles use their gathering time as an opportunity for individuals to journey instead of raising, to spirits, the collective questions. However, the Circle is a unique form and there is a reason that shamanic Circles are prospering in these times. I think we are being asked to use our Circle form as a source of power and wisdom for ushering in significant changes. We will only find out about this if we inquire, as a Circle, of our guiding spirits and the guardians of our planet home.

Journey groups have formed all around the world, where participants journey together and then share their experiences. In a meeting, everyone in the group might perform one personal journey and then you might journey together on behalf of a group member who has a question or challenge in life and seeks guidance.

Some groups add to that a collective journey where all the members journey on a global issue or some aspect of current events. Many groups journey to ask how to honor the change in seasons or the current phase of the moon, or how to create a ceremony together as a community. Each member will receive a unique piece of information that can be woven together to inspire and educate the whole group. There might be similiarities and synchronicities that come up within the participants' journeys underscoring something of particular importance.

THE COLLECTIVE DREAM

As part of a world community, our thoughts and beliefs become part of a collective dream. We have affirmed that the shamanic practitioner can become a master of dreaming. José Stevens emphasizes that it is the nature of any energetic system, at all levels of complexity and awareness, to dream:

> From a shaman's point of view, the material universe we live in is a collective dream and your life story is a local personal dream. Spirit is not attached to these dreams. You could say that Spirit gave birth to the dreamers and then participates in what they dream.
>
> The dreamers, of course, are all the bits and pieces of the physical plane. Each bit and piece has the power to dream at different levels of sophistication. A rock dream is not quite as elaborate as the dream of a butterfly, and the dream of a butterfly is eclipsed in complexity by the dream of a dog. The most sophisticated dreamers on Earth are sentient beings such as human beings and the cetaceans (whales, dolphins). We are capable of dreaming up incredible things. Unfortunately, because of a combination of our amnesia, creativity, free will, and ego orientation, our dreams sometimes turn into nightmares.
>
> In the act of creation, it appears that Spirit decided on a noninterference policy. That is, it created the dreamers and agreed it would abide by whatever dreams they created, knowing of course that in the end, all dreamers would wake up and recognize the basic foundation of love in the universe.

Many who endure extraordinarily challenging lives sometimes curse Spirit for this, believing that it was cruel to create this policy. Yet, if you think it through, Spirit could not have done it any other way without restricting free will. If you lacked this freedom to create any kind of dream you thought of, you might complain that the game was rigged and feel bitter. Nothing less than total freedom to dream and discover is the loving way of Spirit. This is a major understanding on the shamanic path.

From a shaman's point of view, when sentient beings gather together in great numbers, their collective dreams become very strong. For a long time on this planet, dreams were about survival; then came a long period in which the dreams focused on order, laws, control, and collective living. Then came grand dreams of ambition, power, and material gain. These dreams harbor the beliefs that everyone is totally separate, in competition, and that the creative force of the universe either does not exist or exists as some kind of angry, punitive external force. Today these powerful centuries-old dreams are all entwined and carry great momentum for humankind.

The collective dream has developed a kind of personal ego, an identity of its own, based on what it has become, a long story line. This planetary collective dream appears to have great power and seems to gobble up everything in its path. It feeds on the personal dreams of all the people on the planet. What it considers the best food of all is drama, especially drama that is intensely emotion-filled—particularly trauma with lots of anger, fear, jealousy, envy, and violence. Not only does the collective dream feast on these things, it requires them to maintain its remembered identity. So the agreed-upon collective dream keeps trying to incite more incidents of trauma so it can have more food—just like a raging forest fire that hungrily demands more trees for fuel. The dream then reinforces itself every second with more of the same.

Most people's personal dreams are sucked into this vortex, and without realizing it we become contributors to a vast nightmare. Sometimes we dream pleasant things like loving relationships and satisfying work and creating great beauty, but these are not as enticing to the historical collective dream as are the more intense traumas. So sooner or later each person tends to be driven into the great dark dream to be enslaved and apparently victimized. A master shaman would say that human beings have become like sheep or cows filing into the slaughterhouse of the dream. The results are not pretty.

Being a dream, it is subjective in nature, yet it has momentum, and the power of the dream comes from that momentum. In this sense, it is literally being fueled by its dreamers who believe they have no other option than to dream this collective nightmare. Yet we do have a choice.

The shaman's point of view is that a new dream is possible but requires enough dreamers to wake up from their collective nightmare and choose to transform the dream. A few shamans and mystics have managed to wake up from the collective dream, and to some extent they've managed to wake up others enough to sway the dream a little. Mostly these teachers have not been heeded because few human beings are mature enough to know what they've been talking about. A few have taken their lead and used their help to wake up from their own personal contribution to the nightmare at large. Most, however, simply incorporated what the teachers said into the ongoing dream without waking up at all—similar to the way a person might incorporate the sound of a passing siren into their dream.

It is the opinion of many indigenous shamans that now, for the first time, the possibility of humankind waking up from the old negative mass dream exists on a collective level. The possibility now exists for the establishing of a new dream, one that allows the dreamers to wake up within their dream and discover they are dreaming, allowing them to begin to take conscious control of their dream. The new dream can be anything we want, including great cooperation, sharing, loving relationships, peaceful coexistence, grand creativity leading to great beauty and inspiration, mass healing, and living sustainably with Nature.

Hank offers these thoughts from his many years of living with traditional tribal peoples:

The indigenous peoples know that each creature in creation has tasks appropriate to their being. And only when those tasks are performed, and in the right way, can the universe function in life-enhancing ways for all. If any among the multitudinous creatures fails in its tasks, everyone suffers.

This reveals that every thought we think, every action we take, every word we speak, every relationship we engage in, and every emotion we feel, contributes either to the greater good or greater suffering.

As master dreamers, shamanic practitioners have an extraordinary responsibility. As we look at the state of our world today, including our societies, our communities, and our families, it becomes quite obvious that the time has come for us to dream well in a way that contributes to the greater good of all. By doing so, we may work together, and in response, our world will be transformed.

We have incredible potential to create positive changes in our local and global communities, agrees Sandra. In a journey, she once received the following message:

In the future, the stories parents will read to children will not be about one hero or heroine saving the world. The stories written will be how communities of people gathered together to create positive change for the world.

As we begin to journey together in our communities and share our gifts, talents, and messages received, we create a collective energy which over time creates positive change and healing for the planet.

Chapter 14

The Transformational Community

W e have now given you, the reader, an overview of what it means to be a modern visionary—a modern shaman perhaps—as well as what it means to walk upon the path of direct revelation. As you read and absorb our thoughts that follow about the extraordinary community of positively focused souls that has come into being in our time, it is our hope that your inner light will brighten as you affirm with confidence, "Yes . . . this is who and what I am!"

AN INDIGENOUS PROPHECY

At this time, a plethora of well-intentioned books have been published focusing upon 2012, the year that many indigenous traditions such as the Maya, the Inca, the Hopi, and others have predicted as the end time of our world. This trend reveals an ever-increasing awareness in the public psyche that we appear to be coming to the end of our current cycle of ages.

In our research into this compelling issue, we stumbled across something significant that most of the writers have missed entirely—something that has bearing on the current resurgence of interest in the shaman's path of direct revelation.

Nicholas Black Elk (Hehaka Sapa) was an Oglala Sioux medicine man and shaman who is well known for the story he told an anthropologist named John Neihardt—an account that was published as a book titled *Black Elk Speaks*. In this volume, Black Elk tells the story of his life, as well as a great prophetic vision that he was given in his childhood. An instant classic, this book has been in continuous print since its original release in 1932.[1]

Less well known is Black Elk's second book, told just before his death to another anthropologist named Joseph Epes Brown, titled *The Sacred Pipe: Black Elk's Account of the Seven Rites of the Oglala Sioux*. Originally published in 1953, this book contains something that may have great relevance for all of us in our time.

At the book's beginning, Black Elk recounts the mythic story of White Buffalo Calf Woman and of her gifting of the first sacred prayer pipe to the people (the Sioux). At the end of the account, he relates that as the Holy Woman started to leave the lodge where this historical meeting took place, she turned and said to a man called Standing Hollow Horn: "Behold this pipe! Always remember how sacred it is and treat it as such, for it will take you to the end. Remember also that in me there are four ages ... I am leaving now but I shall look back upon your people in every age ... and at the end I shall return."[2]

According to Sioux philosophy, at the beginning of this "cycle of four ages," a buffalo was placed in the west in order to hold back the waters. Every year the buffalo loses one hair, and at the end of each age, he loses one leg. When all its hair and all four legs are gone, the Sioux believe that the waters will rush in once again and the cycle of ages will come to an end—an indigenous prophecy of more than just passing interest considering the polar meltdowns very much in progress and the predicted catastrophic rise in sea levels.

A striking parallel to this myth comes to us from the Hindu tradition where it is the bull (Dharma—a symbol for the divine law) that has four legs, each of which represents an age in the cycle. During the course of these four ages (*yugas*), the true spirituality becomes increasingly obscured until the last age (*manvantara*) closes with a catastrophe.

The Sioux and the Hindus are in accord that the buffalo and the bull are now standing on their last leg and the buffalo is very nearly bald. It is also known that several white buffalo have been born during the past ten years, regarded as a clear sign by many Native American peoples that the current cycle of four ages is now coming to a close.

But Black Elk also predicted just before his death that with the closing of this cycle, the primordial spirituality would re-emerge and be restored, and on this foundation the next cycle of ages will begin again.

This last statement is highly significant because the primordial spirituality *is* the path of direct revelation—it was and is the shaman's path—and interest in shamanism has increased dramatically over the last several decades as part of the widespread spiritual reawakening currently going on in our time—a modern mystical movement that has two sides.

THE MODERN MYSTICAL MOVEMENT

On one side, we find a resurgence of the religious fundamentalism that comes down to us from the Dark Ages: a narrow, literalist perspective that proclaims this world to be the kingdom of a remote, transcendent, authoritarian, father God who can be alternately beneficent and wrathful—and one to be feared. Today, this view has been embraced by misguided religious zealots and self-righteous terrorists who have the fervor, as well as the capacity, to ensure that this world will be their God's kingdom—or nothing.

On the other side, we find the enlightened perspective of the secular humanists who perceive an immanent, omnipresent divine presence or power existing within all of creation. In their more expanded view, this divine pantheistic presence expresses one emotion only—love—and it expresses itself as a universal life-giving and life-sustaining impulse oriented toward the greater good.

In our time this more highly evolved perspective is quietly and definitively gaining acceptance among increasing numbers of well-educated, well-informed, and well-connected individuals, many of whom are in professional and social positions from which they may influence the larger society's ideas and trends.

This view is also gaining ground within the general population, creating a broad social movement that is cutting across socio-economic levels of achievement and status, one that transcends cultural, political, and ethnic boundaries.

The number of people who hold this more enlightened perspective is not known with certainty, but as we have already indicated, fourteen years of sociological research (see endnote for Chapter 13) conducted in the United States by demographer Paul H. Ray and his wife Sherry Ruth Anderson, has revealed that as many as 70 million Americans may fall into this group with another 90 to 100 million in Europe. Ray and Anderson's analysis also suggests that Westerners have arrived at a point in history in which the prevailing mythologies are not working any more.

These hundreds of millions of enlightened souls among us know—without being told—that the time has come to create a new cultural mythos in which we synthesize a whole new set of ways of viewing ourselves and our society, our problems and our strengths, our communities and our world. The numbers of enlightened souls are not small—and they are growing.

Such a shift in the dominant cultural pattern happens only once or twice in a thousand years, and it is significant that this one is occurring during a period of ever-accelerating social change, enabled by a worldwide communication system and technology unlike any seen before. Ray and Anderson's survey reveals these citizens to be socially concerned, environmentally aware, and

spiritually focused creative people who are carriers of more positive ideas and values than in any previous period in history.

These people *are* the Transformational Community, and they
know with absolute certainty that if we continue to do business
as usual and fail to produce a new story, Western civilization may
well collapse, taking the rest of the world with it. This awareness is
producing an increasing sense of urgency, accompanied by a growing insistence on social, political, and economic reform that will
benefit everyone, not just the powerful and the privileged.

THE CYCLE OF AGES

Anthropologists might call this shift in consciousness—this presence of a Transformational Community—a new kind of cultural
revitalization movement, one that is reaching toward the future
rather than retreating into the past. According to historian
Richard Sellin in his book *The Spiritual Gyre,* this revitalization
movement is happening right on schedule. He suggests that our
Western preoccupation with the linear development of our civilization is, in fact, a misconception, and that the *zeitgeist*—the spirit
of the times embodied within the intellectual trends and moral
values characteristic of any age—tends to express itself in cycles
that repeat themselves on a regular basis.[3]

According to Hank Wesselman, the first age of this cycle was
longest: the Upper Paleolithic Period or Late Stone Age that
lasted from around 42,000 to 11,000 years ago:

When cross-referenced with the perspectives of indigenous peoples today, rock art created during the Late
Stone Age reveals that the people's religious practice was
animistic and expressed the conviction that everything,
both animate and inanimate, is invested with its own
personal, supernatural essence or soul. This belief implies
that everything around us is both conscious and aware, at
least to some degree, revealing an immanent intelligence

within Nature with which all humans were once in constant, intimate relationship.

This was the primordial spirituality passed down to us from our Stone Age ancestors, and during those times Nature was God and the religious practitioner was the shaman.

The second age of the cycle was the Neolithic Period, one that lasted for perhaps four thousand years. This age began with the closure of the Stone Age and the end of hunting and gathering as humanity's primary lifeway. The Neolithic Period was characterized by the rise of agriculture, animal domestication, and the establishment of the first permanent, year-round villages and towns.

The religious sphere of the second age in all likelihood still belonged to the shaman, and everything in Nature, both animate and inanimate, was considered to be alive. Yet something else was clearly going on, reflected in the numerous sculptures of pregnant women found at many Neolithic sites. What these represented to those who lived more than six thousand years ago is problematic to us today, but the archetype of the fertile female was obviously preeminent, revealing a concise area of focus within their spirituality.

This second age came to an end with the emergence of the first socially stratified city-states about five thousand years ago among the Sumerians in Mesopotamia, and during this time a new form of spiritual expression emerged: polytheism, which affirms the existence of many high gods and goddesses existing above and beyond Nature. This is a stratified, hierarchical cosmological view, and its appearance reflected an entirely new perception of ourselves, one that developed once we began to live in stratified, hierarchical societies.

This new form of religion became the dominant spiritual focus for the third age—a period that included cultures such as the Akkadians, Babylonians, Hittites, Assyrians, Persians, Anatolians, Egyptians, Myceneans, Phoenicians, Minoans, Greeks, Etruscans, Celts, and of course the Romans. During this age, which lasted perhaps three thousand years, the first stratified religions emerged, managed and run by the first bureaucratized priesthoods. Before this time, there simply was no concept of high gods and goddesses, despite what many well-intentioned writers may claim.

The various high gods and goddesses in these traditions came to symbolize aspects of the human psyche in a supernatural sense, as well as some aspect of the natural world in an ideological sense—such as the Greek father god Zeus, associated with the elemental forces of lightning and thunder; his brother Poseidon, associated with the oceanic realm; and his daughter Athena, a feminine archetype of wisdom and the wise woman as warrior. Among the Romans, these deities were known respectively as Jupiter, Neptune, and Minerva, and with the collapse of the Roman Empire almost two thousand years ago, that third age came to an end.

And with its demise, as before, a new kind of religion came into being: monotheism.

Monotheism's three primary expressions—Judaism, Christianity, and Islam—profess the belief in a single great god who created the universe and everything in it in a singular event, with lesser spiritual beings, angels and archangels, saints and prophets, ranked below. Once again, this belief system reflected a new perspective of ourselves, because as our societies had become more centralized and more hierarchical, with an executive director on top—the king or queen, emperor or president—so had our perception of the supernatural world.

The new religion, monotheism, reflected this by assigning an alternately wrathful, alternately beneficent ruler god, variously called YHWH, Jehovah, Allah, or simply God, as the supernatural executive director or CEO, and this has been the dominant (and dominator) religion in the Western world for our current two-thousand-year age cycle.

Sellin proposes that this fourth age began with a comparatively long theocratic phase in which society relied heavily on religious doctrine and truth was determined by divine direction from the father god, operating through a bureaucratized and politically motivated priesthood. Any informed overview of Western history reveals that such has indeed been the case from the adoption of Christianity by the Romans until the Age of Enlightenment, a period that lasted roughly 1,400 years—a time in which the pagan spiritual practices of the tribal peoples of Europe were ruthlessly suppressed.

The spirit of the times changed considerably at this point. As the guilds gave rise to the infrastructure of the current corporate world-state, the rise of science and intellectualism contributed to the onset of the second stage of our age, a secular phase in which the expansion of our geographical and intellectual horizons, as well as our economic power, occurred on an unprecedented scale. In response, truth was redefined within a new mythology—science—and religion was generally discredited. This relatively shorter phase, dominated by scientific rationalism, has lasted for about three hundred years. The current spiritual reawakening suggests that this phase has now drawn to a close.

With the dawning of the age of Aquarius, Sellin asserts that we are moving into the third and final stage of our two-thousand-year age, a spiritual phase, in which science and spirituality are being synthesized and integrated in an attempt to transcend both previous stages.

We can also observe that the sheer number of people involved in this transformation reveals that this modern mystical movement is not a fad. Rather, this broad social phenomenon heralds the emergence of an authentic Transformational Community, one whose beliefs, values, and trends are already shifting the cultural norms of Western society.

THE NEW SPIRITUAL COMPLEX

The new spiritual complex that is emerging has no name as yet, nor is it focused on the teachings of some charismatic prophet, guru, or holy person. Its singular, distinguishing feature involves the realization that each of us can acquire spiritual knowledge and power ourselves, making the direct, transpersonal contact with the sacred realms that defines the shaman/visionary, without the need for any priest or religious organization to do it for us. In this manner, all people acquire the freedom to become their own teacher, their own priest, their own prophet, and they can receive their spiritual revelations directly from the highest sources—themselves.

As we engage in this ancient human experience, each of us inevitably discovers that our personal consciousness is part of a greater field of consciousness, a deep insight currently being illuminated and confirmed by quantum physics. This is the direct path of the mystic at its absolute best, one that leads the spiritual seeker into the experience of self-realization and spiritual empowerment.

It is not surprising that this new spiritual impulse seems to be integral in nature, drawing on all the world's wisdom traditions, from the East to the West, from animism to Zen. What is surprising is that right at its core a cluster of principles can be found that were embraced at one time by the world's indigenous peoples.

In approaching the idea that principles of indigenous wisdom are involved in the genesis of the new spiritual complex in the West, we are broadly concerned with the general mystical insights that were once held in common by virtually all of the traditional peoples and are thus the birthright of all. We hasten to add that modern spiritual seekers do not seem to be retreating into archaic belief systems, nor, with rare exceptions, are they interested in playing Indian or becoming born-again Aboriginals.

To the contrary, many members of the Transformational Community are seriously reconsidering the core beliefs and values once held by the traditional peoples, and right there, embedded within them all, we find the path of direct revelation.

MODERN MYSTIC BELIEFS

At its inception, the quest of the modern spiritual seeker is intensely personal. Yet as it progresses, it leads us inevitably toward a universal and ultimately altruistic perspective—one that includes a number of mystical beliefs.

For example, ongoing direct experience of the transpersonal worlds leads the seeker to an inescapable conclusion: that everything, everywhere, is interconnected, and that consciousness is the "etheric field" through which this linkage is achieved. This is a core belief that is clearly articulated by the indigenous tribal peoples who were our distant ancestors at one end of the human continuum and at the other end by the quantum physicists and Zen Buddhists of our own time.

Another core belief of the modern mystic concerns the existence of more than one reality. In addition to the everyday, objective physical level in which we all live and have families, friends, and careers on an ongoing basis, there are the nonordinary, subjective levels of the dream worlds or spirit worlds outside the time-space continuum, where the laws of physics and cause and effect do not work in the same way.

This belief leads directly into another: the ability of some individuals to expand their conscious awareness and enter into these alternate realities with ease. This conviction that we can easily access these alternative states reveals why the rediscovery of shamanism has become a major thrust within the Transformational Community. The relative freedom with which the shaman's time-tested methods for achieving mystical states can be learned and practiced, even by nontribal Westerners, stands in stark contrast to the years of rigorous training often required in many of the contemplative disciplines such as meditation and yoga before significant consciousness shifts are achieved.

Another belief held by modern mystics is that by utilizing the shamanic method to journey into these inner worlds, the same levels that Carl Jung called the archetypal realms of the psyche, the seeker may enter into relationship with spirit allies—inner helpers, teachers, and guides who may provide the seeker with access to power and knowledge, protection and support. Among these beings one can find connection with her or his personal Higher Self, variously known as the transpersonal self, the angelic self, the god-self, the overself, or simply the oversoul.

Another related belief concerns the existence of a field of mystical power, perceived by virtually everyone as an invisible essence or vital force that is widely dispersed throughout the universe and highly concentrated in certain objects, places, and living beings. It is becoming generally understood within the movement that everyone can learn how to access, accumulate, and focus this power, and that one's health, well-being, and success in life are ultimately dependent on being able to maintain, and even increase, one's personal supply.

This awareness gives rise to the belief in the existence of a personal energy body—a subjective self-aspect that carries this power as life force and provides the "etheric pattern" or energy body around and within which the physical body is formed and maintained. The ability of some transpersonal healers to manipulate the energy body in restoring and repairing the physical body is a skill that many in the Transformational Community have personally experienced. It is believed that this energetic matrix can be perceived as an aura by those who have psychic awareness and that it can be enhanced by utilizing the energy centers within it called chakras in Eastern thought.

Taken together, these beliefs constitute an emerging worldview that is being embraced by an ever-growing population of well-informed souls. And as we have mentioned already, those who hold the new view believe that it offers an unprecedented promise of hope for all human beings everywhere as well as a firm guarantee of sweeping changes to come.

THE MODERN MYSTICS

Modern spiritual seekers tend to develop in isolation, becoming deeply immersed in personal spiritual studies that are often triggered by spontaneous visionary experiences that society has taught them to conceal. If as many as 43 percent of the general population in the United States has had such experiences (as cited by an anonymous Gallup poll done in 1987), this pool may be even deeper than the 50 to 70 million "cultural creatives" (26 to 30 percent of the population in 2000) that Paul Ray has suggested.

Modern seekers tend to be individualists, people with very full lives who like to gather in local meetings or spend their vacation time attending workshops in which they can acquire direct experience of such practically useful subjects as qigong and reiki, psychic healing and shamanism, meditation and yoga, to name only a few. They then tend to disperse back into the wider society where they utilize what they have learned to benefit themselves, their networks of family and friends, and their communities. The growing body of social research reveals that the Transformational Community exists as an ever-expanding set of overlapping networks that extends across North America and into the international population.

These contemporary spiritual seekers are interested in spiritual liberation, not repressive or rigid dogma, and they tend to be deeply distrustful of any organized religious hierarchy. Because of this, steadily increasing numbers are leaving our mainstream religions in droves, yet this is not an atheistic or anti-religion movement.

Despite their disaffection for and lack of affiliation with organized religions, most transformationals profess belief in some form of universal godlike consciousness, and Jesus of Nazareth is regarded as an important spiritual teacher whether or not the seeker is psychologically Christian.

Although these seekers may achieve a relatively higher density in the large urban centers and in certain geographic regions like California, Paul Ray's research reveals that they are evenly distributed throughout the general population, suggesting that they are everywhere, in every community, and at every level of society.

In their search for authenticity, the transformationals are quietly, yet definitively, gaining a level of spiritual freedom and power that has not been experienced in the West for almost two thousand years. In short, this quietly and steadily escalating social phenomenon has all the appearances of a spiritual revolution.

Seen from this perspective, the resurgence of interest in shamans and their practices may in fact represent the seeds of the next religious tradition in the West—one that will determine much of the Western world's spiritual focus and practice for the next two thousand years and beyond.

Let us now reconsider what we have learned in this book about the shaman and the path of direct revelation. And as we do, be aware that what has been shared with you is very much part of the new story that we all are writing—a new cultural mythos that will require a new, upgraded perception of how we see ourselves and our relationship to the cosmos—as well as a new, upgraded profile of the divinity.

THE PATH OF DIRECT REVELATION

Over the last decade, shamanic practitioner, teacher, and modern mystic Tom Cowan has felt encouraged by discoveries in the field of the "new physics." Science has proven what those engaged in the shaman's journey have known for a long time: that our current religious beliefs are outdated and inadequate. Here Cowan discusses how such discoveries have resulted in the need for a new language to talk about both the subatomic world and our re-emerging awareness of the mystical realms:

For years, those of us involved with the mystical life and its attendant path of direct revelation have been encouraged by ongoing discoveries in the fields of the "new physics." In an age when so many religious faiths and spiritual beliefs are being challenged or proven inadequate from the more evolved perspectives of the modern world, it's always reassuring to find that one's understanding of the universe is shared by others, especially those who view the world from the distinctly different perspectives of biology and physics.

It has been suggested that our current language is ineffectual in describing the subatomic world and what goes on there. The same could be said for our emerging awareness of the mystical realms. It has also been suggested that we need a new language.

All of this is encouraging because language is most definitely our "thing," one that is constantly shifting and changing as we grow, increase, and become more than we were. If we need words that have open-ended meanings, words that haven't even been defined yet, we will create them. If we need poetic symbols or metaphors that are open to various interpretations, we will create them.

This means that our uniquely human creative imagination is going to have to play a greater part in understanding the world (and the universe at large) than it has in the past. And the truth is that the development of our capacity for creative imagination over the past three centuries has been extraordinary, producing a force that may in fact alter the course of human evolution.

For example, an old worn-out analogy of the Newtonian world is that everything is like a pool table where a pool cue hits one ball that in turn hits others that move around the table and bank off the sides and may or may not hit even more balls. My imagination doesn't have to work very hard to grasp this. On the other hand, an electron can get into some kind of echoing warp with another electron and no matter how far apart they travel, they continue to mirror each other's movements and conditions—a known and proven phenomenon in wave-particle physics.

Trying to imagine this makes the inside of my eyes itch. But I'm curiously happier thinking about those mirroring electrons than the dreary clicking of billiard balls. I enjoy playing pool, though I'm not sure it's possible to have a good time with those clone-ish electrons.

What can we do that is like them? Our imagination quivers with the awareness of our unlimited potential; in the end, that may be what makes all the difference. When our spiritual beliefs are grounded in what we might call the primordial spirituality, we relish those things that are mysterious and unexplainable. And the earliest spiritual beliefs, as far as we know, were beliefs about the Powers of Nature.

I'm capitalizing "Powers" so that it's clear these Powers were seen as divine or sacred, and that they had some kind of consciousness about them. They were also mysterious because no one in those cultures that thrived in those primeval millennia had scientific explanations for what was going on with them.

Even today, with the knowledge that we do have, storms, lightning, electricity, fire, and other phenomena retain some element of mystery even when we know the physics behind them. These natural forces retain some unpredictable, uncontrollable mind of their own, and this keeps them in the realm of the mystery. Seen in this light, the need for our creative imagination to understand them becomes obvious, even paramount.

"Imagination" is the buzzword here. According to Aristotle, images are the language of the soul, and I have always felt this explains our human need for spirituality. Imagination can be seen as the creative realm of the soul. So needing a new language, or poetry, or what we might call "imaginative flights of wondering" to understand our world keeps us attuned to the outer Greater Universe and the inner Otherworld in which we live.

The outer Greater Universe can be perceived with microscopes or telescopes and other sleek technological devices for probing way down inside or outside. The inner Otherworld is perceived through the visionary's expanded consciousness through which the Outerworld and the inner Otherworld of myth and dream are revealed to be mirrors of each other, like those twin electrons.

And it's possible that those electrons are analogous to the archetypal forces known (mythically) as the faeries or the devas in the garden that are dancing with the very same physical processes that course through the stems, roots, and buds of plants. Maybe our inner awareness of this is why the primordial spirituality has found a resurgence of interest in our lifetimes.

As scientists continue to expand our perspective about the marvelous, mysterious, complex, and intelligent universe, this knowledge quite naturally allows us to feel those spiritual yearnings of our primal ancestors who, with far less scientific understanding, stood in awe of the beauty, power, and terror of the Powers of Nature.

This was and is the beginning of the path of direct revelation.

Chapter 15

The Return of the Shaman

Shamanism, and by association the visionary path of direct revelation, is an organic practice that has shifted shape throughout the ages and different cultures to address the needs of the times. Hank Wesselman notes that although some researchers claim that shamanic practices are dying, they are, as we've mentioned, truly re-emerging:

> A paper published by Graham Townsley about the current shamanic revival in the journal *Shamanism* reveals how the central momentum of the last few hundred years of history has been *away* from indigenous communities and their worldviews, a trend that has resulted in the waning of the shamanic method among the indigenous peoples.[1]
>
> Anyone who has done time with "the traditionals" in the remoter parts of the world during the past several decades has seen how they are rushing to join what they

perceive as the exciting new world of the future. For indigenous peoples, shamanism begins to look increasingly like old-fashioned hocus pocus, a view instilled in them and fostered by Christian missionaries. In addition, the arrival of modernity with all its glittering gadgets is usually the death knell of their ancient animist beliefs.

And yet, just as these "primitive" worldviews appear to be dying in the new global system's hinterlands, paradoxically they are taking root once again at its center. To our urbanized Western populations, saturated with modern paraphernalia and bored with a world that has been bled of meaning, shamans and their visionary practices of seeking direct revelation of the spiritual realms suddenly seem very appealing.

To the so-called primitive, marginalized, and usually powerless, the promise of the modern is *things*, ease, and security. To the so-called modern person, the promise of the primitive is the one thing he or she lacks—a sense of *meaning and mystery.*

This primitive rush toward the modern and the modern rush toward the primitive has emerged as a feature of our current cultural landscape, and many in the Transformational Community are quietly, yet definitively, reconsidering their personal belief systems and priorities as they engage in spiritual explorations beyond the carefully patrolled borders of our mainstream Western religious traditions.

This is much in keeping with the predictions made more than a half century ago by the Oglala shaman Black Elk just before his death. With the ending of this cycle of ages, the primordial spirituality based in the practice of direct revelation is indeed re-emerging and re-establishing itself, and it will be on this spiritual foundation that the next cycle of ages will be built.

We cannot predict exactly what the practice will look like in the future, yet we can be assured that the shaman's path will continue to be a viable practice for healing and problem-solving, a time-tested and sacred way of life that will nurture and sustain us just as it has for many tens of thousands of years.

MERLIN'S PROPHECY

Historian and master of Celtic shamanism Tom Cowan now draws on the wisdom of an archetypal figure, the wise old shaman Merlin, who in life may have been among the last of the Druids and the mythic advisor and mentor of Arthur Pendragon, the legendary sixth-century king of the Britons:

> With the approach of the end of his days on earth, Merlin gave all of us who would follow a prophetic vision, one that ends with a startling scenario: *Root and branch shall change places, and the newness of the thing shall be thought a miracle.*
>
> Of course there are many ways to interpret old prophecies, but I like to think that this particular image of the tree being inverted is profound in encouraging us to view the transformational changes that are occurring in a positive light. Perhaps this tree is the great archetypal World Tree that connects the many worlds, and now after many centuries, the roots from which we sprang will be fully seen and honored as branches. And the branches that were formerly upper parts of the tree—responsive to the winds and rains of the past ages—will become the new roots and be revitalized in the fertile soil of the Earth, and in so doing revitalize the Earth itself.
>
> We who practice shamanism spend time in the juice and sap of the World Tree, exploring the Upper, Middle, and Lower Worlds of existence. If anyone should be prepared for this transformation, it is us. In that way we are the seed people who will shape spiritual practices for the

future. We will bring "root wisdom" into the light for coming generations, and we will plant the "branch wisdom" of earlier ages into the soil for renewal.

In addition, we are experienced in seeing things from other perspectives, such as upside-down. In faery traditions, there is an image of the inverted tree whose roots become the branches of the underworld beneath the surface of the earth. This image reminds us how we on the surface of the visible earth share energies and life forces with the spirit-folk who live in the invisible places within the earth, in the hollow hills and springs, and behind the waterfalls. In ordinary terms, shamans are bridges who have relationships with the spirit worlds and who can be both branches and roots to carry the life force back and forth between the ordinary and nonordinary realities.

In reflecting on Merlin's and Tom's shared wisdom as well as the shape and the scope of this book as we have created it for you, the reader, we have asked all the contributors, shamans and visionaries, to offer their thoughts about where their work in the world is moving in order that we may continue to be of service to ourselves, our families and friends, our communities and our societies, and to the planet.

In the personal narratives that follow, each of the book's contributors has also written on how they perceive their students to be changing. There is no doubt that what each contributor has shared will change in the coming years. But for now this is what everyone offered in 2009—and in alphabetical order.

So here are our final words from our circle of elders.

Tom Cowan

In my early years of teaching shamanism, I found students were primarily interested in training to become practitioners. As the years went by, I got students who already had a strong practice but who now seek retreat or renewal time. Americans have a great need for novelty, and many students feel they must get something new from each workshop or the workshop is not worth it. But slowly the ones who practice sincerely and intensely come to realize that novelty is not necessary. They are looking for time away from their ordinary lives to deepen their spiritual life. I notice that my own practice must deepen to meet their needs. I cannot just offer new content but must offer what comes from my own life as well. As shamanism becomes a more integral part of students' lives, they seek time in workshops to reflect and meditate on what they already know and do, and they deepen this. Some work can only happen in circles away from ordinary-reality concerns. So I try to tailor my weekend or sessions with that in mind.

I am now getting students in my workshops who are more mystical—the ones who continue their practice, that is. The desire to "know" is not so much a desire to acquire more knowledge but to "know" experientially on cellular or soul levels. In other words, they seek mystical knowledge/experiences rather than practical knowledge such as how to do some shamanic trick. So ritual and journey work should be simple in that it provides an experience that will go into people on a soul level and remain with them. Too much complexity or intellectual content is hard to retain and requires mind-memory rather than soul-memory.

There are still some students for whom "to know" is novelty, who want to learn and know new things. But as the mystical students live their lives in a shamanic way, "to know" or acquiring knowledge is not about newness but about depth. They are content to repeat and deepen already-acquired knowledge rather than acquire new knowledge. They watch themselves change rather than need what they do to change.

Sandra Ingerman

Throughout *Awakening to the Spirit World* I have been sharing how my work has evolved over the years. I have stressed my passion for moving away from methods and technologies to bringing in the feminine principle of shamanism as a way of life.

We are evolving and in a transition time. Every change involves a death. The spiritual is eternal. In this time of great change and uncertainty it is important to infuse spirit into everything we do.

It is time for us to bring back the soul of the world by once again honoring this life-giving force. We need to honor our divine light and our spiritual nature, and we need to honor the spirit that lives in all things, including the elements and the Earth itself. We must honor the spirit of everything we build in the physical world.

This includes living a life of honor and respect for all of life and nature; honoring the cycles of nature; living from a place of awe, wonder, and passion; and being a presence of love and light in our daily lives. The key principle I teach is that we change the world by who we become and by our presence in the world—not by just what we do. This includes learning how to transmute negative states of consciousness that arise throughout the day. And it means we need to be diligent in being aware of our minute-to-minute thoughts in order to change the world and ourselves. Remember that our inner world creates the outer world we live in. And I stress the importance of being a dreamer and the need for us to hold the vision of the world we want to live in. In this way we own our creative potential and gather our efforts together as a global community.

I am a person who does not fall into a complacent state about my work. This means my work, teachings, and writings are always evolving. In this regard I can only write what I am exploring right now, knowing these explorations will lead to new doorways and pathways by the time you are reading this book.

The basis of my exploration is how we can transcend the limitations of the human mind and our collective beliefs. For we do know that the true shamans and mystics were not limited by the collective beliefs of what is possible. My motivation is to be able to help support the global community in creating a world filled with harmony, love, peace, abundance, light, and equality for all. We don't want to use spiritual methods for power over others, manipulation, or psychic abuse. And I will continue to encourage people to work on themselves to attain the emotional maturity to avoid falling into this trap.

I continue to work to create a world that our descendants will sing songs of gratitude about. By working together as a global community we can do this.

Carol Proudfoot-Edgar

In 1989, following a long safari through Africa, I returned home and quit my job at the University of California, Santa Cruz. My experiences in Africa had altered radically my perception of this planet and my place as a pilgrim here.

I did not know what I was going to do, but I knew that the field of psychology (I was an adjunct professor and a counseling psychologist) had a limiting paradigm for individual change and that the place of the animals and the spirit of the land was missing in what I was doing.

Shortly thereafter I was asked to teach the Medicine Wheel Way at Esalen in Big Sur, California. Thus began my journey as both walker and teacher of Earth-based medicine.

In the earlier 1990s, I did extensive training with the Foundation for Shamanic Studies and was appointed a faculty member. These apprentice programs and the courses I taught became the launching platform for my shamanic explorations.

Then in the mid-1990s I was vision questing in Colorado's San Juan Mountains. I encountered a Mother Bear and her cubs. This encounter became the basis of a covenant to walk and teach the path of Bear Medicine.

I have assiduously journeyed, researched, and worked with other women to learn the medicine ways of Bear. I track SheBear in all the realms I am permitted and I know that She tracks me. I am continually amazed and graced by the new teachings, visions, and dreams this Great Spirit brings to me, to others, and with the healing powers of Her ways. It's as though She has been longing and waiting to be heard and to be called. And we have been longing, perhaps unknowingly, to walk and learn from Her.

Work with Bear has now led me to work more with our companion animals, so I am volunteering in animal shelters. I speak of this because I think we are being called to consciously tend all our animal relations: the wild ones and the domesticated ones. We must learn what the animals are seeking to teach us as well as how to take care of their habitats and how to offer healing when needed. All animals have a purpose in the great web, and they are attuned to why the humans are here. They can help us find our way home. They can teach us in what ways "home" is in trouble, and from these teachings we can co-create new ways of living on this Earth.

I stress this issue of learning from the animals because frequently the question has surfaced within me: "If there are no wild animals left, how do we understand the nature of our power animals?" Just as our ancestors, who work with us, once had physical bodies, so too did many of our power animals. We understand them better *because* they live in both embodied and spiritual forms. The capacity for recognizing and receiving information "through" the realms of things hidden is intimately related to being and form through the realms of things seen. We shall be sorely diminished in our embodied selves if the wild beings around us continue to disappear.

Likewise, our companion animals chose us because we have something to learn from them about being human. Part of our humanity is to learn the way of respect and the compassionate tending of animals.

The focus on transformation through relationship to physical form is also manifested in my increased emphasis on enstatic shamanism. Ecstatic shamanism, the major contemporary emphasis, uses methods for journeying outside the body. In other words, *ecstatic* shamanism is the practice wherein the person goes out of the body in order to achieve shamanic states and gain knowledge or the *power to do*. *Enstatic* shamanism is the practice wherein the person plunges inward to achieve shamanic states and gain knowledge or the *power to be*.

José Stevens

The practice of shamanism has been with us since the dawn of time and like all things in this world is in the process of evolution. Yet because of ignorance and deliberate distortion this evolution is not clearly understood and consequently this makes it difficult to know shamanism's true value to the human race. Without shamanism it is my opinion that the human race would never have succeeded as it has and would never have reached its current status on the planet. How would humans have survived without ancient healing techniques, a knowledge of plants, a knowledge of how to read and turn the weather, the intuition to know where to hunt at the proper times and a host of other survival techniques? Purely rational thought and opposable thumbs were advantages but not enough to save a comparably weak simian in the face of daunting odds. In order to truly understand the shamanic tradition and where it is headed we must expand our definition of evolution and see the big picture, the shamanic picture of evolution.

According to our contemporary mainstream perspective it would seem that the impetus to evolution comes from the bottom up, or from the past forward. This would be the strictly scientific approach to looking at the evolution of anything, from nature to technology. However, from a shamanic perspective we could consider that there are larger processes that go beyond technical or economic ones, if you will, spiritual needs that pull the process of evolution forward rather than it being entirely pushed from behind. In other words we could say that Spirit plays a hand in evolution by having an overall game plan that it supports by leading from our so-called future. This would suggest that there is a major cooperation between the natural process of bootstrapping from behind and the natural process of pulling from ahead, thus supporting the old adage, as above so below. We don't bootstrap up without a ladder to give structure to the process. There is a ladder, perhaps one with many options, but nonetheless a ladder that leads us into the future.

Thus there are ways we can understand the evolution of visionary abilities in a shaman within the context of their times and cultures. In the beginning we have someone who shows some proclivity for shamanic skills and has an interest in developing them. Let's say these are like a few simple circuits set up as a foundation. This prospective shaman finds an experienced shaman or perhaps several shamans to train and initiate him/her over a period of many years. Songs are learned, techniques for soul retrieval and healings developed, and ceremonial skills deepened during the training. These in turn create opportunities to advance to new levels of skill. These then are like more advanced circuits with more inputs and outputs. As the older shamans initiate the young shaman, they sing songs and embed prayers into her/him; and these are like designs or vibrations that become part of that person's makeup.

Perhaps, under the supervision of an advanced shaman, the young shaman undertakes a series of diets with various plants—allies that raise power levels and add great knowledge. These plant vibrations now interact with the song vibrations and the prayer vibrations, creating new and different combined vibrations that perhaps have never occurred before.

So the young shaman may eventually spring forth with totally new skills or abilities that have been bootstrapped up by earlier existing components. Because the shaman initiate has a personal essence or soul that is urging the new developments, this essence acts as the force from the future actually pulling forward these new abilities as they are bootstrapped from behind.

This process of bootstrapping and pulling from the future is not simply a random set of developments but is based on the needs of the individual, the needs of the community, and the needs of the present to have another trained shaman with special new skills. Unneeded or unwanted skills would then not be developed. In this way we see that the training and development of a new shaman is not independent of the needs of the community or the world, it is integral to it. In the same way, we find the great new inventions happening just when they are needed the most. We don't invent a device to breathe in space unless we are actually going there and will be needing it. So the skills developed by a new shaman are partly desired by the shaman's personality, partly the deeper intentions of essence, and formed partly by the needs of the community/world. This is why a shaman with a supernatural skill such as flying like Superman does not emerge into the mainstream, because the world does not need it and is not ready for it yet, if ever.

What is more needed is a shaman who can heal cancer or diabetes, clear polluted water, remove radioactive contamination, clean up toxic wastes, and point the way to new energy sources and creative ways of thinking.

When we understand the push/pull dynamics of evolution, we are in a much better position to see the intelligence behind our evolutionary path on this planet. Charles Darwin helped bring the concept of evolution to light, yet he did not see both ends of it. He saw it from one side alone. It is up to us to see the whole evolutionary process and understand where it wants to lead us.

Those who understand such shamanic tools as the Mayan calendar can readily see this big picture at work. After all it is extraordinarily useful to know where we are going in the long run. Random evolution makes little sense in this light. The times now call for new developments in the shamanic tradition. The world has changed and is changing dramatically as we speak.

More than half our planetary population now lives in urban centers, and this calls for developments in urban shamanism, in shamanic practice that is not dependent on long traditional apprenticeships or tradition-bound practices relevant only to the very few. This is not to say that traditional shamanism is dying out. There will always be traditional shamans practicing their trade among their people. What we need now is a worldwide understanding of the shamanic way, an understanding that can be applied by millions of people in the ordinary course of everyday activity. For example, the widespread practices of shamanic prayer, of seeing the world as interdependent, of having great respect for and understanding of the ways of Nature, and of knowing the power of helping spirits and how to use them would be most helpful at this time.

In fact, most astrologers agree that among a variety of developments in the near future will be the return of shamanism as a powerful planetary influence. Yet this shamanism—like our material technology—will be more powerful, more relevant, based on the needs of the world, and infinitely more varied. Whereas at one time only a few scientists and engineers had computers, now the masses have and use them. Thus will shamanism continue its role in influencing the survival and evolution of the human race.

In my opinion the shamanic path on this planet is no accident nor is it an archaic path with no future. Likewise technology has ancient roots and a powerful future. In fact shamanism and technology both have much in common and have cross-fertilized each other for centuries. A simple example would be the ability of shamans to speak with plants that informed them how to grow them in ways to produce more abundant fruits, nuts, and vegetables.

We are not evolving in a vacuum, we are evolving with specific goals given to us by the cosmos. I have no doubt that the shamanic path is designed to help us evolve toward greater unity, universal respect and love for all of nature, and access to infinite power and the consciousness to use it appropriately. Thus the path of shamanism is here to stay and any attempt to eradicate it or ignore it only slows us down on our spiraling path toward enlightenment.

There is no question in my mind that at this time the human race is involved in one of the most important shamanic initiations in its history and a wise choice right now would be to harmonize the evolution of science with our evolving shamanic path.

Alberto Villoldo

We are living at the end of an era. The stories of this era were written when the earth was still flat, when our planet was thought to be at the center of creation, and before the Hubble space telescope showed us that we are one of a billion galaxies in the sky. The old stories have exhausted themselves. We are in need of new life-giving myths that can sustain us and our children for the next thousand years. These myths are beginning to appear. They are the stories of sustainability, of right relationship, of stewardship of the Earth, of everything around us being alive.

The difference between a shaman and a priest is that during ceremony, a priest re-enacts an event that occurred two thousand years ago. A shaman enacts an event that is occurring right now. Shamans are storytellers and mythmakers. In sacred sites throughout the Americas, archeologists find ceramic fragments of vessels that were deliberately shattered during ceremony. In the same way, shamans shatter myths that are no longer useful. They point out that the king has no clothes. And I believe that the new shamans, the new caretakers of the Earth, will come from the West. I believe that we are the ones whom we've been waiting for, the new mythmakers. Perhaps there is no task as important as this one today. Without a guiding myth we are like a ship without a rudder in a storm.

My work is to train Western shamans through my organization, The Four Winds Society. I am not interested in training people to become Indians, as this is impossible, but to learn to heal themselves and the Earth through the practice of shamanic medicine, and to dream a new world into being. We are working with cutting-edge neurologists to discover the brain science underlying shamanic practices. I believe that we can bridge the ancient wisdom with our new understanding of the brain.

Most important, I believe that we have to discover a new personal and collective mythology and begin telling empowering stories about ourselves and our epic journeys through life. I remember one of my early trips to the Amazon. I was then a young anthropologist investigating the healing practices of the shamans of the rainforest, and I'd decided to use myself as a subject. I explained to the jungle medicine man that as a child I'd fled my country of birth because of a Communist revolution. I had seen bloodshed in the streets and been terrified by gunfire in the night. Since then I'd suffered from recurring nightmares in which armed men would force their way into my home and take away my loved ones. At that time I was in my late twenties, yet I'd been unable to enter into a lasting relationship for fear that I'd lose the person I loved, just like in my nightmare.

During one healing ceremony the shaman explained to me that like everyone, I can either have what I want or the reasons why I can't. "You are too enamored of your story," the old man said. "Until you dare to dream a different dream, all you will have is the nightmare."

That evening I learned how I could craft a different story for myself, one in which I'd been tempered by adversity and my experiences had taught me to have compassion for others who were suffering. The first step to dream my new dream was to craft a new story in which I wasn't playing the part of the victim. I then realized that not only was I dreaming my life, but I was also dreaming the entire cosmos into being, just as it was doing with me.

My work today is to dream a greater dream for myself, my family, our students, and the Earth. I do this with other dreamers, who come and gather around a holy fire in the Dreamtime. Each of us brings a small piece of the dream, and when we share it, suddenly we can taste it, feel it, sense it—and occasionally we see it. The reason we dream together is that in the shamanic myth of creation, on the seventh day the Great Spirit said: "For I have created the butterfly, the salmon, and the grasshopper; aren't they beautiful! And now, you finish it . . ." Creation is not complete. It is up to us to finish the task, and have a great time doing it!

Hank Wesselman

As a practicing scientist and academic teacher trained in biology and anthropology, I have observed the participants in my workshops for more than two decades of teaching and three decades of practice. It has been my experience that most of these individualist seekers in my workshops are not religious ascetics who shut themselves away in monasteries and ashrams, nor are they religious extremists who invoke fundamentalist belief systems in search of their own exclusive connection with the godhead. Modern visionaries are not involved in cults, nor are they the least bit interested in turning their power over to some holy so-and-so who claims to have the inside corner on the market of spiritual truth.

In addition, members of my circles tend to reveal a distinct character profile that I find deeply reassuring. Most express a strong sense of social justice and seem to be deeply concerned about the quality of human life at all levels of society. They feel strong support for women's and minority issues. They are concerned for the safety and well-being of both children and the elderly, and they see human relationships as more important than material gain. Social tolerance, personal individualism, and spiritual freedom are highly valued ideals. The reweaving of the social fabric through the rebuilding of families, neighborhoods, and communities are major areas of concern. This is what I mean by "deeply reassuring."

In looking at these values, it quickly becomes apparent that they have little to do with being a liberal or a conservative, a Christian or Jew, Hindu or Muslim, or even a patriot. Yet they have everything to do with being a humanist in the evolved sense of the word. Although the Western world continues to be driven by greed, fueled by denial, motivated by fear, and dominated by competition, members of the Transformational Community appear to be oriented toward democratic, humanistic ideals, and they tend to favor cooperative endeavors that benefit the many.

The transformationals are environmentally savvy, and the importance of balance and harmony lies right at the core of their values. In this respect, they, like the indigenous peoples, have grasped that humans must strive to live in ways that contribute to the greater good rather than pursuing goals that create its opposite. Accordingly, the value of simple, natural living is seen as a high ideal, and the monumental waste being generated at every level of the world capitalist system is regarded with grave concern.

It has been my privilege to spend much quality time with these worthies over the past thirty years; doing so has reinforced my own best qualities so that I have become more like them. Although I continue to function as the spiritual teacher in my ongoing seminars and workshops, I am well aware that I, like them, am a student—a student for life—and I learn as much from them as they take home from me. So to all of them, and to those to come, I offer my unending gratitude and my appreciation.

In closing, allow me to invoke the spirit of the *kahuna nui* Hale Kealohalani Makua, my great Hawaiian friend. With his blessing (and his words), I extend to each of you "the light and the love of the ancestors, the source of life, rejoicing in the power and the peace, braided with the cords of patience, revealing the tapestry of the strongest force in the universe . . . your Aloha."

Acknowledgments

From Sandra Ingerman

There are so many people to thank for their support in helping bring this work into the world.

I want to give thanks to all the wonderful people at Sounds True I have gotten to know and work with. I am deeply grateful to all the support Tami Simon has given me and my work over the years. And I thank Kelly Notaras and Haven Iverson for their editing guidance. Mitchell Clute was the producer for the CD. I thank him for being such a delight to work with.

I give thanks to my agent Barbara Moulton for her continual support and friendship.

Love and appreciation is also offered to Hank Wesselman for his partnership in writing this book. To Tom Cowan, Carol Proudfoot-Edgar, José Stevens, and Alberto Villoldo: thank you so much for the great wealth of your contributions.

And many thanks to The Shamanic Transmissions Band (we had great fun coming up with this name): Sylvia Edwards, Julie

Kramer, Gail Mesplay, John Mullen, Woods Shoemaker, and Kappy Strahan. It was such a privilege to make music together, to join our hearts and spirit together and to infuse the CD for journeying with an abundance of love, light, and joy.

I am in deep gratitude to my husband, Woods Shoemaker; my parents, Aaron and Lee Ingerman; and to my friends and community who love me and support me through the joys and frustrations of writing. Thank you for all you give to me. I thank my students and clients who continue to inspire me. I give thanks to the spirits for the continual teachings of how to live a life filled with joy and meaning and the teachings of how to help others do the same. I give thanks for my life.

From Hank Wesselman

I would like to express my deep gratitude and great affection to Sandra Ingerman, a friend and colleague of almost thirty years whose invitation to co-author this book has created an unprecedented opportunity to collect our thoughts about the new spiritual complex that is taking form at the heart of a new subculture that has been emerging in the Western world over the past several decades.

I also offer gratitude to Michael Harner, whose shamanic teachings helped me enormously when I was still very much embedded in the earlier stages of my initiations. Others who have provided wise guidance and compassionate support across the years include Kahu Nelita Anderson, Lokiriakwanga (Atiko, son of Akiru of the Dassanetch tribe of southwestern Ethiopia), Papa Henry Auwae, Daniel Bianchetta, Larry Dossey, Barbara Marx Hubbard, John Kaumbulu Kimau, Muthoka (son of Kivingo of Kikoko, Kenya) the *kahuna nui* Hale Kealohalani Makua, Eva and Mason Maiku'i and the other members of the Hawaiian Spiritual Warrior Society (Na 'Ao Koa O Pu'ukohola Heiau), Kahu Morrnah Simeona, Lili Townsend, and Sandra Wright.

Thanks also to my literary agents Barbara Moulton and Candice Fuhrman, to my business manager Richard Taubinger, and to Haven Iverson, our editor and guide at Sounds True.

And of course, *aloha nui loa* to my wise, beautiful, and compassionate wife, Jill Kuykendall, and to the wonderful children we created together: Erica and Anna Wesselman. There are as well my allies and friends, advisors and teachers who live on the other side of the mirror . . .

To all of them, to the countless participants in my workshops, and to my students in the university and college classes that I taught across the years, my gratitude with magnitude.

Notes

Preface

1. Some of these dreamlike revelations form the beginning of Hank Wesselman's first book *Spiritwalker: Messages from the Future* (New York: Bantam Books, 1995).

2. See Jean Clottes and David Lewis-Williams, *The Shamans of Prehistory: Trance and Magic in the Painted Caves* (New York: Harry N. Abrams, 1996). See also David Lewis-Williams, *The Mind in the Cave: Consciousness and the Origins of Art* (London: Thames and Hudson, 2002), in which light is shed upon the rock art of Europe through the interpretations of some of the most recent makers of rock art—the !Kung San Bushmen of the Kalahari Desert in southern Africa.

3. See, for example, Richard Katz, *Boiling Energy: Community Healing among the Kalahari !Kung* (Cambridge, MA: Harvard University Press, 1982).

Chapter 1

1. Alberto Villoldo and Erik Jendresen, *Island of the Sun: Mastering the Inca Medicine Wheel* (Destiny Books, 1994).

Chapter 2

1. "Instructions for the Shamanic Journey" is a shortened version from Sandra Ingerman, *The Shamanic Journey: A Beginner's Guide* (Boulder, CO: Sounds True, 2004). If you would like expanded explanations of shamanic journeying with more questions answered, consider reading *The Shamanic Journey*, which includes a drumming CD.
2. For those interested in the "garden journey," see Hank Wesselman's *The Journey to the Sacred Garden* (Hay House, 2003).

Chapter 3

1. Malidoma Somé, *The Healing Wisdom of Africa: Finding Life Purpose through Nature, Ritual, and Community* (New York: Jeremy P. Tarcher/Putnam, 1998).
2. Note from Hank Wesselman: I received this information in an email from someone unknown to me—an unexpected letter that contained these words of an Australian Aboriginal elder. As I read through Miriam Rose Ungunmerr-Baumann's brief statement, I realized that her narrative was filled with power in its simplicity and directness. Miriam Rose's message is clearly for all of us, and it is with gratitude to her, as well as to the sender of the letter, that I share it with you in this book.

Chapter 4

1. The Druids are best known through their association with the conglomeration of tribal peoples collectively known as the Celts, who dominated northern Europe, Ireland, and the British Isles for more than a thousand years. The two primary sources of information that we have about this priestly fellowship are the writings of the Roman general Julius Caesar about the Gauls, and those of a Greek philosopher named Posidonius who made an extended ethnographic field trip into the tribal regions of Gaul early in the first century BC. Virtually everything else written about the Druids is fanciful or

from second-hand sources (such as Tacitus, who drew heavily from Posidonius's original writings—only fragments of which remain today). For information, read Philip Freeman, *The Philosopher and the Druids: A Journey among the Ancient Celts* (New York: Simon & Schuster, 2006).

2. See the writings of James Lovelock, especially *Gaia: A New Look at Life on Earth* (London: Oxford University Press, 2000). See also John Lamb Lash's *Not in His Image: Gnostic Vision, Sacred Ecology and the Future of Belief* (White River Junction, VT: Chelsea Green, 2006).

Chapter 6

1. Sogyal Rinpoche, *The Tibetan Book of Living and Dying*, edited by Patrick Gaffney and Andrew Harvey (San Francisco: Harper SanFrancisco, 1994).

2. See Hank Wesselman, *The Journey to the Sacred Garden: A Guide to Traveling in the Spiritual Realms* (Carlsbad, CA: Hay House, 2003).

3. See Stanislav Grof, *The Adventure of Self-Discovery: Dimensions of Consciousness and New Perspectives in Psychotherapy and Inner Exploration* (Albany: State University of New York Press, 1988). See also Grof, *Psychology of the Future: Lessons from Modern Consciousness Research* (Albany: State University of New York Press, 2000).

4. See Tom Cowan, *Fire in the Head: Shamanism and the Celtic Spirit* (San Francisco: HarperSanFrancisco, 1993).

5. For a similar experience, see Jeremy Taylor, "The Healing Spirit of Lucid Dreaming" in *Shaman's Drum* (Spring 1992), 55–62.

6. Hank Wesselman, *Spiritwalker: Messages from the Future* (New York: Bantam Books, 1995).

Chapter 7

1. See Jean Clottes and David Lewis-Williams, *The Shamans of Prehistory: Trance and Magic in the Painted Caves* (New York:

Harry N. Abrams, 1996). See also David Lewis-Williams, *The Mind in the Cave: Consciousness and the Origins of Art* (London: Thames and Hudson, 2002), in which light is shed upon the rock art of Europe through the interpretations of some of the most recent makers of rock art—the !Kung San Bushmen of the Kalahari Desert in southern Africa.

2. Luis Eduardo Luna and Pablo Ameringo, *Ayahuasca Visions: The Religious Iconography of a Peruvian Shaman* (Berkeley: North Atlantic Books, 1993).

3. Hank Wesselman, *Visionseeker: Shared Wisdom from the Place of Refuge* (Carlsbad, CA: Hay House, 2001).

Chapter 8

1. Barry Bittman, MD, et al., "Composite Effects of Group Drumming Music Therapy on Modulation of Neuroendocrine-Immune Parameters," *Alternative Therapies in Health and Medicine*, vol. 7, no. 1 (2001): 38–47. Visit the Remo Drum Web site (go to remo.com and click on "HealthRhythms") to access this and other studies about the positive health implications of drumming.

2. For an overview of indigenous initiatory experiences, read Joan Halifax, *Shamanic Voices: A Survey of Visionary Narratives* (New York: E. P. Dutton, 1979).

3. For one artist's perception of the oversoul, see Alex Grey's painting of the Universal Mind Lattice in his book *Sacred Mirrors: The Visionary Art of Alex Grey* (Rochester, VT: Inner Traditions, 1990). Hank Wesselman has discussed the nature of this painting with the artist.

Chapter 9

1. Jeremy Naydler, *Shamanic Wisdom in the Pyramid Texts: The Mystical Tradition of Ancient Egypt* (Rochester, VT: Inner Traditions, 2005).

2. Tom Harpur, *The Pagan Christ: Recovering the Lost Light* (New York: Walker and Company, 2005).

3. Raymond Moody, MD, with a foreword by Elisabeth Kübler-Ross, *Life After Life: The Investigation of a Phenomenon—Survival of Bodily Death* (New York: HarperOne, 2001). See also Moody's book with Paul Perry, *Reunions: Visionary Encounters with Departed Loved Ones* (New York: Ivy Books, 1994).

4. See Robert A. Monroe's extraordinary books: *Journeys Out of the Body* (New York: Anchor Books/Doubleday, 1977); *Far Journeys* (New York: Broadway Books, 1985); and *Ultimate Journey* (New York: Broadway Books, 1994).

Chapter 10

1. Nicholas Black Elk with Joseph Epes Brown (editor), *The Sacred Pipe: Black Elk's Account of the Seven Rites of the Oglala Sioux* (Norman, OK: University of Oklahoma Press, 1953, 1989).

Chapter 12

1. Hank Wesselman, *The Journey to the Sacred Garden* has short chapters that children will understand and enjoy. See also his *Little Ruth Reddingford and the Wolf* (with Raquel Abreu) (Bellevue, WA: Illumination Arts, 2004).

Chapter 13

1. Paul H. Ray and Sherry Ruth Anderson, *The Cultural Creatives: How 50 Million People Are Changing the World* (New York: Harmony Books, 2000).

Chapter 14

1. John G. Neihardt, *Black Elk Speaks: Being the Life Story of a Holy Man of the Oglala Sioux* (New York: Washington Square Press, 1932, 1959).

2. Nicholas Black Elk with Joseph Epes Brown (editor), *The Sacred Pipe: Black Elk's Account of the Seven Rites of the Oglala Sioux* (Norman, OK: University of Oklahoma Press, 1953, 1989), 9.

3. Richard Sellin, *The Spiritual Gyre: Recurring Phases of Western History* (Fort Bragg, CA: Lost Coast Press, 1997).

Chapter 15

1. Graham Townsley, "Kamaroa: A Shamanic Revival in the Western Amazon," in *Shamanism*, vol. 14, no. 2: 49–52, (2001).

Further Resources

Books

Cowan, Tom. *Fire in the Head: Shamanism and the Celtic Spirit.* San Francisco: Harper San Francisco, 1993.

Cowan, Tom. *Pocket Guide to Shamanism.* The Crossing Press, 1997.

Cowan, Tom. *Shamanism as a Spiritual Practice for Daily Life.* The Crossing Press, 1996.

Cowan, Tom. *Yearning for the Wind: Celtic Reflections on Soul and Nature* Novato, CA: New World Library, 2003.

Ingerman, Sandra. *A Fall to Grace.* Moon Tree Rising Productions, 1997.

Ingerman, Sandra. *How to Heal Toxic Thoughts.* Sterling, 2007.

Ingerman, Sandra. *How to Thrive in Changing Times,* 2010.

Ingerman, Sandra. *Medicine for the Earth.* New York: Three Rivers Press, 2001.

Ingerman, Sandra. *The Shamanic Journey: A Beginner's Guide.* Boulder, CO: Sounds True, 2004, 2006. Contains expanded explanations about journeying plus a drumming CD.

Ingerman, Sandra. *Soul Retrieval: Mending the Fragmented Self.* San Francisco: Harper SanFrancisco, 1991.

Ingerman, Sandra. *Welcome Home: Following Your Soul's Journey Home.* San Francisco: Harper SanFrancisco, 1993.

Stevens, José Luis. *Praying with Power: How to Use Ancient Shamanic Techniques to Gain Maximum Spiritual Benefit and Extraordinary Results Through Prayer.* London: Watkins Publishing, 2005.

Stevens, José Luis. *Secrets of Shamanism: Tapping the Spirit Power Within You.* New York: Avon Books, 1988.

Stevens, José Luis. *Transforming Your Dragons: How to Turn Fear Patterns Into Personal Power* Rochester, VT: Watkins-Bear and Company, 1994.

Villoldo, Alberto. *Courageous Dreaming.* Carlsbad, CA: Hay House, 2008.

Villoldo, Alberto. *Dance of the Four Winds.* Rochester, VT: Destiny Books, 1994.

Villoldo, Alberto. *The Four Insights.* Carlsbad, CA: Hay House, 2007.

Villoldo, Alberto. *Mending the Past and Healing the Future with Soul Retrieval.* Carlsbad, CA: Hay House, 2006.

Villoldo, Alberto. *Shaman, Healer, Sage: How to Heal Yourself and Others with the Energy Medicine of the Americas.* New York: Harmony, 2000.

Villoldo, Alberto. *Yoga, Power, and Spirit.* Carlsbad: CA: Hay House, 2007.

Wesselman, Hank. *The Journey to the Sacred Garden: A Guide to Traveling in the Spiritual Realms.* Carlsbad, CA: Hay House 2003. Book with CD.

Wesselman, Hank (with Raquel Abreu). *Little Ruth Reddingford and the Wolf.* Bellevue, WA: Illumination Arts, 2004. A book for children.

Wesselman, Hank with Jill Kuykendall. *Spirit Medicine: Healing in the Sacred Realms.* Carlsbad, CA: Hay House, 2004. Book with CD.

Wesselman, Hank *Spiritwalker* trilogy: an overview on how a mainstream scientist became a mystic and a shaman.

Wesselman, Hank. *Spiritwalker: Messages from the Future.* New York: Bantam Books, 1995.

Wesselman, Hank. *Medicinemaker: Mystic Encounters on the Shaman's Path.* New York: Bantam Books, 1998.

Wesselman, Hank. *Visionseeker: Shared Wisdom from the Place of Refuge.* Carlsbad, CA: Hay House, 2001.

Audio

Ingerman, Sandra. *The Beginner's Guide to Shamanic Journeying.* Boulder, CO: Sounds True, 2003.

Ingerman, Sandra. *Miracles for the Earth.* Boulder, CO: Sounds True, 2004. Sandra's audio program includes a guided visualization for transfiguration with toning.

Ingerman, Sandra. *Shamanic Meditations.* Boulder, CO: Sounds True, 2010.

Ingerman, Sandra. *Soul Journeys.* Boulder, CO: Sounds True, 2010.

Ingerman, Sandra. *The Soul Retrieval Journey.* Boulder, CO: Sounds True, 2004. This audio lecture on CD discusses illness from a shamanic perspective.

Wesselman, Hank with Jill Kuykendall. *The Spiritwalker Teachings: Journeys for the Modern Mystic.* Captain Cook, HI: Shared Wisdom, 2008. This six-CD audio program, with accompanying booklet, is available from sharedwisdom.com.

Video

Listen with Your Heart: Sandra Ingerman on Shamanism, Healing, and Nature produced and filmed by Victor Demko (thecenterforhealingarts.com), 2008.

Websites

Tom Cowan: riverdrum.com has Tom's teaching schedule, recommended books on shamanism, Celtic shamanism, and Celtic spirituality, descriptions of Tom's books, and an archive of his essays on various topics called "River Currents."

Carol Proudfoot-Edgar: shamanicvisions.com. On this website, Carol includes articles she has written describing specific healing methods involved in the practice of Bear Medicine.

Sandra Ingerman: sandraingerman.com. On this website, Sandra includes articles she has written on all her work, including "Soul Retrieval" and "An Abstract on Shamanism," which include a discussion about the diagnosis of emotional and physical illness from a shamanic perspective. You can also read her monthly column, "The Transmutation" here.

Shamanic Teachers: shamanicteachers.com includes a list of international shamanic teachers and practitioners who have trained with Sandra Ingerman.

José Stevens: the powerpath.com includes many of José free articles about shamanism (as well as e-books) are located on this site.

Alberto Villoldo: the fourwinds.com. This site includes information on Alberto's Healing the Light Body School as well as his expeditions to Peru.

Hank Wesselman: sharedwisdom.com is the website of Hank Wesselman, PhD, and Jill Kuykendall, RPT. In addition to their ongoing teaching schedule of workshops, travel events, and presentations, Hank writes a free monthly column and a newsletter updated regularly with articles, blogs, and anthropological knowledge, and visitors can also learn about Jill's work with Soul Retrieval.

About Shamanic Practitioners

Shamanic healing is a spiritual method of healing that deals with the spiritual aspect of illness. There are some common causes of illness in the shaman's worldview. A person may have lost his or her power, causing depression, chronic illness, or a series of misfortunes. In this case, the shaman journeys to restore that person's lost power.

Or, a person may have lost part of their soul or essence, causing soul loss, which sometimes occurs during emotional or physical trauma such as accidents, surgery, abuse, war, natural disasters, divorce, or death of a loved one. Soul loss can result in dissociation, post-traumatic stress syndrome, depression, illness, immune deficiency problems, addictions, unending grief, or coma. Soul loss can prevent us from creating healthy relationships and the life we truly wish to live. It is the role of the shaman to track down the parts that have fled and been lost due to trauma by performing a soul-retrieval ceremony.

Another cause of illness from a shamanic perspective would be spiritual blockages or negative energies a client has taken on due to the loss of his or her power or soul. These spiritual blockages also cause illness, usually in a localized area of the body. It is the role of the shaman to extract and remove these harmful energies from the body.

A shaman heals both the living and the deceased. In healing those who died, the shaman performs a psychopomp ceremony to help those who have died cross over to a comfortable and peaceful place. The ceremony may also include clearing a person, home, or land of spirits that are in a state of unrest.

Because shamanic healing deals with the spiritual aspect of illness, there is no way to predict the results that will manifest emotionally or physically. Shamanic healing does not replace the need for traditional psychological and medical treatment.

There are different ways that practitioners work. One way is for the shamanic practitioner to only provide spiritual healing and follow-up treatments if necessary. Another option: after the healing work, the client continues with the shamanic practitioner on the process of integration.

The purpose of continuing the work would be to find ways to restore balance and harmony in your life and create a positive present and future for yourself through the use of spiritual practices and ceremonies. Life without passion and meaning can result in despair. With shamanic practices, you can explore how to create a meaningful life. Examples of the type of work that shamanic practitioners can help with are included in my second book, *Welcome Home*, and have to do with what I call "life after healing."

Some people feel they have their own support systems in psychotherapy and with other spiritual practices; they do not feel they need such follow-up work with a shamanic practitioner.

It is important that you find what you need to support the shamanic healing work that has been done. The practitioners on this list can supply support if you need it.

Guidelines for Finding a Practitioner

1. On the website list, go to the state where you live and find someone you can see in person. Long-distance work can be done with shamanic healing; however, I find the best results occur when the client sees the practitioner in person, unless there is a critical situation that prevents the client from traveling.
2. Talk to the practitioners near you and choose a person you feel comfortable working with.
3. Find a practitioner who is flexible in their fees.
4. Make sure the practitioner is accessible and does follow-up work if you need it.

It is important to understand that the shamanic practitioner works in partnership with his/her helping spirits, which do the diagnosis and advise on what healing ceremony should be done.

Today, in a psychologically sophisticated culture, many clients show up telling shamanic practitioners what healing work needs to be done. This is not how shamanic healing works. The shamanic practitioner listens to the problem the client presents and then consults with his or her healing spirits for the spiritual diagnosis and the proper healing method.

Also, please understand that all shamanic practitioners have different styles of working. A good shamanic practitioner follows the directions of their helping spirits, who know what is best for the client.

A message from Sandra Ingerman about finding a shamanic practitioner:

> One of my visions has to been to seed local communities with well-trained shamanic teachers and practitioners. My vision is also to create an alliance of international teachers and practitioners who cooperate and collaborate together. In this regard, I created a website, shamanicteachers.com, which lists an alliance of teachers and practitioners I have trained.
>
> From the website, here is some information about finding a shamanic practitioner that you might find helpful:
>
> *Please note:* shamanicteachers.com is limited to shamanic teachers and practitioners who have trained with me. I invite you to visit the websites of the other contributors; they also have their own training programs and work with clients.
>
> If you would like to find a circle of people in your community who practice journeywork together, please visit shamanicteachers.com and click on "drumming circles." Alternatively, you can visit shamaniccircles.org.

About The Society
for Shamanic Practitioners

The Society for Shamanic Practitioners has members throughout the world. The Society is focused on the here and now and is interested in documenting how shamanism is changing and how it is being used as it interfaces with the twenty-first-century world.

We are an alliance of people deeply committed to the re-emergence of shamanic practices that promote healthy individuals and communities.

To keep up with the changing times, the Society of Shamanic Practitioners:

- Creates an alliance of diverse shamanic practitioners, which functions as a circle of peers.

- Gathers and disseminates knowledge about shamanic practice.

- Promotes the importance of personal responsibility in doing the inner work necessary to live and practice with integrity.

- Focuses resources and shamanic energies to bring healing and unity to the world.

- Provides a forum for sharing ideas about integrating shamanic practice into contemporary society, clinical practice, institutions, and efforts to heal the earth.

- Encourages a dynamic exchange around how people use spiritual practice.

- Creates grassroots communities that support each other.

- Supports education through an annual conference, regional gatherings, and small focused retreats.

- Maintains a repository of stories and clinical case studies of successful shamanic interventions.

- Facilitates research evaluating the outcome of shamanic healing.

For more information, please visit shamansociety.org.

Index

About the Authors

© JACKIE MATHEY

Sandra Ingerman, MA, is the author of *Soul Retrieval: Mending the Fragmented Self; Welcome Home: Following Your Soul's Journey Home; A Fall to Grace; Medicine for the Earth: How to Transform Personal and Environmental Toxins; Shamanic Journeying: A Beginner's Guide; How to Heal Toxic Thoughts: Simple Tools for Personal Transformation;* and *How to Thrive in Changing Times.* She is also the author of lecture programs for Sounds True, including *The Soul Retrieval Journey, The Beginner's Guide to Shamanic Journeying, Miracles for the Earth, Shamanic Meditations: Guided Journeys for Insight, Vision, and Healing,* and *Soul Journeys: Music for Shamanic Practice.*

Sandra teaches workshops internationally on shamanic journeying, healing, and reversing environmental pollution using spiritual methods. She has trained and founded an international alliance of Medicine for the Earth teachers and shamanic teachers. Sandra is recognized for bridging ancient cross-cultural healing methods into our modern culture, addressing the needs of our times. Sandra is a licensed marriage and family therapist and professional mental health counselor. She is also a board-certified expert on traumatic stress with additional certification in acute traumatic stress management.

For information on Sandra's work, to see her articles on shamanism, and to read her monthly column "The Transmutation News" you can visit her website at sandraingerman.com. "The Transmutation News" is translated into seven languages besides English.

To find a local shamanic teacher or shamanic practitioner who has trained with Sandra, please visit shamanicteachers.com.

© DANIEL BIANCHETTA

Hank Wesselman, PhD, is an environmental and evolutionary biologist who did his undergraduate and masters degree in zoology at the University of Colorado at Boulder. Hank served in the U.S. Peace Corps in the 1960s, living among people of the Yoruba tribe in Nigeria, where he first became interested in indigenous spiritual traditions. He went on to receive his doctoral degree in anthropology from the University of California at Berkeley, and in that capacity he has conducted research with an international group of scientists for much of the past thirty-seven years, exploring eastern Africa's Great Rift Valley and Ethiopia in search of answers to the mystery of human origins. His expeditionary fieldwork has allowed him to spend much of his life with tribal peoples rarely, if ever, visited by outsiders, among whom he first encountered traditional shamans.

Hank is also a shamanic practitioner and teacher, now in the twenty-eighth year of his apprenticeship. The books in his autobiographical trilogy—*Spiritwalker, Medicinemaker,* and *Visionseeker* —have been translated into thirteen languages and reveal the nature of his initiation into the shaman's world, documenting his investigations into a hidden reality that most of us have heard about but few have experienced directly. In addition to his scientific papers and monographs, Hank is also the author of *The Journey to the Sacred Garden*, a book with CD; *Spirit Medicine* (with Jill Kuykendall), a book with CD; *The Spiritwalker Teachings* (with Jill Kuykendall), a six-CD set with booklet; and *Little Ruth Reddingford and the Wolf* (with Raquel Abreu), a story for children.

Hank has taught for the University of Hawai'i at Hilo's West Hawai'i campus, the University of California at San Diego, California State University at Sacramento, American River College and Sierra College in Northern California, and Adeola Odutola College and Kirigi Memorial College in western Nigeria. He currently offers training workshops at many internationally recognized centers such as the Esalen Institute in California and the Omega Institute near New York.

Hank and his family live on their farm in Honaunau on Hawai'i Island. Visit their website at sharedwisdom.com.

About the Contributors

Tom Cowan has been a shamanic practitioner for more than twenty-five years. He has studied with and taught for the Foundation for Shamanic Studies. He is the author of several books on shamanism and Celtic spirituality including *Fire in the Head: Shamanism and the Celtic Spirit; Shamanism as a Spiritual Practice for Daily Life;* and *Yearning for the Wind: Celtic Reflections on Nature and the Soul.*

Tom is a minister in the Circle of the Sacred Earth and is on the board of directors of the Society for Shamanic Practitioners. He offers shamanic training workshops and spiritual retreats in North America, Central and Eastern Europe, Ireland, Scotland, and England. He lives in New York's Hudson River Valley. His website is riverdrum.com.

Carol Proudfoot-Edgar has taught shamanism since 1992. In addition, her specialties include Bear Medicine, Spirits of Place, and developing women's circles and Teachers. For twelve years she has led a group of women physicians in integrating shamanism into both their personal and professional lives. She has been a teacher for the Department of Integrative Medicine at the University of California, San Francisco. In addition, she considers one of her primary roles to be that of ceremonialist.

Carol is an explorer who perceives her work to be that of assisting individuals to probe beyond the known realities and to venture outside the usual parameters for contextualizing and manifesting the future. Carol says that through such explorations, "Spirit can meet us, and together we can construct a web of compassion and joy" that can hold and support the divine nature of every being and element on this great Earth planet.

Since 1995, Carol has been involved in developing nonprofit organizations that will coordinate the efforts of individuals seeking to bringing change that is grounded in shamanic consciousness. She is especially interested in using technology to further coordinate work around the globe. Her websites contain a broad range of her shamanic material and listing of Circles working together: shamanicvisions.com, shamaniccircles.org.

José Luis Stevens, PhD, is the president and co-founder of Power Path Seminars, an international consulting firm based in Santa Fe, New Mexico. He is an international lecturer, organizational consultant, and executive coach to professionals in a wide variety of fields. He uses his knowledge of shamanism and indigenous wisdom to advise and assist leaders to make difficult life decisions and to develop life strategies.

José and his wife, Lena, have completed a ten-year apprenticeship with a Huichol *maracame* (shaman) in the Sierras of Central Mexico; in addition, they currently study intensively with Shipibo healers in the Peruvian Amazon and Incan shamans in the Andes. José often speaks on the subject of the indigenous wisdom of shamans and how this knowledge applies to the modern world. He is on the board of the Society for Shamanic Practitioners and is co-founder of the nonprofit Center for Shamanic Education and Exchange.

José is a licensed psychotherapist with more than thirty-five years of experience specializing in understanding personality. He is the author of ten books and numerous articles, including *The Power Path: The Shaman's Way to Success in Business and Life*; *Transforming Your Dragons*; *Secrets of Shamanism*; and *Praying With Power: How to Use Ancient Shamanic Techniques to Gain Maximum Benefit and Extraordinary Results Through Prayer*. Learn more at thepowerpath.com.

Alberto Villoldo, PhD, is a medical anthropologist and psychologist who has studied the spiritual practices of the Amazon and the Andes for more than twenty-five years. While at San Francisco State University, he founded the Biological Self-Regulation Laboratory to study how the mind creates psychosomatic health and disease.

Founder of The Four Winds Society, he instructs individuals throughout the world in the practice of energy medicine. Alberto has written numerous bestselling books, including *Shaman, Healer, Sage; Yoga, Power, and Spirit: Patanjali the Shaman,* and *Courageous Dreaming*. See his website, thefourwinds.com, for more.